DECARCERATION

Community Treatment and the Deviant — a Radical View

Second edition

Library of Congress Cataloguing in Publication Data

Scull, Andrew T.
  Decarceration: community treatment and the
deviant.

  (Crime, law, and deviance)
  Bibliography: p.
  Includes index.
  1. Community-based corrections – United States.
  2. Community-based corrections – Great Britain.
  I. Title. II. Series.
  HV9304.S38   1984   364.6   83-17724
  ISBN 0 – 8135 – 1034 – 1
  ISBN 0 – 8135 – 1035 – X (pbk.)

Selections reprinted by permission of the publisher, from Closing
Correctional Institutions *edited by Y. Bakal (Lexington,
Mass.: Lexington Books, D.C. Heath and Company, 1973).*

First edition published in USA by Prentice-Hall, Inc.,
1977, as *A Spectrum Book.*

First revised edition published in Great Britain by
Martin Robertson and Co., Ltd., 1984, and in the
United States by Rutgers University Press, 1984.

Printed in Great Britain

H/86

Contents

Preface to the Second Edition
Acknowledgments

Part One   Introduction   1

1   Deviance and the dynamics of control   3
2   Capitalism and the modern social control
    apparatus   15
3   The decarceration of the bad: criminals
    and delinquents   41
4   The demise of the asylum: decarcerating the mad   64

    Part Two   Conventional explanations for decarceration:
                their limitations and inadequacies   77

5   The "technological fix"? Psychoactive drugs
    and community treatment   79
6   Social science and social policy: the critique
    of the total institution   95

    Part Three   Social control and welfare capitalism   121

7   Structural sources of the failure of the nineteenth
    century decarceration movement   123
8   "Success" in the twentieth century: welfare
    capitalism and the changing exigencies of domestic
    pacification and control   134

    Part Four   Afterword: 1983   161

Bibliography   191

Index   219

For Nancy

Preface to the Second Edition

Analysing major changes in social control styles and practices is always a complex task, never so fraught with risks as when one attempts a critical assessment of large-scale transformations while they are still in their formative stages. Perhaps only the intellectual *chutzpah* of youth could have prompted me to undertake such an ambitious project. And there can be no doubt that, with the wisdom of hindsight (to say nothing of the further unfolding of events over the past eight or nine years), I should want to modify my original arguments in some important respects. The appearance of this new edition of *Decarceration* provides a welcome opportunity to discuss recent developments and to outline some of these qualifications and partial retractions. This I have done in the new Part Four. At the same time, however, I hope it is not immodest to suggest that the republication of the original text is testimony to the continuing impact of my attempt to develop a historically informed macrosociological perspective on the structure of social control in contemporary England and the United States.

As this book went to press, I learned of Peter Sedgwick's tragic and untimely death. His passing is a great sorrow to those of us who were privileged to have him for a friend, and a great loss for those victimized by poverty and mental disorder, for whose interests he was a passionate, clear sighted and untiring advocate.

Andrew Scull
October 1983

Acknowledgements

I owe a major intellectual debt to Steven Spitzer, who first suggested that my ideas on this subject were worth committing to paper, and who has since provided advice, criticism, and suggestions of great value. I should like, too, to thank Peter Sterling for unstintingly giving of his time and knowledge. Without their help, this would have been a much poorer book. I am also grateful to several other colleagues and friends — Magali Larson, Jan Smith, Paul Rock, John Moffett, and Fred Block — for their comments and suggestions. A number of people — among them David Mechanic, John Wing, George Brown, and Keith Hearn — provided me with references and material; and the staff of the libraries of the College of Physicians in Philadelphia and the Institute of Living in Hartford, Connecticut facilitated my researches into nineteenth century materials. I thank them for their kindness. I should also like to acknowledge the editorial suggestions and encouragement of Michael Hunter at Prentice-Hall. Some of the arguments developed here first appeared as "The Deinstitutionalization of the Mentally Ill: A Critical View." *Politics and Society* 6 (Summer 1976).

Research on which portions of this manuscript are based was assisted by grants from the American Philosophical Society and from the University of Pennsylvania. I am grateful to them, too.

My greatest debt, as always, is to my wife, Nancy.

PART ONE

Introduction

"Decarceration" is a word which has not yet entered the dictionary. But it is increasingly being used to designate a process with momentous implications for all of us. It is shorthand for a state-sponsored policy of closing down asylums, prisons, and reformatories. Mad people, criminals, and delinquents are being discharged or refused admission to the dumps in which they have been traditionally housed. Instead, they are to be left at large, to be coped with "in the community."

We are told by those who run programs of this sort that keeping the criminal and the mentally disturbed in our midst is "humane." We are informed that it is a "more effective" means of curing or rehabilitating such people. And, miracle of miracles, we learn that this approach is also "cheaper"! With an alternative which embraces such an array of virtues, who can be surprised to learn that mental hospitals are emptying faster and faster, and that with each passing day the convicted felon's chances of going to prison grow more remote?

On closer examination, it turns out that this whole enterprise is built on a foundation of sand. The contention that treatment in the community is more effective than institutionalization is an empty one. There is massive ignorance about what "community treatment" actually involves, and about the likely effects of abandoning institutional controls. The claim that leaving deviants at large "cures" or "rehabilitates" them is just that—a claim. Little or no solid evidence can be offered in its support. Instead, it rests uneasily on a cloud of rhetoric and wishful thinking. Most people's conception of the "humane" does not embrace placing senile men and women in the hands of rapacious nursing home operators or turning loose the perpetrators of violent crimes, under conditions which guarantee that they will receive little or no supervision. Yet, as decarceration has been implemented, this is what has been happening. Much of the time, it appears as if the policy makers simply do not know what will happen when their schemes are put into effect. Nor do they seem very concerned to find out. Often, they do not even know where those they have dumped back on the rest of us are to be found.[1]

What has the new approach meant in practice? For thousands of the old, already suffering in varying degrees from mental confusion and deterioration, it has meant premature death. For others, it has meant that they have been left to rot and decay, physically and otherwise, in broken down welfare hotels or in what are termed, with Orwellian euphemism, "personal-care" nursing homes. For thousands of younger psychotics discharged into the streets, it has meant a nightmare existence in the blighted centers of our cities, amidst neighborhoods crowded with prostitutes, ex-felons, addicts, alcoholics, and the other human rejects now repressively tolerated by our society. Here they eke out a precarious existence, supported by welfare checks they may not even know how to cash. They spend their days locked in or locked out of dilapidated "community-based" boarding houses. And they find themselves alternately the prey of street criminals (who may themselves have been "decarcerated"), and a source of nuisance and alarm to those "normal" residents of the neighborhood too poverty-stricken to leave. For the criminal and the delinquent, "community corrections" (as it is called) has meant a further erosion of the sanctions imposed on their conduct. Not only are they steadily less likely to be caught in the first place, but if they do have the misfortune to be apprehended and convicted, their chance of receiving a prison term grows ever more remote. Instead, they find themselves released on probation, "supervised" by men coping with caseloads of one and two hundred persons. This allows the probation officer to give each case an average of ten or fifteen minutes' attention per week.

Excluded from the more desirable neighborhoods by zoning practices and organized community opposition, the decarcerated deviants are in any case impelled by economics—the need for cheap housing and to be close to a welfare office—to cluster in the ghettos and the decaying core of the inner city. As for the criminal, he is also attracted by the tokenism of police operations in these areas and by the willingness of the wider (white) society to leave ghetto residents to fend for themselves. Decarceration thus forms yet one more burden heaped on the backs of those who are most obviously the victims of our society's inequities. And it places the deviant in those communities least able to care for or cope with him.

In the circumstances, moral panics are an ever-present possibility. Aroused by stories of released mental patients who "urinate or defecate in public, expose themselves to women and children, ride up and down in automatic elevators, become helplessly drunk and shout obscenities. . ."[2] and by the knowledge that burglars and muggers are being left to walk the streets, inhabitants of black and inner city areas may well resort, in time, to vigilante action. There is, after all, a strong subterranean tradition of such activity in America. And should this happen, who is to guard the ex-inmate against his neighbor? It may well turn out that the protection an institution offers the community from the *deviant* and the protection it offers the deviant from the *community* are of equal importance.[3]

Decarceration is something which vitally affects us all. An adequate socio-logical understanding of its nature and sources is clearly an urgent necessity. It is this understanding that I hope to provide here.

[1]. Senate Select Committee on Aging 1971: 1106; *San Francisco Chronicle,* November 29, 1973.

[2]. The *New York Times,* March 18, 1974,: 17: © by the New York Times Company. Reprinted by permission.

[3]. Paul Rock, Personal communication to the author.

CHAPTER ONE

Deviance and the dynamics of control

A myth is, of course, not a fairy story. It is the presentation of facts belonging in one category in the idioms belonging to another. To explode a myth is accordingly not to deny the facts but to re-allocate them.

GILBERT RYLE
*The Concept of Mind**

I

In recent years, a state-sponsored effort to de-institutionalize deviant populations has become a central element in the social control practices of a number of advanced capitalist societies. In varying degrees, control of such deviant groups as criminals, juvenile delinquents, and the mentally ill has increasingly become "community-based." Plans have been devised (and to some extent have already been carried out) to eliminate mental hospitals and juvenile reformatories; the resident population of such institutions has fallen off dramatically; the prison as the dominant response to the criminal has likewise come under mounting attack; and in the face of a steadily escalating crime rate and an ever larger population formally "deserving" imprisonment, a variety of approaches have been initiated to hold the number imprisoned down to its former level. Yet despite the enormous importance of this change in social policy, surprisingly little effort has been made to unravel the reasons for its appearance. Usually it is discussed simply in passing. Only rarely does one come upon extended discussions of the problem.

Our concern in this book will be to provide just such a sustained examination of the sources of this major shift in social control styles and practices, treating the whole issue in comparative and historical

*New York: Harper & Row, Publishers, Inc. Used by permission.

perspective, and focusing particularly on the United States and England. Some space, particularly in Part One, will be devoted to an examination of the policy of decarceration as it has been applied to the control of crime and delinquency. Our major focus, however, will be on this change as it has affected the handling of the mentally disturbed, not only because the policy has been pursued most rapidly and universally with this "problem population," but also because what conventional accounts of the sources of the decarceration movement we do have are most carefully elaborated and have their greatest surface plausibility with reference to this subgroup. I want to begin in this chapter, though, by placing my concern with systems of social control in a general sociological context.

II

Agencies of social control (though not, as I shall show, their relationships with the larger social order) have increasingly come to be defined as one of the focal points of research in the sociology of deviance. In part, this is simply a reflection of the fact that these agencies are such a ubiquitous feature of modern societies and that they dispose of such large quantities of resources and people. Inevitably, then, attention comes to be focused on what it is they claim to be doing and what they in fact achieve. But more than that, a great deal of recent writing on deviance has viewed the systems and agents of social control as deeply and irretrievably implicated in the process by which others become deviant.

Among adherents of the so-called labeling or societal reaction school, the existence of reciprocal relationships between deviance and control has come to seem almost axiomatic. Indeed, work in this tradition has consisted in large part of the elaboration and documentation of the ironical notion that "the very effort to prevent, intervene, arrest and 'cure' persons of their alleged pathologies may . . . precipitate or seriously aggravate the tendency society wishes to guard against."[1] This perspective is undoubtedly badly flawed—a point to which I shall return shortly. Nevertheless, one must recognize that the labeling approach, in rendering social control so sharply problematic, represented a considerable theoretical advance in the sociology of deviance.

For many years, sociologists had taken deviance merely as a "given." From this common sense perspective, social problems were seen as generating societal responses, but only rarely as reflecting those responses. In such a context, there was something clearly liberating and intellectually challenging about the emergence of a more skeptical viewpoint. No longer content simply to buttress conventional images of deviance with pseudoscientific trapping, a number of writers began to display a greater willingness to question the traditional notion that the societal reaction to deviance represented no more than a benign and defensive response to individual pathology. Their more critical orientation produced a pronounced shift away from an obsessive concern with the attributes of individual deviants towards a more wide-ranging interest in social process. This approach forced deviance to be considered as inseparable from the wider social context within which it occurred, and suggested that it was susceptible to analysis in terms of the conventional apparatus of sociological inquiry.

The first major proponent of this new viewpoint was Edwin Lemert. In his work in the late 1940s and early 1950s he began to delineate and develop a distinction between "primary" and "secondary" deviation, a distinction which has been of central importance to the work of recent labeling analysts. For Lemert, "primary deviation . . . is polygenetic, arising out of a variety of social, cultural, psychological, and physiological factors, either in adventitious or recurring combinations."[2] Although such deviance is quite common, it also has only very marginal implications for the individual and society. Under some circumstances, however, there occurs some sort of more or less organized societal reaction to some of this primary deviation, a reaction usually involving elements of stigmatization, punishment, and actual or symbolic segregation of the offender. The general effect of these reactions is to produce marked changes in the social situation in which the person finds himself, and, in consequence,

> . . . early or adult socialization is categorically affected. [The reactions] become central facts of experience for those experiencing them, altering psychic structure, producing specialized organization of social roles and self-regarding attitudes. . . . In effect, the original causes of the deviation recede and give way to the central importance of the disapproving, degradational, and labeling reactions of society.[3]

As we can readily see, this early formulation of labeling theory remained rather vague and general. Moreover, at first sight Lemert's argument seemed to lead to an increased concern with analysis at the social-psychological level. And not just at first sight; for much of the labeling literature displays just such a concern with analyzing the process of becoming deviant on the social-psychological level, emphasizing the sequences of interaction through which deviant identities are built up and sustained. A glance at the central concepts employed simply reinforces that impression, besides revealing the perspective's profound debt to George Herbert Mead and the symbolic-interactionist view of society.[4] Consider the following tools of analysis: stigma, degradation, mortificacation of self, discretion, and drift; typing and stereotyping, the reconstitution of self and retrospective reconstruction of identity; perceptions, reputation, the moral career—the social-psychological connotations of these terms are all-pervasive. Much of the time, it appears that the reader is meant to watch, fascinated and overwhelmed by the richness and detail of the ethnographic description the sociologist provides, as the neophyte deviant passes through a public degradation ceremony. This ceremony, by imposing a grossly stigmatizing "master status"—that is, a status with a generalized symbolic value—ushers him firmly into his new role. The very process of being caught and publicly labeled as "deviant" thus sets in motion a relentless self-fulfilling prophecy. For, once acquired, it is very difficult to relinquish the deviant status, both because of the reluctance of the wider community to accept the deviant back into its ranks, and because the experience of being singled out and publicly branded in this way usually culminates in a deviant world view. In this fashion, the societal reaction allegedly produces a kind of role imprisonment which locks the deviant into a symbolic jail.[5]

As well as demonstrating a concern with these dramatic face-to-face confrontations between the deviant and the normal, the labeling approach also provoked a shift in research and analytical perspective more directly related to our present concerns—a much greater interest in at least some aspects of the formal social control apparatus. An orientation which viewed deviance as primarily a consequence of the reactions of others, and which directed attention to the ways society unintentionally creates or aggravates deviance in the very process of attempting to control it, could scarcely avoid examining the agencies making up this formal social control apparatus, in view of the looming presence of such agencies in modern society. And, in fact, many of the societal reaction theorists have come to see the deviant's interaction with and processing by formally constituted agencies of social control as perhaps the single most vital context in which unorganized "primary" deviation comes to be stabilized. In essence, this reflects their conclusion that it is these "macrocosmic, organizational forces of social control through which public and private agencies actively define and classify people, impose punishment, restrict or open access to rewards and satisfactions, set limits to social interaction and induct deviants into special, segregated environments."[6] Put somewhat differently, it is the societal reaction, as expressed through the activities of these agencies, which produces a crystallization of the moral order, giving visible, concrete shape and form to the abstraction that is deviance. And it is in these contexts that "deviants come under the regulation of hierarchy, impersonality, specialization and systematic formal rules."[7]

Certainly a considerable literature now exists on control agencies, including studies of the police and the criminal justice system, the juvenile justice system, prisons, agencies for the blind, and hospitals for the mentally retarded and the mentally ill.[8] Although some were written before the rise of labeling theory, the bulk of these studies were done in the 1960s and were more or less explicitly guided by the societal reaction perspective. But the issue is no longer the question of *whether* the agencies have been subjected to sociological scrutiny (though even the strongest critics of the societal reaction approach would concede its contribution in making this initial step); it is, rather, the *adequacy* of that scrutiny. And here the perspective's defenders are on much weaker ground.

Existing literature on control agencies focuses primarily on "the direct impact on the processed deviants of organizational settings and programs."[9] Attention tends to be narrowly fixed on the role of the agencies in selecting and processing the deviant population, with particular interest in how their activities in these respects serve to redefine and remake the identity of individual deviants.[10] We have already noted the tendency of those working in the labeling tradition to play down the importance of the deviant's own actions and to claim that his status is ascribed rather than achieved, that is, that his status depends primarily upon conditions external to the individual. Consistent with this general orientation, and when considering the impact of control agencies, these same workers have argued that the organized penalties of and reactions to such agencies increase (perhaps even create) and condition the forms taken by deviance.

In some of his earliest writing in this area, Lemert had argued that

. . . not only do reform and rehabilitative institutions in our society fail to demonstrate scientifically that their work actually accomplishes what is claimed for it, but their staffs would be hard put to prove that their efforts did not have effects opposite from what was intended. Many of the social welfare policies of post-Elizabethan England and nineteenth century United States created as many pauperized individuals as they eliminated. . . . Some observers are inclined to the belief that treatment in our mental hospitals precipitates psychoses in many patients and fixes and exaggerates the emotional disturbances of others. Certainly it is not hard to show that our penology and administrative policies towards criminals are important factors in recidivism.[11]

The studies of particular agencies which we have listed above have for the most part been attempts to find empirical support for this position. In the process, however, they have moved from the modest claim initially made by Lemert, hedged as it is with qualifications, towards a far more radical position, one which sees the agencies rather than the deviants as the basic source of trouble. The deviant is now seen as "the put-upon victim, with the social control agents the villain of the piece."[12]

A few of the more perceptive labeling theorists have themselves become somewhat uncomfortable with the implicit romanticizing of the deviant. Lemert, for example, has recently complained of his work being distorted so as to accent "the arbitrariness of official action, stereotyped decision-making in bureaucratic contexts, bias in the administration of law . . ." and so on.[13] He seems tempted to attribute these "distortions" to the vulgarization of labeling theory and its assimilation to popular causes, reacting to "the preeminence and intrusion of large-scale, bureaucratized organizations in the lives of the individuals."[14] But in a deeper sense, as he himself begins to recognize elsewhere in the same essay, the crudeness was built into the approach from the outset, and has merely become more salient and noticeable with time and as work within the perspective has sought to encompass concerns that were originally peripheral (such as the institutional arrangements which order political process or the nature of bureaucratic agencies of social control).

To see this, one must begin by recalling labeling theory's origins in the symbolic-interactionist view of society. Expressed in the dramaturgic metaphor, it is this which led to the overriding concern with deviant identity and to the crucial but as yet only partially liberating notion of control as an independent factor in shaping and producing deviance. But along with this undoubted advance came an adherence to a vision of social life as episodic, and an analytical approach which largely confined itself to interpersonal transactions in an ahistorical and noninstitutional context.[15]

In keeping with this orientation to the world, recent work on deviance "is chiefly distinguished by a phenomenalism and an emphasis on *Verstehen* [that is, by a stress on developing purely descriptive accounts of observable phenomena, and by an effort to put oneself in the place of the group being studied in order to describe the world from its subjective point of view] which propel the analysis towards the study of small bounded settings. Both features engender an ingrained distrust of approaches which are thought to reify, systematize, or abstract."[16] To remove one's analysis from concrete, observable settings, it is argued, leads almost certainly to falsification and distortion.[17]

The view of social life as process and the stress on interaction have produced, on the one hand, an emphasis on "the vagueness, ambiguity and fluidity of everyday life . . .," and on the other, "a radical version of pluralism which defines society as an agglomeration of small worlds which lacks overall structure."[18] Carried to an extreme by adherents of the ethnomethodological/phenomenological cult, this approach has led to a neglect or even a denial of the relevance of structural factors—such as the division of society into classes or the nature of its political and economic organization—and, in Gouldner's vivid phrase, to "an almost Nietschian hostility to conceptualization and abstraction."[19] While it is true, of course, that society is made up of individuals, and therefore that all relations between social institutions take place through individuals, this does not mean that these relations can be undertood solely in terms of individual encounters.[20] Yet societal reaction theorists often speak and act as though this *were* possible, ignoring the larger social contexts within which the encounters they are busy describing are embedded.[21] The trouble lies in the inability of their basic conceptual framework to "encompass the structural arrangements which organize the contexts of defining encounters. [In consequence], the largest describable unit is the group of labeling agents who are bound by face to face links. Relations *between* groups, and relations which do not impinge on the deviant directly remain unsurveyed . . .";[22] and the crucially relevant features of the social context are dealt with only insofar as they are built into the descriptions of the individuals observed.[23]

We can now appreciate more clearly why the societal reaction theorists' attempts to grapple with the nature and functioning of the social control apparatus have failed. Almost exclusive attention to the impact of organizations on the individual results in only passing attention to the structure of the organizations themselves and in almost total

neglect of the overarching structural context within which particular
agencies of social control operate. In turn, this narrowness of vision
inevitably leads to work which depicts social control as arbitrary. For
want of a larger perspective, the actions of the agencies come to be seen
either as free-floating and apparently perverse, or as determined simply
by the immediate interests of the first line controllers. Put less abstractly,
"Of course there are definers and defined but what do the definers
represent? What interests are they defending? How do their actions
reinforce the existing nature of capitalist society? No answers to such
questions are provided: the definers are a group of free-floating
'baddies'."[24]

When the labeling theorists *do* attempt to grapple with why the social
control apparatus takes the form that it does and what makes for transformations in the nature of social control, their work remains flawed by
the same tendency to "trivialise the unexaminable features of the larger
world."[25] Their treatment of this area begins with a simple observation
about the relationship of deviance to place, time, and context. In Erikson's formulation, "Deviance is not a property *inherent in* certain forms
of behavior; it is a property *conferred upon* these forms by the audience
which directly or indirectly witnesses them."[26] In the ensuing discussion
of the rules which govern audience reaction, it was natural enough that
attention should be shifted towards a consideration of *how* the rules
which ascribe deviant status were first created.

For all the obvious relevance of the subject, however, and despite a
number of statements stressing its importance to the field,[27] the number
of such studies undertaken by societal reaction theorists remains surprisingly small: Apart from Becker's study of the Marihuana Tax Act
(replicated by Dickson[28] with somewhat different results), the literature
is confined to an account of the rules covering drug use in America[29] an
analysis of the "creation" of juvenile delinquency,[30] and an examination
of the rise and decline of the Prohibition Movement.[31] But the more
important problems lie in the way the subject is approached. Becker's
work has undoubtedly been the most influential in this area. But the
only type of "rule creator" he discusses is the "moral entrepreneur" who
operates by starting a "moral crusade." The very term "rule creator"
reveals the personalistic approach that dominates his analysis, matched
by neglect of a detailed examination of the *social context* within which
new forms of deviation come to be defined and new forms of social
control emerge. Seeing new forms of deviance "as emerging out of the
matrix of an unanalyzed society, he does not see deviance as deriving
from specified master institutions of this larger society, or as expressing

an active opposition to them."[32] Instead, he rests content with a simplistic distinction between crusading reformers and professional reformers, and with an even cruder discussion of their respective "interests" — while the crusader pictures his mission as "holy," the enforcer "may not be interested in the content of the rule itself, but only in the fact that the existence of the rule provides him with a job, a profession, and a raison d'être."[33] In all these respects he is no worse (though no better) than his fellows; for "it is most difficult to discover in the writings on deviancy a description of legislation and rule-making which is more than anthropomorphic conspiracy theory."[34] With all the talk of entrepreneurs and crusades, one is left, in Lemert's apt and acid epigram, with no more than "a type of *reductio ad personam* theory. . . ."[35]

This outcome is doubly unfortunate. For one might have hoped that, if nowhere else, a consideration of the rule making process (which after all requires that attention be given to the political arena and to the distribution of power) would have served to force deviancy theory to move beyond "a critique of caretaking establishments"[36] towards a consideration of the nature of the social and political order within which rules are generated. Instead, the labeling theorists continue to apply an interactionist viewpoint where a structural analysis is called for. The acknowledgment of the role of power remains formal rather than substantive, with little effect on theory or analysis. And the ritual acknowledgment that those who label (or who construct and impose new labels) are more powerful than those who are labeled represents a dismal substitute for the analyses of power structures and their impact.[37] Thus "the larger whole which might lend unity and order to the fragments has been left untouched."[38]

It is my contention, then, that adequate theoretical work in this area clearly demands that we develop an historically informed macrosociological perspective on the interrelationships between deviance, control structures, and the nature of the wider social systems of which they are both a part and an essential support. Much of the discussion presented in this chapter has unavoidably been somewhat abstract. But abstract polemics about the merits of an alternative approach are no substitute for a practical demonstration of its analytic utility. The latter is what I hope to achieve here. As it examines the contemporary effort to decarcerate many deviant populations, the remainder of this book will seek to demonstrate the superiority of explanations which focus directly on the complex dialectical interplay between transformations in the social control apparatus (and thus in the shapes and forms of deviance) and changes in the wider social system.

The remainder of Part One will continue laying the factual and analytical groundwork for the discussions which follow in Parts Two and Three. Chapter Two will provide an historically grounded overview of the main features of the social control apparatus in England and America and of their development and structural supports, prior to the adoption of a policy of de-institutionalization. We shall pay particularly close attention to three highly interrelated aspects of this development: the progressive institutionalization, bureaucratization, and professionalization of systems of social control. Moving to a consideration of more recent developments, Chapters Three and Four will describe the process of decarcerating the bad (criminals and delinquents) and the mad (those officially stigmatized as crazy).

Part Two examines in detail and refutes the standard accounts of why decarceration is taking place. Such accounts are shown to rest on two central arguments, one of which emphasizes the advent of psycho-active drugs, while the other stresses the therapeutic bankruptcy of the institutional approach to the management of deviance.[39] Chapters Five and Six, respectively, show these explanations are radically implausible and unsatisfactory.

Part Three attempts to avoid the pitfalls inherent in these earlier analyses, and to demonstrate that this far-reaching change in social control styles and practices can be explained both more completely and more parsimoniously by reference to deep-seated changes in the nature and functioning of modern capitalist societies. Chapter Seven examines the reasons for the failure of influential figures in nineteenth century England and America, who had come to despair of the institutional approach, to secure the adoption of a policy of decarceration; this despite their considerable political skills and the powerful intellectual arguments they mustered in its behalf. By pointing out the structural forces which inhibited the adoption of such an approach, these historical materials demonstrate how closely changes in the character of the social control apparatus are linked to changes in the nature of the social system within which it is embedded. Chapter Eight seeks to reinforce this central insight by demonstrating how the state's receptivity in the modern era to a policy of decarceration can be traced back to fundamental transformations in the social organization of advanced capitalism. The pervasiveness, intensity, and mutually reinforcing character of the pressures to adopt a policy of decarceration are shown to be intimately connected to the rise of welfare capitalism. And, finally, I demonstrate that such a perspective allows us to comprehend a number of crucial aspects of the decarceration movement which conventional accounts either ignore or are forced to claim are simply fortuitous.

1. Matza 1969: 80.
2. Lemert 1967: 40.
3. Lemert 1967: 63, 17.
4. Briefly, this is a perspective which stresses that individuals are continuously engaged in constructing their behavior in the course of their daily activity, and do so primarily with reference to their definitions of the situations in which they act. In other words, individuals act in terms of the symbolic meanings they attach to wants and encounters. The emphasis on grasping the process of interpretation leads to a characteristic focus on the present, the contingent, and the subjective, and to a consistent down-playing of the role of the wider social and political context.
5. This portrait of the deviant as "a passive nonentity who is responsible neither for his suffering nor its alleviation—who is more sinned against than sinning," (Gouldner 1968: 106) runs like a connecting thread through the societal reaction literature. Theoretically, this concentration on deviance as status, as something ascribed rather than achieved, has been distinctly unfortunate (see Taylor, Walton, and Young 1973: Ch. 5). Practically, as we shall see, it has been of enormous significance. For it has provided an invaluable ideological account of the failings and ill effects of institutions like prisons. mental hospitals, and juvenile reformatories, smoothing the way towards an abandonment, or at least a major modification of this segregative control system, and enabling this development to be presented as motivated by concern for the deviant as well as for the community as a whole.
6. Lemert 1967: 41.
7. Rubington and Weinberg 1968: 111.
8. Skolnick 1966; Sudnow 1965; Cicourel 1968; Clemmer 1938; Sykes 1958; Scott 1969; Edgerton 1967; Goffman 1961; Mechanic 1962; Scheff 1966; Belknap 1956.
9. Schur 1971: 98.
10. In many ways, this concern with the manner in which control systems act as "forcing houses for the changing of persons" (Goffman 1961: 12) can be seen as an extension into a new setting of the fascination with the social psychology of deviance which I have analyzed above. Perhaps as a consequence of this bewitchment with the intricacies of interpersonal process, many of these writers apparently "cannot discuss abstract bureaucratic process in language other than that of personal morality" (Rock, "The Sociology of Deviancy," 1974: 145).
11. Lemert 1951: 68
12. Lorber 1967: 309; see also Gouldner 1968: 107.
13 Lemert 1972: 16; see also Howard Becker's (1974) somewhat unconvincing reply to his critics.
14. Lemert 1972: 16–17.
15. Gouldner 1970: 379.
16. Rock, "The Sociology of Deviancy" 1974. For an analysis of this tendency by someone who views it as a largely favorable development, cf. Matza 1969. In what follows, I am heavily indebted to the sophisticated discussion in Rock's essay.
17. Cf. Cicourel 1968.
18. Rock, "The Sociology of Deviancy," 1974: 141.
19. Gouldner 1970: 391. Cf. Douglas 1970:20: "Life is too immensely complex, too uncertain, too conflictful, too changing for any set of abstract and predetermined rules to specify activities that will have results seen as adequate by the individual actors."

20. Rock, "The Sociology of Deviancy" 1974: 143.

21. Compare, for example, the lack of concern with institutional structures and the wider social setting evident in the following:

> People act, as Mead and Blumer have made clearest, *together*. They do what they do with an eye on what others have done, are doing now, and may do in the future. One tries to fit his own line of action into the actions of others, just as each of them likewise adjusts his own developing actions to what he sees and expects others to do. The result of all this adjusting and fitting in can be called a collective action, especially if it is borne in mind that the term covers more than a conscious collective agreement to, let's say, go on strike, but also extends to having a school class, having a meal together or crossing the street, each of these seen as something being done by a lot of people together (Becker 1974: 44).

22. Rock, "The Sociology of Deviancy," 1974: 144.

23. See, for example, Becker 1974: 45 for an extension of the analogy of individual interaction on the face to face level to the structural level, something he apparently perceives as essentially nonproblematic. For an excellent critique of the methodological individualist standpoint, which this represents, see Lukes 1968; 1973: esp. Ch. 17.

24. Taylor and Taylor 1968: 30.

25. Rock, "The Sociology of Deviancy," 1974: 139.

26. Erikson 1964: 11.

27. See Schur 1971: 105–106; Becker 1963: Ch. 7.

28. Dickson 1968.

29. Lindesmith 1965.

30. Platt 1969.

31. Gusfield 1963. There have been, however, important contributions in this area from those not sharing a labeling orientation—see, for example, Hall 1935; Chambliss 1964.

32. Gouldner 1968: 107.

33. Becker 1963: 156.

34. Rock, "The Sociology of Deviance," 1974: 144.

35. Lemert 1972: 19.

36. Gouldner 1968: 107.

37. Compare, for example, Howard Becker's constant references to "moral entrepreneurs" and to the trite notion that upper class male entrepreneurs are more likely to succeed in imposing "their" definitions on others, as evidence that he deals with the issue of power and does not exempt the powerful from scrutiny (Becker 1974). His examples of "power relationships" in the same paper ("parents and children," "welfare worker and client," "teacher and student") are similarly revealing (Becker 1974: 49).

38. Rock, "The Sociology of Deviance," 1974: 143.

39. The first of these "explanations," of course, applies only to the case of the mentally ill; the latter is alleged to be more generally applicable.

CHAPTER TWO

Capitalism and the
modern social control apparatus

*Mr. Podsnap: "I see what you are driving at. I knew it from the first. Centraliza-
tion. No. Never with my consent. Not English."*

CHARLES DICKENS
Our Mutual Friend

*One of the effects of civilization (not to say one of the ingredients in it) is, that the
spectacle, and even the very idea of pain, is more and more kept out of the sight of
those classes who enjoy in their fullness the benefits of civilization.*

JOHN STUART MILL
Civilization

This chapter will take the form of a brief and necessarily schematic
look at the origins of the modern approach to the problems posed by
"the dangerous classes." Throughout, the discussion will emphasize the
development of three analytically distinct but empirically closely inter-
connected features which I take to distinguish deviance and its control
in modern society from the shapes which such phenomena assume elsewhere. These are: (1) the substantial involvement of the state, and the
emergence of a highly rationalized and generally centrally administered
and directed social control apparatus; (2) the treatment of many types
of deviance in institutions providing a large measure of segregation
from the surrounding community (something which still remains the
case, despite the advent of the decarceration movement); and (3) the
careful differentiation of different sorts of deviance, and the subsequent
consignment of each variety to the ministrations of "experts"—which
last development entails, as an important corollary, the emergence of
professional and semiprofessional "helping occupations." Throughout
Western Europe and North America, all these features of the modern

social control apparatus were substantially a product of the eighteenth and nineteenth centuries.

As both Rusche and Kirchheimer and Michel Foucault have shown,[1] there is a sense in which the first moves towards reliance on the institution lie still further back in time. During the mercantile period, the initial growth of capitalist enterprise in the context of a competitive European state system produced structural pressures towards a more intensive exploitation of the labor of the domestic population.[2] Deviant groups—vagrants, minor criminals, prostitutes, paupers, beggars, lunatics, orphans, and so forth—represented those most readily subjected to state control; and, at least in the centers of the most advanced economic activity of the period, control assumed an increasingly institutional form.

The earliest manifestation of this tendency was the establishment of the Bridewell, or house of correction, in London in 1555. By the end of the sixteenth century, Amsterdam, the center of the society with the most highly developed capitalist system in Europe at this time, had begun to develop its own variants of the workhouse, the Zuchthaus and the Spinnhaus. And subsequently, this innovation spread to the other major centers of commercial activity—to Bremen in 1609; to Lubeck in 1613, Bern in 1614, Basle in 1616, Hamburg in 1622, Danzig in 1636, and to Bristol in 1696. Perhaps the most famous of all were the French Hôpitaux Généraux, the first of which was founded in Paris in 1656.

One should be careful, however, not to exaggerate the significance of these first tentative steps towards a system of segregative control. In the first place, the degree of direct state involvement through a centrally directed, bureaucratically organized administrative apparatus was comparatively negligible. More often, either individual inmates or entire establishments were leased to entrepreneurs who hoped to exploit the deviants' labor power.[3] Second, institutions in this period coped with only a small fraction of the total number of deviants, and although they were present in most European societies, their influence within each society clearly remained geographically circumscribed. Throughout most of Europe, in the seventeenth and even in the eighteenth century, control of deviants was still an essentially communal and family affair.

In this, as in other respects, the methods for coping with the unfortunate and the morally disreputable remained those inherited from the Middle Ages. As in medieval times, most of what we now think of as the separate elements composing this class—such groups as the poor, the aged and the impotent, lunatics, the sick and physically handicapped, vagrants and beggars, and minor criminals — were in no sense rigorously distinguished from one another. Rather, they were for the most part lumped together in a single ill-defined, amorphous entity, and responded to in essentially similar ways.

In the medieval period, the dependent had relied heavily on a haphazard and often ineffectual tradition of Christian charity and almsgiving. Poverty, particularly if it were voluntarily assumed, was a status invested with considerable religious significance and meaning. But neither the Church nor private individuals made any serious effort to match aid to need or to provide an organized response to specific problems of dependency. To the contrary, such a measured, calculated response was quite foreign to a society where the impulse to give was governed largely by the need to ensure one's own salvation; this sort of response began to emerge only with the decay of ecclesiastical responsibility in this area. The family was held liable to provide for its own; and, with the aid of temporary assistance or a more permanent subsidy from the community, it generally did so. Only a few exceptionally burdensome cases, and those without family or friends to call on for support, might find themselves gathered up under one roof — "the sick, aged, bedridden, diseased, wayfaring men, diseased soldiers, and honest folk fallen into poverty" clustered within the walls of one of the many small medieval "hospitals."[4] Sometimes such places took a lunatic too violent to be left at large. Others so afflicted might find themselves in the local gaol.

Small structures serving as gaols were scattered somewhat haphazardly through the countryside. Nominally, all such prisons were the king's. Practically speaking, the degree of central intervention, responsibility, and control was minimal, more often nonexistent, even as late as the eighteenth century. Frequently housed in ramshackle buildings, gaols were private speculations run on behalf of municipalities, of ecclesiastical dignitaries, or (very often) of private individuals, all of whom attempted "to make a living out of their prisoners by means of fees, lodging charges, and the sale of drink and victuals."[5] The inmates, for whose maintenance the state assumed little or no responsibility, found themselves crammed together in a single heterogeneous assemblage. As well as lunatics and debtors, some were there "as a means of securing the payment into the Exchequer of debts due to the Crown,"[6] while others were held as punishment for various minor infractions. But most were in custody simply to ensure their appearance at their trials or their executions. For, far from imprisonment being a major form of punishment, until the nineteenth century most crimes, and all serious crimes, were dealt with by some combination of fines, corporal punishment, mutilation, or death (for which transportation overseas was frequently substituted in later years).[7]

While the administration of gaols changed little until the nineteenth century,[8] elsewhere one can perceive the origins of a major departure from medieval precedent in the handling of the poor, dangerous, and disreputable sections of the community as early as the sixteenth century. Throughout Europe in this period, the efforts of centralizing monarchs to augment state power produced a series of clashes between state and Church. In England this conflict led to a decisive subordination of the latter to secular political authority, and greatly accelerated the diminution of the Church's role in civil society. The dissolution of the monasteries and the redistribution of monastic lands were both symptoms and causes of this decline, a decline which rendered a Church-based response to the indigent increasingly anachronistic and unworkable. At the same time, demands for the maintenance of internal order were, if anything, more acutely felt than in the past. The growing commercialization of agriculture, reflected in the spread of enclosures, was spawning a volatile "army" of vagrants, beggars, and idlers, who were no longer needed on the land. And the threat these groups posed to the central royal authorities' power was heightened by the still-precarious nature of royal control, both vis-à-vis potential challengers from within, and in the context of the ever intensifying international rivalries of the emerging European state system. Forced to attend to the demands of internal order, the Tudor monarchs found themselves increasingly compelled to supplement religious with secular control of the poor.

Completion of this process came with the passage of the great Poor Law Act of 1601 (43 Elizabeth c. 2), marking the official recognition of the final breakdown of ecclesiastical responsibility for the indigent and its replacement by the principle of secular involvement. As a last resort, parishes were now empowered to levy taxes for the support of the indigent. But even here, little effort was made to separate and define the various classes of the needy who were deserving of aid. Provision of relief continued to be unhampered by bureaucratic rules concerning eligibility, and was administered primarily at the parish level.

As many as 15,000 separate administrative units were this involved in the management of the poor; and this pervasive emphasis on localism was further reinforced by the custom of restricting aid to those belonging to one's own parish, a practice which received statutory recognition in the 1662 Act of Settlement (14 Charles II c. 12). Yet despite this wide scope for the exercise of local discretion, most parishes continued to provide for the derelict in essentially similar ways. Of all the funds expended for such purposes during this period, "by far the largest amounts were dedicated to used which we may fairly describe as house-hold relief . . . for the support at the subsistence level of needy and worthy poor, legally resident in the parish.[9] Efforts were made to keep even such groups as the senile, the crippled, the blind, and lunatics in the community, if necessary providing their relatives or others prepared to care for them with permanent pensions for their support.

Relief practices in colonial America, not surprisingly, differed little from these. The political, economic, and cultural dependence of the colonies was reflected in "a fundamental unity of policy between England and America. . . . Differences were present, of course, because of varia-tions between the two countries, but even they did not make for major deviations from the English pattern."[10] In Virginia and Maryland, for example, where there was an established (Anglican) church, provision for the poor and dependent was administered, as in England, on a parish level through church vestries and officials; New England, on the other hand, lacking an established church, conferred similar duties on the town selectmen or overseers of the poor. Both places, however, operated in a typically informal fashion. In the words of an early Massa-chusetts statute, "every township shall make competent provision for the mayntenance of their poore according as they fynde most convenient and suitable for themselves by an order and generall agreement in a publike town meeting."[11] Until well into the eighteenth century, "it was usual to deal with each case individually as it arose. And it was usual, also, to present the case to the entire town in regular town meeting, there to be discussed, frequently to be haggled over, and finally disposed of by some temporizing step."[12] In this way local com-munities provided for their own while relying, like their English counterparts, on settlement laws to exclude the needy outsider.

Although imprisonment was rarely used as a form of punishment, jails were found scattered throughout the colonies. Towns expelled their criminals and vagrants, or else made use of the standard penalties of corporal punishment, fines, mutilation, and death. Town jails were places of pretrial detention, receptacles for debtors, and a means of ensuring that those convicted of serious offences were still around for the infliction of sentence. A glance at their architecture suffices to indicate the virtual impossibility of a more extensive use of such structures, such as for the lengthy confinement of convicted offenders as a form of correction: "even those constructed after the middle of the eighteenth century were rather crude frame structures, highly combustible and ill-adapted for the safe confinement of offenders."[13]

Major changes in this shared reliance on an essentially noninstitutional approach to the control of deviance did not begin to be discussed and implemented until the eighteenth century. This increased emphasis on providing for the indigent and disreputable by institutional means was most marked in the English capital. Defoe, listing 27 "Public Gaols" and 125 "tolerated prisons" (a general term for all types of institutions for deviants), commented: "There are in London, notwithstanding we are a nation of liberty, more public and private prisons, and houses of confinement, than in any city in Europe, perhaps as many as in all the capital cities of Europe put together."[14] Long-established institutions such as Bethlem were now considerably enlarged,[15] and were supplemented by a large number of new institutions, many of them charitable foundations. Hospitals provide one of the most notable examples of the growing tendency to isolate the indigent from the rest of society. In this period they were used almost exclusively by the poor. Between 1719 and 1751, seven hospitals were added to the ancient foundations of St. Bartholemew's, St. Thomas's, and Bethlem in London alone. Others were founded in major provincial cities such as Liverpool, Manchester, and Leicester. Similarly, workhouses, first established on an experimental basis in a few towns in the 1630s, spread rapidly, following the more successful example of the Bristol workhouse founded in 1696. In England "by the middle of the eighteenth century the urban community of market town size or above, which had no workhouse, was a rarity . . .," and "from about 1760 onwards" these institutions were increasingly housed in buildings constructed with their specific purposes in mind.[16]

Colonial America lacked an urban center even approximating London's size and importance. Indeed, "from an eighteenth century standpoint, American towns were more comparable to English provincial cities than to London."[17] Like their English equivalents, though, Philadelphia, New York, and Boston, and increasingly the smaller towns as well, began to adopt the institutional approach. The first almshouse was built in Boston in 1662, and was followed by others combining the features of a poorhouse, workhouse, and house of correction in Philadelphia (1731), New Orleans (1734), and New York (1736). The first American hospital was founded in Philadelphia in 1751, followed by a second in New York in 1771. Towards the end of the century, the Walnut Street jail in Philadelphia was extensively rebuilt and reorganized, and as the use of capital and other sanguinary forms of punishment declined, it served as the model for a whole series of similar structures from Maryland to Massachusetts.

Thus, by the late eighteenth century, both England and America had begun to abandon the old informal methods for coping with the deviant. And even though it remained the case that only a minority of this class were to be found in institutions at the turn of the century, nevertheless the capital and intellectual investment in institutional responses—workhouses, houses of correction, jails, hospitals, and asylums—was already by no means negligible, albeit on a scale which was soon to be dwarfed as the central government in England and the states in the new American Republic insisted on allocating ever increasing funds to sustain and expand such places.

By modern standards, most eighteenth century institutions possessed a peculiarly mixed character. Workhouses, for example, despite their name and the intentions of their founders, became dumping grounds for the decrepit and dependent of all descriptions.[18] Prisons mixed young and old, men and women, debtors and felons, furious maniacs and condemned murderers, in a single heterogeneous mass. A number of more specialized institutions did exist by now—such as the charity asylums and private madhouses coping with an increasing proportion of English lunatics.[19] But in general, the distinctions between the various categories making up the disreputable classes continued to be very imprecise.[20]

In the initial phases of the transition towards an institutionally based control system, the English government did no more than provide the Justices of the Peace, the key figures in the local administrative structure, with permissive powers to build asylums, prisons, and workhouses.[21] But when the latter proved reluctant to implement these acts, the central authorities, after a considerable delay, built demonstration penitentiaries of their own,[22] and moved to compel the construction of prisons, asylums, and workhouses,[23] all of which then became subject to ever tighter central supervision and direction. By the 1820s and 1830s many Americans were exhibiting a similar enthusiasm for the institution as the solution to the problem of deviancy; and in the 1840s and 1850s the states undertook a massive building program, setting up a host of

penitentiaries, asylums, workhouses, orphan asylums, juvenile reformatories, and the like.[24]

To a far greater degree than their eighteenth century precursors,
these products of assorted nineteenth century "reform" movements
resembled instruments for segregative control as we know them today.
Indeed, the direct line of inheritance to our own present-day total
institutions extends even to the nineteenth century buildings many of
them continue to use. The greatly increased emphasis on classification,
both within and between institutions, amounted to a qualitative change
vis-à-vis eighteenth century institutions. Careful efforts were made to
distinguish the criminal and the crazy, children, the sick, and the
deserving and the undeserving poor. Internal classificatory schemes
became a vital feature of the "well-ordered asylum" of the period.
And along with the specialization of the social control apparatus came
its professionalization: Gaolers were transformed into prison wardens;
madhouse keepers into alienists or psychiatrists; the local militia were
replaced by a bureaucratically organized police force; the parish vestry-
men by paid Poor Law Guardians.

One common explanation of these changes attributes them in a
relatively direct and uncomplicated fashion to the rise of an urban
industrial society. As Mechanic puts it, "Industrial and technological
change . . . , coupled with increasing urbanization brought decreasing
tolerance for bizarre and disruptive behavior and less ability to contain
deviant behavior within the existing social structure."[25] The increased
geographical mobility of the population and the anonymity of existence
in the urban slums were combined with the destruction of the old
paternal relationships that went with a stable hierarchically organized
rural society. Furthermore, as they huddled together in the grossly over-
crowded conditions which accompanied the explosive, unplanned growth
of urban and industrial centers, the situation of the poor and dependent
classes became simultaneously more visible and more desperate. There
emerged the new phenomenon of urban poverty "among concentrated
masses of wage earners without natural protectors to turn to in
distress."[26]

All of this seems to lend credence to the view that the structural preconditions for the effective operation of a system of amateur parochial
relief were fast disappearing. Yet, although they were no longer concerned with individuals but with an amorphous mass, and convinced
that many of the poor were "undeserving," the new class of entrepreneurs
could not wholly evade making some provision for them, if only because
of the revolutionary threat they posed to the social order. The asylum,
and analogous institutions such as the workhouse, together with the

replacement of amateur by professional administration, allegedly constituted their response to this situation.

A major problem with this line of argument is that even in England the process of urbanization was simply not so far advanced as this would suggest when pressures developed to differentiate and institutionalize the deviant population. In the early stages of the Industrial Revolution, "cotton was the pacemaker of industrial change, and the basis of the first regions which could not have existed but for industrialization, and which expressed a new form of society, industrial capitalism.[27] Although technical innovations introduced into the manufacturing process in the latter half of the eighteenth century and the application of steam power soon resulted in factory production, the technology of cotton production remained comparatively simple; and much of the industry remained decentralized and scattered in a variety of local factories, as likely to be located in "industrial villages as concentrated in large urban centers."[28] Consequently, although large towns absorbed an increasing proportion of the English population, city dwellers remained a distinct minority during the first decades of the nineteenth century, when pressures to establish asylums, prisons, and workhouses on a compulsory basis were at their strongest.

London, which already had a population of 840,000 in 1801, grew to contain more than a million people by 1811, but it remained unique and exceptional. In 1801, there were only six other cities with a population of more than 50,000; by 1811, there were eight; by 1821 there were twelve, including three which had passed the 100,000 mark.[29] As Table 2-1 shows, at the turn of the century, only 17% of the population lived in towns of 20,000 and more. It was 1851 before a third of the population did so, and almost the end of the century before towns of this size and above finally contained an absolute majority of the English population.

TABLE 2-1
**Percentage of the Population of England and Wales
Living in Cities of 20,000 and More People**

1801	1811	1821	1831	1841	1851	1861	1871
16.94	18.11	20.82	25.05	28.90	35.00	38.21	42.00
			1881	1891			
			48.00	53.58			

SOURCE: Adapted from Adna F. Weber. *The Growth of Cities in the Nineteenth Century: A Study in Statistics.* New York: Columbia University Studies in History, Economics and Public Law No. 11, 1899, p. 47.

If all this casts doubt on the notion that it was urban poverty as such which forced the adoption of an institutional, bureaucratic response to the deviant, the difficulties one encounters with this line of reasoning are still more acute when it is applied to the American experience. Although there were wide regional variations in the level of economic development and the degree of urbanization, even the most highly "urbanized" regions, New England and the Mid-Atlantic states, remained overwhelmingly rural when the movement to institutionalize deviants began to take hold. In 1790, 3.7 million out of the 3.9 million people in the United States were rural dwellers, and the two largest cities contained fewer than 50,000 people.[30] After the turn of the century, growth was rapid, particularly in the North East, reflecting the fact that "Americans underwent a revolution in the organization of their economic lives between 1815 or 1820 and 1860. . . ."[31] While "the greatest developments in American manufacturing were to come in the decades immediately after the Civil War, yet the rate of growth was astonishingly swift before 1860. . . ."[32] By that date, more than a third of the population of New England and the Mid-Atlantic states consisted of urban dwellers: New York's population exceeded a million, and Philadelphia's was almost 600,000.[33] But this means that urban growth occurred simultaneously with, or even slightly later than, the adoption of an institutional approach to the handling of deviance; so that it is only by exaggerating the degree and accelerating the timing of the former development that one can use it to explain the latter.[34]

Instead, I would contend that many of the transformations underlying the move towards institutionalization can be more plausibly tied to the growth of the capitalist market system and to its impact on economic and social relationships.[35] In the first place, prior to the emergence of a capitalist system, economic relationships did not manifest themselves as purely market relationships — economic domination or subordination was overlaid and fused with personal ties between individuals. But the market destroyed the traditional ties between rich and poor and the reciprocal notions of paternalism, deference, and dependence which characterized the old order, producing profound shifts in the relationships between superordinate and subordinate classes, and of upper class preceptions of their responsibilities towards the less fortunate.

Indeed, one of the earliest casualties of the developing capitalist system was the old sense of social obligation towards the poor.[36] In Mantoux's words, in a capitalist social order, "[the employer] owed his employees wages, and once these were paid, the men had no further claim on him."[37] In rural as in urban areas this process proceeded apace, nowhere more rapidly than in the United States, where notions of obligations towards the poor had always been more fragile than in England. (America, after all, lacked a feudal aristocratic class, which encouraged a swifter and more complete supremacy of the bourgeois and commercial classes.)[38]

At the same time, the "proletarianization" of labor and the detachment of the lower orders from the means of providing at worst for the bare minimum of their own subsistence, together with the tendency of the primitive capitalist economy to oscillate unpredictably between conditions of boom and slump, greatly increased the strains on a family based system of relief.[39] There is, for all its simplification and rhetorical flourishes, a profound and bitter truth to Marx's comment that the advent of a full-blown market system "has pitilessly torn asunder the motley feudal ties that bound man to his 'natural superiors,' and has left no other nexus between man and man than naked self interest, than callous cash payment. . . . In one word, for exploitation veiled by religious and political illusions, it has substituted naked, shameless, direct, brutal exploitation."[40] And while the impact of urbanization and (in England) industrialization was at this stage geographically limited in scope, by the latter part of the eighteenth century almost all regions of England had been drawn into a single national market economy;[41] and the same period in the United States saw a continuing steady "movement of people out of self-sufficiency into the market economy."[42] The impact of the universal market of capitalism was felt everywhere, forcing "the transformation of the relations between the rural rich and the rural poor, the farmers and their labour force, into a purely market relationship between employer and proletarian."[43]

These changes in structures, perceptions, and outlook which marked the transition from the old paternalistic order to a capitalist social system provided a direct source of bourgeois dissatisfaction with the traditional, noninstitutional response to the indigent. More indirectly, the decay of the traditional social structure associated with the transition towards this new type of economy was reflected in a sizable expansion of the proportion of the population in temporary or permanent receipt of poor relief;[44] an expansion that took place at precisely that point in time when the growing power of the bourgeoisie was reducing the inclination to tolerate such a state of affairs to its lowest ebb. In this situation, the latter readily convinced themselves that laxly administered systems of household relief promoted poverty rather than relieved it.[45] Increasingly, therefore, they were attracted towards an institutionally based response to the indigent which (in theory at least) would permit close oversight of who received relief, and, by establishing a regime sufficiently harsh to deter all but the truly deserving from applying, would render the whole system efficient and economical.[46]

Moreover, just as the vagrancy laws of the sixteenth century had begun to produce "the discipline necessary for the wage labor system,"[47] so too the conditions in the new institutions mimicked the discipline necessary for the factory system. The quasi-military authority structure of the total institution seemed ideally suited to be the means of establishing "proper" work habits among these marginal elements of the workforce who were apparently most resistant to the monotony, routine, and regularity of industrialized labor. As William Temple put it, "by these means, we hope that the rising generation will be so habituated to constant employment that it would at length prove agreeable and entertaining to them."[48] Bentham's Panopticon, with which both English and American "reformers" exhibited a considerable fascination, was, in his own words, "a mill to grind rogues honest and idle men industrious . . .,"[49] an engine of reformation which would employ "convicts instead of steam, and thus combine philanthropy with business.[50] And undoubtedly, one of the attractions of places like asylums and prisons was the promise they held out of instilling the virtues of bourgeois rationality into those segments of the population least amenable to them.

There were, of course, other factors lying behind the move towards an institutionally focused, centrally regulated system of social control. For the moment, however, I intend to leave further analysis of what these were on one side. Instead, I want to turn to the question of how and why the previously amorphous class of deviant behaviors became differentiated into what were now seen as distinct species of pathology, each requiring specialized treatment in an institution of its own.

The establishment of a market economy, and, more particularly, the emergence of a market in labor, provided the initial incentive to distinguish far more carefully than heretofore between different categories of deviance. If nothing else, under these conditions stress had to be laid for the first time on the importance of distinguishing the able-bodied from the non-able-bodied poor. One of the most basic prerequisites of a capitalist system, as both Marx and Weber have emphasized, was the existence of a large mass of wage laborers who were not simply "free" to dispose of their labor power on the open market, but who were actually forced to do so. In Marx's words: "Capital presupposes wage labour and wage labour capital. One is the necessary condition of the other. . . ."[51] But to provide aid to the able-bodied threatened to undermine, in a radical fashion, the whole notion of a labor market.

Parochial provision of relief to the able-bodied interfered with labor mobility.[52] In England, where labor was plentiful, it encouraged the retention of a "vast inert mass of redundant labor," a stagnant pool of underemployed laboring men in rural areas where the demand for labor was subject to wide seasonal fluctuations.[53] It distorted the operations of the labor market and, thereby, of all other markets, most especially on account of its tendency, via the vagaries of local administration, "to create cost differentials as between the various parts of the country."[54] Finally, by its removal of the threat of individual starvation, such relief had a pernicious effect on labor discipline and productivity,[55] an outcome accentuated by the fact that the "early laborer . . . abhorred the factory, where he felt degraded and tortured. . . ."[56]

Instead, it was felt, want ought to be the stimulus to the capable, who must therefore be distinguished from the helpless. Such a distinction is deceptively simple; but in a wider perspective, this development can be seen as a crucial phase in the growing rationalization of the Western social order and the transformation of prior *extensive* structures of domination into the ever more intensive forms characteristic of the modern world. It forms part, that is, of the changeover from an approach which viewed the domestic population as a largely unchangeable given from which an effort was made to squeeze as large a surplus as possible, to a perception of it as modifiable and manipulable human material whose yield could be steadily enlarged through careful management and through improvements in use and organization designed to qualitatively transform its value as an economic resource. As Moffett has shown, during this process "the domestic population came increasingly to be regarded as an industrial labor force — not simply a tax reservoir as formerly — and state policies came increasingly to be oriented to forcing the entire working population into renumerative employment."[57] The significance of the distinction between the able-bodied and the non-able-bodied poor thus increases *pari passu* with the rise of the wage labor system.

The beginnings of such a separation are evident even in the early phases of English capitalism. The great Elizabethan Poor Law of 1601, for example, classified the poor into the aged and impotent, children, and the able but unemployed,[58] and a number of historians have been tempted to see in this and in the Statute of Artificers (1563) a primitive labor code of the period, dealing respectively with what we would call the unemployed and unemployable, and the employed. But, as Polanyi suggests, in large measure "the neat distinction between the employed, unemployed and unemployable is, of course, anachronistic since it implies the existence of a modern wage system which was absent [at this period]."[59] Until much later, the boundaries between these categories remained much more fluid and ill-defined than the modern reader is apt to realize. Moreover, although it is plain that the Tudors and Stuarts had no scruples about invoking harsh legal penalties in an effort to compel the poor to work,[60] these measures were undertaken at least as much "for the sake of political security" as for more directly economic motives.[61]

Gradually, however, economic considerations became more and more dominant. As they did so, it became increasingly evident that "no treatment of this matter was adequate which failed to distinguish between the able-bodied on the one hand, the aged, infirm, and children on the other."[62] The former were to be compelled to work, at first through the direct legal compulsion inherited from an earlier period. More and more, however, the upper classes came to despair of the notion "that they may be compelled to work [by statute] according to their abilities,"[63] and to be attracted towards an alternative method according to which, in the picturesque language of John Bellers, "The Sluggard shall be cloathed in Raggs. He that will not work shall not eat."[64] The superiority of this approach was put most bluntly by Joseph Townsend:

> Hunger will tame the fiercest animals, it will teach decency and civility, obedience and subjection to the most perverse. In general, it is only hunger which can spur and goad [the poor] on to labour; yet our laws have said they shall never hunger. The laws, it must be confessed, have likewise said, they shall be compelled to work. But then legal constraint is attended with much trouble, violence, and noise: creates ill-will, and can never be productive of good and acceptable service: whereas hunger is not only peaceable, silent, unremitting pressure, but, as the most natural motive to industry and labour, it calls forth the most violent exertions.[65]

Thus, the functional requirements of a market system promoted a relatively simple, if crucial, distinction between two broad classes of the indigent. Workhouses and the like were to be an important *practical* means of making this vital theoretical separation, and thereby of making the whole system efficient and economical. However, although work-houses were initially intended to be just that, institutions to remove the able-bodied poor from the community in order to teach them the whole-some discipline of labor,[66] they swiftly found themselves depositories for the decaying, the decrepit, and the unemployable. And an unintended consequence of this concentration of deviants in an institutional environment was that it produced an exacerbation of the problems of handling at least some of them.[67] More specifically, it rendered prob-lematic the whole question of what was to be done with those who could not or would not abide by the rules of the house—such groups as criminals, orphans, and the mad.[68] The adoption of an institutional response, therefore, greatly increased the pressures to elaborate the distinctions amongst and between the deviant and the dependent.[69]

Such a differentiation of deviance provided one of the essential social preconditions for the establishment of a number of newly organized professions and semiprofessions claiming to possess specific expertise in the management of each type of deviance. The state-supported institu-tions which emerged to cope with the different varieties of deviant behavior permitted, or perhaps it might be more accurate to say, formed the breeding ground for this emerging "professionalism." On the one hand, they provided the incentive, in the form of a guaranteed market for the experts' services; and on the other they provided a context within which, isolated from the community at large, the protoprofessions could develop at the very least empirically based craft skills in the management of particular forms of deviance.[70] These skills could then be used as the basis for claims to monopolize particular lines of "dirty work," and, in the case of the more successful occupations, as the foundation for assertions of professional autonomy,[71] freedom from outside "lay" interference.

None of the "dirty workers" were as successful as psychiatrists in this regard, in part because the latter firmly cemented their ties to the "respectable" profession of medicine and thus were able to minimize the stigma of close association with the poor and powerless. But the common pattern of the growth of specialized "helping claims" and the organiza-tion and consolidation of those who allegedly possessed expert knowledge is clear.[72] Other factors contributed to the tendency to professionalize social control in this period. Bureaucratically organized specialists were generally more efficient at controlling the morally disreputable. More than that, however, they also formed a buffer between the dominant classes and those the latter sought to control, deflecting antagonisms, and obscuring the links between social control and class domination. And their availability meant that the propertied classes no longer had to discharge personally the sordid task of supervising the dangerous classes, as had remained the case throughout the eighteenth century.[73]

The emerging professions made much of their ability, not simply to manage deviants, but to rehabilitate them: Madmen were to be cured, criminals reformed, delinquent children saved.[74] The functions of such ideologies for the "experts" need no elaboration. But the receptivity of the English and American elites to such ideas illustrates another, and more subtle, connection between changes in the nature of the social control apparatus and changes in the wider social structure. On the most general level, this receptivity reflected the growing secular rational- ization of Western society at this time; a development which, following Weber, I would argue took place under the dominant, though not the sole, impetus of the development of a capitalist market system. More specifically, it reflected the penetration of this realm of social existence by the values of science, the idea that "there are no mysterious incalcul- able forces that come into play, but rather that one can, in principle, master all things by calculation."[75] Linked to this change in perspective was a fundamental shift in the underlying perceptions of various forms of deviance: the growth of a secular emphasis on crime rather than a religious one on sin; a transformation of the paradigm of insanity away from an emphasis on its demonological, nonhuman, animalistic qualities towards a naturalistic position which viewed the madman as exhibiting a defective *human* mechanism, and which therefore saw this condition as at least potentially remediable. More speculatively, in view of the elective affinity of a market system and the restorative ideal (the former emphasizing the notion of a free, rational, self-determining individual; the latter the repair of a damaged human mechanism so that it once more fulfilled these preconditions for competing in the market), one is tempted to suggest that the greatly increased salience of the notion of rehabilitation reflected an indirect impact of the market on social con- sciousness.[76]

How the various specialists in the control of deviance were able to exploit this favorable cultural environment to secure for themselves recognition as "experts" need not concern us here.[77] What *does* matter for our present concerns is one important consequence of the fact *that* they were able to do so. That is, the way the emergence of assorted "experts" in the control of various forms of deviance, and the elaborate ideological accounts of their work these groups produced, helped to complete and lend an aura of objectivity to the process of rigidification of the various subcategories of deviance.[78]

In a sense, one had here a self-reinforcing system. For the key element in most of the new occupations' claims to expertise lay in their development of new administrative techniques, more efficient means of managing large numbers of people incarcerated for extended periods of time. The essence of the new approach developed by these running asylums, prisons, workhouses, and even orphan asylums, lay in its emphasis on order, rationality, and self-control; and much of its appeal to the bourgeoisie derived from the high value it placed on work as a means to these ends. All of this could only be accomplished in an institutional setting. Just as the separation of deviants into such specialized institutions helped to create the conditions for the emergence of occupational groups laying claim to expertise in their management and rehabilitation, so, too, the nature and content of the restorative ideal which the latter fostered reinforced the commitment to the institutional approach. Thereafter, the existence of both the institutions and their associated bureaucratic administrators testified to the "necessity" and "naturalness" of distinguishing among types of deviants in particular ways.

A vital feature of this radically new social control apparatus was the degree to which its operations became subject to central control and direction. As both the Weberian and the Marxian analyses have stressed, precapitalist social formations are overwhelmingly localized in their social organization. And as we have seen, the mechanisms for coping with deviance in pre-nineteenth century England and America placed a corresponding reliance on an essentially communal and family based system of social control. The assumption of direct state responsibility thus marked a sharp departure from these traditional emphases.

Although the administrative rationalization and centralization which are crucial elements of this transformation are not only or wholly the consequence of economic rationalization, yet it seems inescapable that the advance of the capitalist economic order and the growth of the central authority of the state are twin processes intimately connected with each other. "On the one hand, were it not for the expansion of commerce and the rise of capitalist agriculture, there would scarcely have been the economic base to finance the expanded bureaucratic state structures. But on the other hand, the state structures were themselves a major economic underpinning of the new capitalist system (not to speak of being its political guarantee)."[79] In a very literal sense, institutional control mechanisms were impracticable earlier, because of the absence both of the necessary administrative techniques and also of the surplus required to establish and maintain them.

The creation of more efficient administrative structures, which was both precondition and consequence of the growth of the state and of large-scale capitalist enterprise, possessed a dual importance. On the one hand, it allowed for the first time the development of a tolerably adequate administrative apparatus to mediate between central and local authorities, and thus to extend central control down to the local level. On the other, it provided the basis for the development of techniques for the efficient handling of large numbers of people confined for months or years on end, lacking which basis, institutional methods of social control could scarcely have achieved the importance that they did. Financially speaking, state construction and operation of institutions for the deviant and dependent was very costly,[80] requiring the development of large stable tax revenues and/or the state's ability to borrow on a substantial scale. These, in turn, were intimately tied to the expansion of the monetary sector of the economy and the growth of the sophisticated credit mechanisms characteristic of capitalist economic organization.[81]

As part of the drive to solidify their own political control, the central authorities sought to extend a single moral order throughout the state, seeking thereby to homogenize the domestic population and eliminate or greatly reduce the significance of purely local allegiances. In this respect, the state simply accentuated the tendency of the developing national and international markets to produce a diminution, if not a destruction, of the traditional influence of local groups (especially kinship units) which formerly played a large role in the regulation of social life.[82] But there was a paradox here. For capitalism, which did so much to undermine and destroy traditional social restraints, was at the same time far more sensitive than its predecessors to social disorder.[83] The growth of more and more sophisticated markets was thus inextricably linked to demands for new and more efficient means of controlling potential sources of disorder. Most particularly, the growth of a single national market and the rise of allegiance to the central political authority to a position of overriding importance undermined the rationale of a locally based response to deviance, based as that was on the idea of settlement and the warning out of strangers. As local communities came to be defined and to define themselves as part of a single overarching economic and political system, it made less and less sense for one town to dispose of its problems by passing them on to the next. There was a need for some substitute mode of exclusion. All of these factors contributed to "the monopolization of all 'legitimate' coercive power by one universalist coercive institution . . . ,"[84] and to the development of a state-sponsored system of segregative control.[85]

To summarize briefly, what was crucial about the late eighteenth and the first half of the nineteenth century was the coincidence in this period of both the need and the ability to organize the necessary administrative structures and to raise the substantial sums required to establish an institutionally based control system. Ultimately, one must view the move toward this type of social control apparatus as a reflection of the underlying transformations of the social structure I have analyzed here. The initial optimism about rehabilitation proved unfounded. And yet, if prisons, asylums, and "reformatories," and the activities of those running them, did not transform their inmates into upright citizens, they did at least get rid of troublesome people for the rest of us. For all the criticisms which might be leveled at them, they remained a convenient way to get rid of inconvenient people. The community readily got used to disposing of the dangerous and derelict in institutions where, as one nineteenth century observer put it, "they are for the most part harmless because they are kept out of harm's way."[86] Finally, the treatment of those so confined served as an omnipresent example, a reminder of the awful consequences of inability or refusal to conform.[87] Until quite recently, and with only comparatively minor modifications and additions,[88] the social control of the deviant in both England and America continued to rest firmly on these nineteenth century foundations.

1. Rusche and Kirchheimer 1968; Foucault 1965.

2. See Furniss 1965; Heckscher 1955 Vol. II: esp. 145–172.

3. See Rusche and Kirchheimer 1968: 43ff.

4. Clay 1909: 13. One should remember that the medieval hospital was "an ecclesiastical, not a medical, institution . . . for care rather than for cure."

5. Pugh 1968: 387.

6. Pugh 1968: 5.

7. The importance of the prison as a revenue producer rather than a form of punishment is indicated by the case with which one could mitigate the pains of confinement or even terminate it altogether (assuming adequate financial resources), openly by the payment of compositions or "ransomes" and covertly by bribes. See Pugh 1968: 387.

8. On the failure of efforts to rationalize the distribution of goals, see Pugh 1968: 343-344. Through the eighteenth century, "private gaols still existed in the hands of bishops and other ecclesiastical potentates, of manorial lords and other territorial dignitaries, who clung to them as income-yielding properties." Webb and Webb 1922: 3.

9. Jordan 1959: 256.

10. Mencher 1967: 39.

11. Plymouth Colony Records, 1642, cited in Kelso 1922: 92.

12. Kelso 1922: 93.

13. Barnes n.d.: 44. For example, the county jail at Philadelphia in 1685 occupied one half of a rented farmhouse, while the family who owned the building continued to live in the other half (Barnes 1927:70).

14. Defoe 1724-1725: 321.

15. Bethlem or Bedlam was a small medieval hospital founded in the thirteenth century which came to specialize in the treatment of lunatics. Its inmate population fluctuated between 25 and 45 in the seventeenth century (Jordan 1960: 189-190); it now expanded to take almost three hundred (Defoe 1724-1726: 329-330).

16. Oxley 1974: 84. On eighteenth century hospitals, see George 1965: 61; also Abel-Smith 1964.

17. Shryock 1960: 46.

18. Oxley 1974: 91ff.; Grob 1966: 5-6.

19. Cf. Scull 1974: Ch. 2; Parry-Jones 1972.

20. As late as 1812, for example, Edward Wakefield, one of the leading English lunacy reformers, could seriously propose the erection of a network of asylums designed to contain within a single structure "lunatics, and idiots . . . cripples, blind persons, and those who may be afflicted with disgusting diseases . . ." See Wakefield 1812.

21. For workhouses, the key acts were 9 George I c. 7: 1723 (which gave individual parishes the right to erect workhouses); and 22 George III c. 83, Gilbert's Act of 1782, which allowed parishes to combine for this purpose. For prisons, the major statute was George III c. 46, 1791; and for asylums, Wynn's Act, 48 George III c. 96, 1808.

22. Milbank Prison, begun in 1812 and completed in 1821; and Pentonville, opened in 1842.

23. Workhouses by the Poor Law Amendment Act of 1834 (4 and 5 William IV c. 76); prisons by an 1835 Act (3 and 6 William IV c. 38): and asylums by an 1845 Act (8 and 9 Victoria c. 126).

24. In David Rothman's words, the enthusiasm for the institution was such that "one can properly label the Jacksonian years 'the age of the asylum.' " Rothman 1971: xiv.

25. Mechanic 1969: 54.

26. Perkin 1969: 162.

27. Hobsbawm 1968: 56.

28. Hobsbawm 1968: 58-65.

29. Halevy 1949: 257.

30. North 1961: 17.

31. Meyers 1957: 87.

32. P. Jones 1956: 37.

33. North 1961: 206.

34. There is also of course, the awkward problem that at a comparatively early date rural areas in both England and America exhibited a marked enthusiasm for the asylum solution. See Scull 1974: Chs. 3 and 4; Rothman 1971.

35. The relationships I am about to outline here are somewhat obscured in the United States by the process of cultural diffusion. Frontier areas in nineteenth century America

acquired asylums and prisons within a few years (two or three decades at most) of their appearance on the Eastern seaboard. Perhaps the most influential recent treatment of the rise of institutional processing of deviance in America has seen this as undermining any attempt to explain this change is structural terms (see Rothman 1971: xvi–xvii). But this is surely a mistake. Western immigrants in this period exhibited a thoroughgoing intellectual and social dependence on the most advanced Eastern states. In Meyers' words: "Once the current [of settlement] has set toward a given spot for a time, vestiges of a barbarous life rapidly disappear. Emigrants bring with them the wants, habits, and institutions of an advanced society" (Meyers 1957: 46). This desire for the trappings of "civilization" naturally included such relatively novel items as asylums and penitentiaries (see W. D. Lewis 1965: 55ff., 72ff.).

36. See Townsend 1786; Hobsbawm 1968: 88.

37. Mantoux 1928: 428.

38. As well as the more obvious historical reasons for this, the deficiency reflected the structural position of the American colonies in the emerging capitalist world economy of the seventeenth and eighteenth centuries: "The American colonist represented the external or foreign aspects of mercantilism, and his function was the creation of profits for the mother country rather than the establishment of a cohesive internal social structure."
Less attached to the inherited system of responsibility for the lower orders which the English bourgeoisie were in the process of trying to dislodge, Americans could adopt enclosure and other principles of a commercialized agriculture without the long struggle the former were forced to engage in. From an early date, the American landed class were land *merchants* rather than *landlords*, "primarily concerned with the profits to be made from speculation, tenancies, and production." Mencher 1967: 131–132; see also Hacker 1940: 94–95.

39. See Polanyi 1944: 92ff.; Hobsbawm 1968: Chs. 3 and 4. In England, as Furniss (1965: 209) emphasizes, "the economic conditions of the laborer were altered radically during the course of the eighteenth century and . . . the change had the effect of placing him more and more at the mercy of market conditions." For a discussion of the sources of this proletarianization of the lower orders, stressing the decline of nonwage sources of subsistence (common lands, a small plot of one's own, etc.) and the growing vulnerability of the laborer's position, see Furniss 1965: esp. 211–221. On widening class differences in late eighteenth century America, and the emergence of a working population living on the edge of subsistence and deeply vulnerable to the shifting fortunes of the market economy, see Mencher 1967: 133–137. Here, of course, such problems were greatly accentuated by large-scale immigration, such as the great influx of Irishmen after 1830. See Pessen 1969: 60–61; Handlin 1968: 45.

40. Marx and Engels 1968: 37–38.

41. Hobsbawm 1968: 27–28. As Keith Thomas (1971:796) points out, "Agriculture, after all, was the first sector of the British economy to become thoroughly capitalized and developed in a 'rational' manner." See also, in this regard, Mantoux 1928: 74: "The modern factory system is not responsible for the creation of the proletariat, any more than for the capitalist organization of production. It only accelerated and completed a process long since begun."

42. North 1961: 54.

43. Hobsbawm and Rude 1969: Ch. 2. See also Mencher 1967: 132: "From the start American society conformed to the social ideal. . . . No people had so literally absorbed the notion of the social contract as the early Americans."

44. By 1803, "over a million people, one in nine of the [English] population, were said to be in receipt of poor relief, casual or permanent." Perkin 1969: 22. In the United

States, as many as 500,000 were unemployed at the height of the depression following the Napoleonic War, and a large number of the substantial economic downturn of 1829. Mencher 1967: 137.

45. The English found ample ideological justification for this conclusion in the work of Malthus and others. See Malthus 1798: esp. Ch. V; MacFarlan 1782: 34–36; Temple 1770: 258; Mantoux 1928: 70; Rimlinger 1966: 562–563. By and large, American ideas and practices "closely resembled the dominant British trends . . .," and "assistance policy showed striking parallels with the formula of the English Poor Law Commission . . .;" (Mencher 1967: 131) though Malthusian ideas, less obviously applicable in a society where land and resources were abundant, were less popular here.

46. As Furniss (1965: 107) points out, "this is the one strong note which sounds through the writings of the eighteenth century reformers, the demand for rigorous life conditions to discipline the laborer and purge his character of the evil habits of 'luxury' and 'sloth'. . . ." William Temple (1770: 151–269), for example, placed much emphasis on a proposal for a "workhouse to perform the double service of administering punishment for idleness and providing training in habits of thrift and industry." For other advocates of the workhouse as part of a general scheme to discipline the poor, cf. Alcock 1752; Bailey 1758; Massie 1758; Potter 1775; cf. also Poor Law Report 1834. In America, states like New York, Massachusetts, New Hampshire, and Pennsylvania produced a series of state reports during the 1820s on the problem of the poor which echoed those themes.

47. Marx 1967 Vol. 1: 737; also Chambliss 1964.

48. Temple 1770: 266ff.

49. Bentham to Brissot in Bentham 1843 Vol. X: 226. For British examples of this fascination, see Stark 1810; Wakefield 1812. In America, a number of prisons, the most famous being the Western Pennsylvania Penitentiary at Pittsburg, were built on a modified version of the Panopticon plan: see McKelvey 1936: 14.

50. Stephen 1900 Vol. 1: 203. Rusche and Kirchheimer (1968) rightly emphasize the importance of the desire to exploit inmates' labor as a factor in the rise of imprisonment as a dominant mode of punishment. In the early stages of industrialization, prisons could break even or perhaps show a profit via the exploitation of convict labor (see W. D. Lewis 1965; Webb and Webb 1922: 82–83), a possibility which subsequently disappeared as production requirements became more rigorous, "rendering it every day increasingly difficult to make any actual profit out of the demoralized and indiscriminately collected gaol inmates . . ." (Webb and Webb 1922: 88–89). The problem was compounded by the fact that incentives were needed to get skilled labor performed properly; but this tended to make the living conditions of some prisoners better than the lot of many on the outside; and capitalists and free labor increasingly complained of unfair competition (see W. D. Lewis 1965; Webb and Webb 1922: 88).

51. Marx 1967 Vol. 1: 578; also 714–716, and 716–733. For Weber's view, see 1961: 172–173; and 1930: 22. See also Polanyi 1944: 77; Mantoux 1928: 445.

52. MacFarlan 1782: 176ff.; Smith 1937: 135–140.

53. Redford, cited in Polanyi 1944: 301. See also Polanyi 1944: 77–102; Webb and Webb 1927; Hobsbawm 1968: 99–100.

54. Polanyi 1944: 301. MacFarlan (1782: 178) complained that relief to the able-bodied "renders the price of labour in England very unequal, in some places so low as to afford little encouragement to industry; in others so exorbitantly high as to become ruinous to manufactures. . . ." This complaint was echoed by the Poor Law Commission Report (1834: 43): "A manufacturer in Macclesfield could be ruined in consequence of the defective administration of the Poor Laws in Essex." A further problem, according to

Mantoux (1928: 450), was that "manufacturers where normal wages were paid proved unable to compete with establishments which employed assisted paupers."

55. MacFarlan 1782: 169ff.

56. Polanyi 1944: 164–165. On working class hatred of the factory system and the reluctance of workers to enter the factory, see Mantoux 1928: esp. 419ff.; Thompson 1963.

57. Moffett 1971: 187 et passim.

58. Marshall 1926: 23. For parallel developments in Western Europe, cf. Mencher 1967: 24ff. For an early example of such differentiation in the American colonies, see Stokes 1903: 73–74.

59. Polanyi 1944: 86. Rusche and Kirchheimer comment: "In theory these systems represented a marked advance . . ., but in practice they rarely achieved success" (1968: 38–39). On the theoretical distinction's lack of application in practice, see Rusche and Kirchheimer 1968: 63ff. (for England and Western Europe) and Rothman 1971: Ch. 1 (for America).

60. See Dobb 1963: 233ff.

61. Marshall 1926: 17.

62. Polanyi 1944: 94.

63. MacFarlan 1782: 105.

64. Bellers 1696. Similar ideas were current in the United States. For example, the Yates Report of 1824 in New York State recommended a withdrawal of all public support from able-bodied paupers aged between 18 and 50, a more drastic policy than that of the English Poor Law Commission. Mencher 1967: 148.

65. Townsend 1786. Cf. also Malthus 1826 II: 339: "When nature will govern and punish for us, it is a very miserable ambition to wish to snatch the rod from her hands and draw upon ourselves the odium of executioner."

66. One may note here that there existed a systematic contradiction between the desire to employ the workhouse as a means of deterring the lazy (and thus as a reinforcement for the whiplash of hunger), and the efforts to use it to resocialize or train an industrial workforce. For the system of positive and negative sanctions which the latter goal required as incentives to manipulate behavior ran directly counter to the stress of the former on maintaining conditions of less eligibility. As the working class in general became more inured to conditions of work in a factory system, so the problem of obtaining a disciplined workforce steadily declined in significance. In parallel fashion, the role of the workhouse as a resocializing institution received less emphasis, while its importance as a deterrent to the able-bodied and a depository for the decrepit increased.

67. MacFarlan 1782: 97ff.; Franklin 1754: 3; Grob 1966: 20; Boston Prison Discipline Society Report Vol. 2, 1827: 19.

68. The kinds of problems which were created can be imagined by considering the case of the New York City almshouse. In 1795, there were 622 inmates (though its nominal capacity was less than half that number), including, besides orphans, work-shy vagrants, and so forth, "14 blind entirely, 8 or 10 nearly so, 28 afflicted with lunacy, insanity, idiotism," as well as many impotent old people "subject to Rheumatism, Ulcers, and Palsies and to Fits which impair their Reason and elude all the force of Medicine" (City Council Minutes, cited in Pomerantz 1938: 332). In Massachusetts, the town almshouse and jail mixed together the poor, orphans, vagrants, drunkards, idiots, and maniacs, except that "it was common to provide a separate room for the furiously mad, as their ravings made life intolerable for the rest" (Kelso 1922: 113).

69. For primitive mid-eighteenth century examples of this process, see Marshall 1926: 49ff. On the necessity of such a classification, see MacFarlan 1782: 2-3. The increasing numbers of the poor

> . . . are thought to arise chiefly from the want of proper general views of the subject, and of a just discrimination of the characters of those who are the object of punishment or compassion. Thus, while at one time the attention of the public is employed in detecting and punishing vagrants, real objects of charity are exposed to famine, or condemned to suffer a chastisement they have not deserved; at another time, while an ample provision is made for the poor in general, a liberal supply is often granted to the most slothful and profligate. Hence arise two opposite complaints, yet both of them well-grounded. The one of inhumanity and cruelty to our distressed fellow creatures; the other, of a profusion of public charity, and an ill-judged lenity, tending to encourage idleness and vice.

For an elaborate late eighteenth century classification and differentiation of the various elements composing the poor, see Bentham 1797; see also Mencher 1967:127.

70. The contrast I want to stress here is between skills largely learned by a process of trial and error and transmitted through apprenticeship, and those resting on an elaborate rational-scientific cognitive base. Ideological smokescreens notwithstanding, the former remains the basis for most controllers' claims to expertise.

71. Freidson 1970.

72. Cf., for example, Rothman 1971: 207ff.

73. In this regard, see Allan Silver's analysis of the origins of the modern police force: The older system of relying in emergencies on a hastily assembled militia under the direct command of local landowners was "inefficient [and] . . . directly exposed the propertied classes to attack." Lacking the military tradition of a landowning aristocracy, commercial and industrial capitalists were in any event "much less eager to take up the tasks of self-defense. . . . [However,] not only did the manufacturing classes wish to avoid personal danger and inconvenience while protecting their property, but they also saw that . . . the use of social and economic superiors as police exacerbated rather than mollified class violence" (Silver 1967: 9-10).

74. For America, see Rothman 1971; for England, Scull 1974: Ch. 6.

75. Weber 1946: 139. For a superb recent treatment of this "disenchantment of the world," both physical and social, and the transition to a naturalistic perspective, see Thomas 1971.

76. Note here the obvious links between the rise of imprisonment as the dominant response to crime and the ideological hegemony of "rationalism" of the Benthamite market variety. For utilitarians, "the most consistent champions of this type of rationality, even morals and politics, came under these simple calculations. Happiness was the object of policy. Every man's pleasure could be expressed (at least in theory) as a quantity and so could his pain. Deduct the pain from the pleasure and the net result was his happiness. . . . The accountancy of humanity would produce its debit and credit balances, like that of business" (Hobsbawm 1968: 79). Imprisonment allowed a punishment of graduated intensity to meet the gravity of the crime — an infinitely variable "price" which the offender had to "pay." The desire to rehabilitate as well as to isolate the deviant reinforced pressures to differentiate this human material into manageable subgroups for subsequent processing, as well as to differentiate between inmates within an institution so as to allow the creation of an intimate tie between the inmate's position in this classificatory system and his behavior. See Boston Prison Discipline Society 2nd Annual Report, 1827: 47; Webb and Webb 1922: 62; Scull 1974: 371-375; Goffman 1961: 361-362.

77. For the case of psychiatry, see Scull 1975a; on the police, Silver 1967; and on the social work "profession," Lubove 1971.

78. The clearest case of all is that of psychiatry, under whose aegis the vague cultural construct of madness was transformed into what now purported to be a formally coherent, scientifically distinguishable entity which reflected and was caused by a single underlying pathology.

79. Wallerstein 1974: 133.

80. Hence the importance as a transitional arrangement of the system of the state contracting with private entrepreneurs to provide jails, madhouses, and the like. Under this method, the state allows the "deviant farmer" to extort his fees in whatever way he can, and turns a blind eye to his methods; in return, the latter relieves the state of the capital expenditure (and often many of the running costs) required by a system of segregative control.

81. On taxes, see Wallerstein 1974; on "national debts," Hamilton 1947.

82. On the resultant fears for the durability of the social order, see Rothman 1971. Rothman describes these fears well, but neglects to connect them systematically to the commercialization of society.

83. In Polanyi's words: "The market system was more allergic to rioting than any other economic system we know. . . . In the nineteenth century breaches of the peace, if committed by armed crowds, were deemed an incipient rebellion and an acute danger to the state; stocks collapsed and there was no bottom in prices. A shooting affray in the streets of the metropolis might destroy a substantial part of the nominal national capital" (Polanyi 1944: 186–187).

84. Weber 1968 Vol. I: 337.

85. Such a transfer of the locus of power and responsibility necessarily took place in the face of fierce local resistance. In part this opposition emanated from a parochial defensiveness against the encroachments of the state. And in part it reflected the uneven spread of the new perceptions of crime, insanity, and so forth. In England these factors produced a protracted but finally successful struggle to assert central control, lasting from the eighteenth to the mid-nineteenth century. (For the case of crime and prisons, see Webb and Webb 1922: on insanity and asylums, Scull 1974: Ch. 4; on the poor and workhouses. Oxley 1974: esp. 82; Edsall 1971; Mencher 1967: 121ff.) In the United States they had more lasting consequences. The fragmentation of the political structure impeded the achievement of direct central control, so that a greater measure of local autonomy in this area persists to this day. Responsibility for prisons, jails, mental hospitals, and so forth remains primarily at the state (and sometimes county or city) level even now; Mencher 1967: 238.

86. 25th Annual Report of the Hanwell Lunatic Asylum, Middlesex, England: 36.

87. Some of these places, of course, purported to be humanitarian institutions. The true character of even these "humane" parts of the control system is perhaps hinted at in the comment of one of their supervising agencies, which expressed concern lest "any sane person should . . . be condemned to the *living death* of incarceration, in some private hospital for the insane:—a fate next in horror to being buried alive" (Pennsylvania: Annual Report of the Board of Commissioners 1876: 6; emphasis in the original). For a more extensive analysis and documentation of conditions in nineteenth century asylums, see Scull 1974: Ch. 7.

88. For example, probation and parole, aftercare for the mentally ill, and so forth. Some have been tempted (e.g., Rothman 1971) to overestimate the importance of these changes, seeing them as part of a transformation of the system and as coterminous with

contemporary moves towards deinstitutionalization. On the contrary, when one disregards the surface similarities and looks at what those who introduced and administered these programs actually did, "there is no evidence that they were advocating a substitution of community type programs for incarceration. Probation was always considered an adjunct of the court. Parole was part of the indeterminate sentence paradigm . . ." (Miller 1974: 108–109) and its spread was "probably due largely to its success in furthering prison discipline" (*U.S. Attorney General's Survey of Release Procedures, 1939*, cited in Messinger 1968: 60).

CHAPTER THREE

The decarceration of the bad: criminals and delinquents

The new reformers create the illusion that a specific penal practice is bound up with a specific penal theory, and that it is sufficient to demolish the latter in order to set the former under way. . . . We are actually turning things upside down, however, if we take at its face value the imaginary power of doctrine over reality, instead of understanding the theoretical innovation as the expression of a necessary or already accomplished change in social praxis. *

GEORG RUSCHE AND OTTO KIRCHHEIMER
Punishment and Social Structure

A growing chorus of politicians, liberal social scientists, and high-level managers of the social control apparatus (those seemingly in the best position to know) have informed us that prisons, juvenile reformatories, and asylums are now "decaying institutions," the product of an earlier "humanitarian" and well-intended reform movement which somehow went wrong. For such people, the failure of repeated efforts to ameliorate the quality of incarceration in these institutions has finally produced a belated recognition that, since "we inherit, in essence, a two-hundred-year history of reform without change,"[1] perhaps the whole notion of improving the institution rests on a fundamental misconception. Rather than trying to upgrade prisons and asylums, we ought to get on with the work of emptying them.

Decarceration, deinstitutionalization, diversion—under whatever name the process currently masquerades—the movement to return the bad and the mad to the community has led many to anticipate (or even announce) the advent of the therapeutic millennium. In tones of hushed

*Reprinted from G. Rusche and O. Kirchheimer, *Punishment and Social Structure*. New York: Columbia University Press, 1939. By permission of the publisher.

reverence, and in a language which neatly juxtaposes the sacred and the profane, we are told that

> nothing succeeds like an idea whose time has come. The institution as a means of coping with the problems of specific sectors of our population seems at this point to have run its course. Whether one is aged, below par intellectually or emotionally, delinquent, alcoholic, or drug-addicted, the source — and the remedy — of the problem lie in the communities where such people come from. By bringing them back into the community, by enlisting the good will and the desire to serve, the ability to understand which is found in every neighborhood, we shall meet the challenge which such groups of persons present, and at the same time ease the financial burden of their confinement in fixed institutions.[2]

"[Dealing] with problems in their social context," we must aim at "reintegrating the offender into the community . . . [while] avoiding as much as possible the isolating and labelling effects of commitment to an institution."[3]

Like the quest for the Holy Grail,

> the road back to community dealing with the problems of the young, the retarded, and the mentally disturbed will not be easy. But the destination is a degree of community participation and effectiveness which has all but departed our lives as people living together. Part of the powerlessness and frustration which so many sense at this juncture will be resolved in this trend, to the benefit not only of inmates or clients or patients or criminals now in institutions — but of the community as a whole.[4]

This marvelous panacea will thus usher in a new Golden Age.

There is a curious historical irony here, for the *adoption* of the asylum, whose *abolition* is now supposed to be attended with such universally beneficent consequences, aroused an almost precisely parallel set of millennial expectations among *its* advocates. In Rothman's words:

> The asylum was to fulfill a dual purpose for its innovators. It would rehabilitate inmates and then, by virtue of its success, set an example of right action for the larger society. There was a utopian flavor to this first venture, one that looked to reform the deviant and dependent and to serve as a model for others. The well-ordered asylum would exemplify the proper principles of social organization and thus [by reawakening the public to the virtues of the eighteenth-century community] insure the safety of the republic. . . [5]

Advocates of decarceration like to picture themselves as "committed to humanizing the correctional process [or the care of the mentally ill] and reducing its costs."[6] (Almost magically, these are no longer incompatible goals.) Much of their propaganda presents the deviant as the near-helpless victim of society's labeling processes, and exhibits the superficial and sentimental sympathy for the underdog so effectively criticized by Gouldner.[7] The institution is irredeemably evil; the community unequivocably good: "Keeping youngsters out of institutions, even if the community is not geared to serve them, is all to the good."[8] After all, community care is "flexible, adaptive," while the institution, that symbol of nastiness, is "traditional, static."[9]

While rhetoric of this sort abounds, there are in practice almost no sustained and intellectually serious efforts to argue for, let alone scientifically demonstrate, the superiority of a community-based approach. Two substitutes are employed: On the one hand prisons and asylums are subjected to a searching scrutiny which demonstrates they are ill-equipped to perform their nominal tasks of rehabilitating and reintegrating their inmates. I shall consider these arguments at length in Chapter Six. On the other hand, drawing particularly on the work of David Rothman (where such materials abound), an effort is made to conjure up a mythical "Golden Age": an innocent, robust society uncorrupted by bureaucracy, where neighbor helps neighbor and families willingly minister to the needs of their own troublesome members, while a benevolent and indulgent squirearchy looks on, always ready to lend a helping hand. In Alper's words:

> There was a simpler time not so very long ago—in this country and in others with similar economic and social organizations—when the problems of the mentally retarded and disturbed, the aged and the troubled young, were dealt with in the communities where each of these people lived. A greater continuity or integration of the entire age spectrum seems to have prevailed in those days: those who were old were not euphemistically and evasively dubbed as in their "golden" years, and those who were deficient in intelligence or emotional balance were not only tolerated but accommodated.[10]

Apparently, eliminating our prisons, reformatories, and mental hospitals will lead us back towards this glorious Paradise Lost.[11]

In this chapter and the next I shall examine the extent to which movements towards community-based corrections and noninstitutional "treatment" of the mentally ill sustain, or at least provide some empirical basis for, these flights of fancy. How far has the movement to decarcerate prisoners, delinquents, and mental patients actually gone in England and the United States? For criminals and juvenile delinquents, this is by no means an easy question to answer. Indeed, "no one today can have more than an impressionistic view of the extent to which community alternatives are replacing incarceration, and it will be years before we can know the answer to even this preliminary question which requires only a relatively simple 'counting' type of research."[12] A number of factors contribute to this state of affairs. Part of the problem, particularly in the United States, lies in the persistence of a relatively high degree of fragmentation and decentralization in the criminal justice apparatus, with decision making being so widely dispersed among a variety of competing and overlapping administrative units—counties, cities, states and at the federal level—that arriving at even a rough estimate of the number being diverted out of the institutional sector becomes a virtual impossibility.[13] The task is made still more difficult by the degree to which many of the operations of the criminal justice system necessarily remain obscure and largely invisible, beyond the reach of straightforward observation and measurement from the outside.

For example, police discretion about whether or not to arrest has always provided one low visibility method of dropping or diverting cases from the criminal justice system.[14] The very informality and lack of record-keeping which is the essence of this process means one can do little more than guess about the scope and long-term trends in its use. The proportion of individuals diverted away from custodial alternatives may be raised by treating their offenses as misdemeanors rather than felonies, thus "justifying" (if only by semantic sleight of hand) a greater reliance on noninstitutional mechanisms such as fines and probation[15]— a development accentuated by the spreading acceptance of the practice of plea-bargaining on both formal and informal levels. Similarly, the process of reclassifying whole categories of offenses and offenders (modifying, even largely eliminating penalties for marijuana use and possession; relabeling heroin addiction as a medical problem and transferring jurisdiction over addicts from jails to methadone clinics), although not undertaken exclusively with the intention of reducing the size of the population committed to custodial institutions, clearly has such an effect.

All of these factors intensify the complexity of measuring the extent to which processes operating at the preconviction phase are contributing to the trend toward noninstitutional responses. But difficulties of definition and measurement are also present in the postconviction phase. Diversion at this stage in the system relies heavily on a number of techniques and dispositions—probation, suspended sentences, parole— which in most cases have long been part of the criminal justice system. With the exception of the use of parole in England (which did not begin until 1968), the change has been one of degree and numbers, and of the fact that these techniques are now increasingly being employed in place of, rather than simply to supplement, incarceration. In other words, the rise of "community corrections" has meant not so much the introduction of radically novel approaches, but rather the transformation of traditional mechanisms so as to promote the return to the outside world of many who would previously have been incarcerated, and to develop special incentives designed to speed up this process.[16]

If evidence of the overall *size* of the decarceration process is difficult to come by, evidence that it is occurring on a considerable scale clearly is not. Such changes reflect "the remarkable consensus [which has emerged] across the political spectrum"[17] and across national boundaries in support of deinstitutionalization. In England and in the United States (on both the federal and the state levels) official advocacy and pressure for a return of the criminal and delinquent to the community are continuing to grow. Where fifteen or twenty years ago, the ideal was to commit nondangerous offenders to minimum security prisons where intensive efforts at rehabilitation would be undertaken,[18] there is now a stress on employing community options "whenever it appears that such disposition does not pose a danger of serious harm to public safety."[19] The most "progressive" penal systems are in the forefront of this rush to decarcerate. And even in England, where the implementation of the new approach has lagged somewhat, the most recent official review of the treatment of so-called "young offenders" (those between 17 and 21) has lent its weight to the argument that "a shift is needed in emphasis, and therefore in deployment of resources, from custodial treatment to treatment in the community . . ."—[20] a view which qualified observers predict will, "[in] the future . . ., inform the direction of [English] penal policy for adults as well."[21]

In the United States, federal pressures designed to accelerate the movement towards noninstitutional alternatives have not been confined to mere verbal exhortations. Particularly since the creation of the Law Enforcement Assistance Administration, efforts have been under way to manipulate federal funding and support for state and local law enforcement so as to provide sizeable financial incentives for the development of community corrections' programs.[22] Partly in response to these pressures, and partly as a reflection of local initiatives, "there is an increasing tendency to fine offenders, to name their felonies misdemeanors so they can be sent to county jails, and even to ignore their crimes rather than committing them to prisons and reformatories."[23] In many jurisdictions, the use of probation on first conviction for lesser felonies and misdemeanors is becoming almost standard.[24] As early as 1967, the Task Force on Corrections of the President's Commission on Law Enforcement and the Administration of Justice reported that "some jurisdictions are using probation for as much as 70 percent of their *felony* convictions."[25] More recent data from California indicates that the percentage of superior court defendants sent to prison fell from 23.3 percent in 1965 to 9.8 percent in 1969, while the proportion placed on probation rose from 51 percent to 68 percent in the same period.[26] States have evolved a whole series of "new procedures or incentives to raise the number, the percentage, or the seriousness-of-offense level of the offenders who leave the system early; new screening devices to select those who will leave; or new places, programs or opportunities for those who do leave."[27] For example, a series of programs has been designed in an effort to minimize pretrial detention, and there have even been programs to suspend prosecution altogether provided the defendant demonstrates he can and will hold a job.[28] In addition, a number of categories of deviance—such groups as alcoholics and addicts—formerly dealt with by the criminal justice system have increasingly been recognized as especially useful candidates for diversion, and more and more frequently are now dealt with outside that system.[29]

Prison statistics do reflect at least some dimensions of the transformation in social practices now under way. As Table 3–1 shows, the

TABLE 3 – 1
U.S. Prison Population and Prisoner Rate
per 100,000 people, 1950 – 1971

Year	Prison Population	Prisoner Rate/ 100,000	Year	Prison Population	Prisoner Rate/ 100,000
1950	166,165	109.5	1961	220,149	120.8
1951	165,680	107.3	1962	218,830	118.3
1952	168,233	107.1	1963	217,283	115.7
1953	173,579	108.7	1964	214,283	112.6
1954	182,901	112.6	1965	210,895	109.5
1955	185,915	112.5	1966	199,654	102.7
1956	189,575	112.7	1967	194,896	99.1
1957	195,414	114.1	1968	192,682	96.0
1958	205,493	118.8	1969	196,007	97.6
1959	207,446	117.7	1970	196,429	96.7
1960	212,953	118.6	1971	203,843	NA

SOURCE: U.S. Census Bureau, *Statistical History of the United States from Colonial Times to the Present; Statistical Abstract of the United States—1970, 1972.* Washington D.C.: Government Printing Office.

TABLE 3-2
Persons Placed on Probation (All Offenses) in Florida

Year	Placed on Probation	Year	Placed on Probation
1964–65	3,430	1969–70	9,328
1965–66	4,117	1970–71	13,730
1966–67	6,275	1971–72	24,243
1967–68	6,564	1972–73	36,285
1968–69	7,046	1973–74	49,424

SOURCE: Florida Parole and Probation Commission, 34th Annual Report, 1974: 20.

increasing emphasis on noninstitutional controls has been accompanied by a marked decline in the rate of imprisonment over the past decade and a half. The decline is even more impressive than it appears at first sight, for it has occurred in a period when official crime rates have been climbing extremely rapidly (the number of reported index crimes increased 176 percent between 1960 and 1970); and despite a large rise in the number of reported arrests (between 1960 and 1970 arrests increased by 31 percent).[30] Moreover, it reflects a sizeable decline in the absolute number of prisoners, rather than simply being a statistical artifact of the fact that existing prisons have been filled to overflowing, creating a fall in the rate of imprisonment as the number of prisoners necessarily stagnates while the population as a whole continues to grow.[31]

Figures recently released by the Florida Parole and Probation Commission provide a more dramatic example of the kinds of changes which have been introduced. Beyond all dispute, these data reveal that from the late 1960s onwards, probation and parole began to be used in an historically unprecedented way. Considering first the data presented in Tables 3-2 and 3-3, it is apparent that between 1964–1965 and 1973–74, the numbers placed on probation in a twelve month period rose overall from 3,430 to 49,424, an increase amounting to a staggering

TABLE 3-3
Disposition of State Felony Convictions in Florida

Year	Prison	Percent	Probation	Percent
1966–67	3,208	53.7	2,761	46.3
1967–68	3,288	53.2	2,893	46.8
1968–69	3,453	50.8	3,333	49.2
1969–70	3,584	43.8	4,589	56.2
1970–71	4,972	37.8	8,122	62.2
1971–72	5,651	27.6	14,820	72.4
1972–73	4,502	20.2	17,800	79.8
1973–74	5,022	21.3	18,502	78.7

SOURCE: Florida Parole and Probation Commission, 34th Annual Report, 1974: 14.

1,340 percent. Confining our attention simply to the more serious cases, state felony convictions, the same trend is apparent. Between 1966–67 and 1973–1974, the number sent to prison in any given year rose from 3,208 to 5,022, an increase of some 56 percent; while the numbers released on probation rose from 2,761 to 18,502, an increase of over 560 percent! Nor is there any tendency for this explosive rate of growth in the use of noninstitutional techniques to level off. Complaining that its employees are "overlooked, over-worked, over-extended, and under-paid," the Commission comments that pressures to step up the rate of release continue: "Dangerously, we are being encouraged to release the inmate who has been considered marginal in his or her rehabilitation potential. . . . The projections are these: As of January 1, 1975, Florida will have some 11,000 persons inside penal institutions. It will have 56,000 — give or take a few — under supervision in the communities of the state."[32] Figure 1 provides startling visual confirmation of this qualitative transformation in penal practices, and suggests how far, in some jurisdictions at least, the noninstitutional approach to the management of the criminal has already gone. Within a ten year period, while the number in prison at any one time has risen by only 62 percent, from 6,969 in 1965 to 11,335 in 1974, the number on probation and parole has grown by very nearly *500 percent,* from 8,840 to 52,412.

By the mid 1960s available institutional resources for sequestering juvenile delinquents were coming under severe strain. Under the impact of crime and arrest rates climbing even faster than their adult equivalents, and despite the fact that even in 1967 four times as many delinquents as were committed to reformatories were already placed in community programs,[33] massive new outlays to finance a greatly expanded network of institutions seemed unavoidable. The 1967 Presidential Crime Commission found that "only 17 per cent of the nation's [juvenile] institutions are operating at less than capacity; the other 83 percent are at or in excess of their capacity."[34] By 1975, the Commission projected that the number of juvenile delinquents incarcerated would rise by a further 70 percent, ten times the estimated increment in the state and federal prison load in the same period.

Faced even earlier by a rapidly diminishing or nonexistent reserve of space in existing "training schools" and the like, a number of states had, almost simultaneously in the early 1960s, introduced a program of "diagnostic parole" (i.e., intensive screening of all commitments to juvenile courts for eligibility for parole). Confronting similarly "acute population pressures in overcrowded institutions," Wisconsin had begun

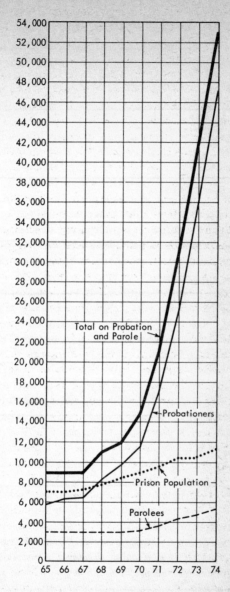

Figure 1 Numbers on probation, parole, and in prison in Florida, 1965-1974. SOURCE: Florida Parole and Probation Commission, Annual Report 1974: 2. Tallahassee, Florida, 1974.

experiments using foster homes for juveniles who would formerly have been incarcerated, and by the mid-sixties the numbers involved in this program were already equivalent to the population of "at least one institution."[35] The Crime Commission proposed a rapid and wide-ranging expansion of these and similar programs to divert as many juveniles as possible from the criminal justice system, a recommendation which won widespread acceptance, at least on the semantic level. Backed by massive funding from the Law Enforcement Assistance Administration, "the Youth Development and Delinquency Prevention Administration of the Department of Health, Education and Welfare . . . has given special priority to the development of what are called *youth services systems*. These are systems at the local level designed specifically to cut down drastically on the number of youth entering the juvenile justice system or being dealt with by means of traditional correctional programs."[36] But how successful the Youth Services Bureaus have been in practice in securing such early diversion remains problematic, the subject of little more than informed speculation, since no hard data exist with which to answer even this limited problem.[37]

By contrast with the fog of confusion and imprecision which envelops much of this federally sponsored activity, two projects developed and implemented at the state level — the California Probation Subsidy Program and the Massachusetts decision to close all state-run facilities for juvenile delinquents — are at one and the same time (a) perhaps the two most intensive efforts to move towards a "community-based" correctional system; (b) relatively closely studied and well documented;[38] and (c) apparently successful — at least in terms of reducing the size of the deviant population confined in total institutions at state expense. These programs are, I think, worth discussing in some detail, both because there have been a number of efforts elsewhere to emulate them, and because they reveal a number of interesting facets of the movement to decarcerate criminals and juveniles.

Certainly the most spectacular single example of the shift towards community treatment has been the complete shutting down of all juvenile training schools and reformatories for delinquents in the state of Massachusetts. This was a process the final and most important stages of which took place almost overnight. The initial plans were drawn up only three to four weeks before their implementation, and "the final decision to go ahead took place only days before [the closure] began."[39]

Such a momentous change of policy obviously had much deeper roots than this. In the years prior to their closure, the Massachusetts institutions exhibited in particularly marked form the faults of their brethren throughout the United States. Like reform schools elsewhere, those in Massachusetts were overcrowded and run by an often brutal custodial staff, which was effectively insulated and "protected from review, promotion, or devotion by civil service or political cronyism. . . . Annual costs per child ranged as high as $11,500, twice the national average. . . ." Yet despite this, and for all the "liberalism" of the state's political elite, Massachusetts allegedly possessed "one of the worst systems in the country," characterized among other things by a recidivism rate in the neighborhood of 80 percent. Such a combination of costliness, brutality, and failure (a combination characteristic of segregative control institutions since their inception) is virtually guaranteed to produce periodic scandals and associated campaigns in the mass media for "reform." Between 1965 and 1969, based on a series of press exposés of conditions in the state's reformatories, just this sort of campaign developed, culminating in the forced resignation of the director of the Division of Youth Services.[40]

Historically, the outcome of similar "crusades" for reform has been the introduction of a series of merely cosmetic changes, while on the more fundamental level business proceeds as usual. And indeed the first charges introduced in response to this latest campaign suggested that the ancient tradition of "reform by word-magic" was alive and well. Semantic changes abounded: The *Division* of Youth Services was transformed into the *Department* of Youth Services; and, in the words of one of the bureaucrats imported to supervise the new regime, the 1969 Reorganization Act "set a new professional tone for the agency, using key words such as therapy, prevention, community services, purchase of services, and research."[41] As if evil were to be abolished and the good to triumph through the exercise of words alone! But where in the past verbal sleight of hand and a few changes of personnel would have sufficed, by the end of the sixties, in the context of an intellectual climate of marked antipathy towards institutional responses to deviance, and in the face of the threat of further massive increases in costs as the number of juveniles confined continued relentlessly upward, more radical changes now ensued.

"Between 1969 and 1973 the Department of Youth Services closed all the state reform schools and replaced them with a regionalized system of community-based group homes and other treatment programs, largely operated by private groups."[42] Under its new director, Jerome Miller, the department at first moved cautiously. Although convinced that a system based on incarceration was "insane" and destructive, and that "any alternative will be better than what we have"[43] (a position widely

held by those advocating decarceration), he began by attempting to
modify somewhat the conditions in the institutions nominally under his
control. The English psychiatrist, Dr. Maxwell Jones, who had promoted
the notion of turning mental hospitals into "therapeutic communities,"
was imported to introduce his concept into a new setting — with disastrous results, including "staff polarization and mass runaways."
Simultaneously, in the late spring of 1970, the Bridgewater maximum
security unit was closed and its inmates distributed to ordinary training
schools. No effort was made to provide an alternative unit for the most
troublesome cases, "and Miller actively began to advocate that there
was no need for one." Meanwhile, his first small-scale effort to develop a
community-based program provoked so much community opposition
that it was temporarily abandoned.[44]

The following year, still pursuing a strategy of gradualism, the
department slowly began to phase out the Shirley Industrial School.
Once more the program dissolved in turmoil. Staff resistance took
various forms: covert sabotage, such as encouraging their charges to
abscond; and more overt resistance in the form of letters to the press
and to state legislators — all of which provoked "increased opposition
from the local communities and pressure from the legislature."[45] Yet
the executive branch continued to back the moves to decarcerate
juveniles.

Fresh from this stunning series of administrative "triumphs," the
departmental leadership "abandoned gradualism, for it only provided
more time and excuses [another observer might say 'reasons'] for political opposition to form."[46] Instead, the plan to close the reformatories
now proceeded by strategy, political maneuver, and surprise. Staff
morale, solidarity, and organization were systematically destroyed by a
conscious policy of changing and rotating administrators between the
various institutions; and deliberately fostered chaos and anarchy were
employed to further paralyze potential internal sources of resistance —
tactics facilitated by a strong tradition of institutional autonomy which
precluded organized, system-wide opposition. Reinforcing these moves,
a massive public relations effort was launched, using techniques which
would have graced Madison Avenue. Staff were assigned to travel
through the state disseminating propaganda about the evils of the old
system and the promise of the new. Descriptions of the changes the
department planned to make were intentionally left vague, allowing the
reformers to appear to be offering all things to all men. In this way,
proponents of the new system could gather maximal support for their
proposals, "while depriving . . . opponents of a focus for opposition."

Media coverage of the final stages of the shutdown was carefully orchestrated: "Numerous newspaper articles and several television networks covered the series of events, and the department was described by them as a bold, action-oriented agency willing to take risks to ameliorate the deplorable conditions of training schools for youthful offenders. In professional circles, this action was described as a new breakthrough in providing services for youth in trouble."[47]

All this activity was designed to forestall (or at least neutralize) opposition from those working within and committed to the traditional system, while also inhibiting the development of organized opposition from a community portrayed as willing to have deviants returned to its midst. Miller himself claimed that he expected what he called "this public educational process" would mean that "the public will move dramatically" in support of decarceration. But in case such a shift in sentiment failed to occur (which it did), he advised that "administrators must be cool and in a sense manipulative, and must use the laws as creatively as possible."[48] Miller then demonstrated what he had in mind. During the January 1972 legislative recess, when political counteraction was least likely, he suddenly and without warning used his discretionary powers as commissioner to empty and officially close all juvenile institutions.[49]

Only *after* taking this action did the department begin the task of creating community-based alternatives. Almost proudly, the current Assistant Commissioner concedes that this was standard operating procedure. As he puts it, "destroying a system *before* creating alternatives to it was a characteristic mode of action for the department."[50] In consequence, under the pressure of sheer necessity, delinquents had to be placed wherever room could be found for them. Much of the "community placement" came to depend upon the activities of private entrepreneurs who stepped in to take advantage of the new market the state was in the process of creating. Gradually the situation stabilized. "Groups began to come up with proposals; resources were found; and the children filled these placements at an accelerated rate." Meanwhile, the small remnant of delinquents — 35 or 40 — whom even the department considered too dangerous to release, were likewise handed over to a private agency (which, ironically enough, housed its operations in one of the old detention buildings the state had just vacated).[51]

As we noted in Chapter Two, the fragmentation of the United States' political structure has consistently stood in the way of the secular pressures towards ever increasing rationalization and centralization characteristic of the Western social order in general. This has produced, among much else, a far greater degree of local autonomy in the administration of the social control apparatus than is characteristic of other modern societies. The California Probation Subsidy Program both illustrates how this persistent localism and political fragmentation leads, in principle, to obstruct efforts to implement decarceration, and demonstrates how the pressures to circumvent such obstacles are beginning to be reflected in social policy.

In California, as elsewhere in the United States, the courts, in whose hands rests control over how many offenders are sent to prison, are agencies funded at the county level; whereas the prison system is financed by the state. In consequence (a) "the State had virtually no control over its own correctional intake, hence [none over] workloads and expenditures . . ."; and (b) the courts had every incentive to commit offenders to state "correctional facilities" (a form of control costing the counties nothing), rather than to channel them into noninstitutional alternatives such as probation (which were primarily or exclusively paid for by their employers, the counties). By the mid-1960s, as crime, arrest, and conviction rates continued to rise sharply, existing prisons and reformatories were filled to and beyond capacity, with every indication that the situation would steadily worsen. Official forecasts of state correctional populations made in this period showed that unless sentencing patterns changed dramatically, new admissions to the Department of the Youth Authority and the Department of Corrections would double within a decade. Plans were discussed for the construction of one new prison or juvenile reformatory in California every year for at least ten years, at a capital cost alone of some $90 million, without allowing for inflation. As the implications of these figures sank in, it became increasingly clear that "a new balance . . . had to be achieved if a financial crisis in corrections was to be averted. . . ."[52]

It was in this context that a new program known as "probation subsidy" suddenly began to win support right across the conventional political spectrum. Earlier attempts to expand the number of offenders placed on probation had largely failed, but in 1961 a small experimental Community Treatment Program had been introduced for juveniles.[53] Inadequate and incomplete data from this program were now used in support of a greatly expanded version of this approach, which was applied to adults as well as juveniles.[54] Allegedly, "everyone benefited" as community treatment expanded — citizens as well as criminals — and proponents of the Probation Subsidy Program proclaimed the "cost effectiveness and the fiscal soundness of the program they represented, as well as [its] humanitarian values."[55]

TABLE 3-4
First Commitments to Prisons and Juvenile Institutions
in California, 1965–1971

Fiscal Year	California Youth Authority	Department of Corrections	Total Commitments
1965–66	5,831	5,834	11,665
1970–71	3,441	4,650	8,091
% decrease	41.0	20.3	30.6

SOURCE: Robert Smith. *A Quiet Revolution—Probation Subsidy.* Washington, D.C.: U.S. Department of Health, Education, and Welfare, 1971: 52.

In essence, the Probation Subsidy Program can be viewed as a relatively elaborate means of encouraging counties to divert offenders away from state correctional institutions and of prompting judges to increase the proportion of offenders placed on probation. "Oversimplifying, the subsidy provides state funds to the counties for not committing cases to state institutions. The more cases not committed, the greater the subsidy."[56] Passed unanimously by the state legislature, the program became operative in July 1966.

The idea of providing "bribes" on a sliding scale to encourage the use of alternatives to incarceration has proceeded to have a striking effect

TABLE 3-5
California Superior Court Defendants Convicted
and Adults Granted Probation, 1960–1969

Year	Number Convicted and Sentenced	Number on Probation	Percent on Probation
1960	24,800	11,000	44.4
1961	28,000	12,600	45.0
1962	27,000	11,400	42.2
1963	28,400	13,500	47.5
1964	27,800	14,200	51.1
1965	30,800	15,700	51.0
1966	32,000	16,800	52.5
1967	34,700	20,300	58.5
1968	40,500	25,000	61.7
1969	50,600	33,200	65.6
% change	104	202	

SOURCE: Adapted from Robert Smith. *A Quiet Revolution—Probation Subsidy.* Washington, D.C.: U.S. Department of Health, Education, and Welfare, 1971: 53.

on the state supported institutional population in California.[57] At the outset, it was hoped that a 25 percent reduction could ultimately be made in statewide commitment rates, and projections made regarding the decrease in rates assumed it would take five years to reach this point. "In fact, the State goal was achieved in the second year of operation," and rates have continued to fall since then.[58]

Meanwhile, as Table 3–5 shows, a sharp rise in the number of adult offenders convicted and sentenced in Superior Court was more than matched by an even more dramatic rise in the proportion being placed on probation. As a result, per capita rates for incarceration are now "lower than they were in 1965, prior to the probation subsidy . . .": and the massive prison and reform school construction program envisaged in 1964 is now dismissed as unnecessary.[59]

No decarceration programs of comparable scope and intensity have as yet been implemented in England. Indeed, a glance at the figures presented in Table 3–6 for prison populations there reveals that the number of adult criminals and "young offenders" (those between 17 and 21) in prison continued to rise throughout the 1960s and into the 1970s. Clearly the diversion movement (with respect to criminals at least) has lagged considerably in the English context, as compared with the American experience.

TABLE 3 – 6
Average Daily Prison and Borstal Population in England and Wales, and Rate of Imprisonment per 100,000 of the General Population, 1951 – 1972

Year	Prison Population	Rate/ 100,000	Year	Prison Population	Rate/ 100,000
1951	21,370	48.8	1962	31,063	66.6
1952	23,680	53.9	1963	30,896	65.9
1953	23,610	53.5	1964	29,600	62.7
1954	22,421	50.6	1965	30,421	64.0
1955	21,134	47.6	1966	33,086	69.2
1956	20,807	46.8	1967	35,009	72.8
1957	22,602	50.3	1968	32,461	67.1
1958	25,379	56.3	1969	34,667	71.4
1959	26,623	58.7	1970	39,028	80.2
1960	27,099	59.2	1971	39,708	81.3
1961	29,025	62.8	1972	38,328	77.9

SOURCE: Data from Central Statistical Office, *Annual Abstract of Statistics* 1952–1973. London: H.M.S.O.

Yet once again it is important to place the raw statistics on prison populations in perspective. As in the United States, the 1960s and 1970s in England have been a period in which both crime and conviction rates have been spiralling rapidly upwards. This continuing increase means, of course, that the numbers potentially "eligible" for incarceration have been rising much more quickly than has the general population; so that rates of imprisonment like those presented in Table 3–6, which fail to allow for this factor, are to that extent misleading. To put it another way, under the conditions which currently prevail, the absolute size of the prison population (and even its size relative to the total population) may continue to rise even as the proportion of convicted criminals being imprisoned falls.

Although the evidence is far from decisive on this point, it does suggest that this is indeed what has been happening recently, particularly among adult criminals. Two caveats need to be borne in mind, however. First, the trends we are examining are relatively recent, so while there are grounds for believing that they are not simply a temporary phenomenon, a certain hesitancy is warranted about too casual a projection of them into the future. Secondly, official criminal statistics are notoriously hazardous data with which to work, particularly in the longer term, when there are likely to have been changes in official definitions and recording practices—with the obvious difficulties this creates concerning comparability. And unfortunately, the period we are concerned with encompasses just such a change: The Theft Act of 1968 (which came into effect on January 1, 1969) involved a major recodification of a substantial segment of the criminal law. Still, the very size of the change in the proportion of those convicted being sent to prison (consistently around 24–25 percent between 1960 and 1967, and fluctuating between 17 percent and 18 percent since then) seems to imply that the decline is real, rather than being simply a statistical artifact. And one's confidence in the correctness of this interpretation is strengthened when one looks at data on adult offenders only (those over 21 years old) over a slightly longer time period. In 1958, of every 1,000 adult men convicted of indictable offenses, 396 were imprisoned; by 1970, the proportion had fallen to 216 per 1,000; and by 1972 to only 197 per 1,000—or by more than fifty percent—[60] a change which clearly reflects an increasing reliance on noncustodial dispositions. Meanwhile, in another move which had and will have an impact on prison populations, a parole system was introduced in England and Wales for the first time in 1968. Since then the proportion of prisoners being released on parole before the expiration of their original sentence, while still low by American standards, has grown steadily.[61]

TABLE 3-7

**Convictions for Indictable Offenses, Prison Admissions (Male),
and Admissions as a Percentage of Convictions, 1960–1971
(England and Wales)**

Year	Convictions	Admissions	Admissions as a Percentage of Convictions
1960	163,482	40,329	24.7
1961	182,217	44,135	24.2
1962	203,775	50,767	24.9
1963	211,718	51,950	24.5
1964	205,262	51,326	25.0
1965	218,435	54,385	24.9
1966	232,854	60,169	25.8
1967	242,208	58,643	24.2
1968	257,327	47,650	18.5
1969	304,070	53,159	17.5
1970	322,898	59,957	18.6
1971	321,836	58,442	18.2

SOURCES: Convictions from Central Statistical Office, *Annual Abstracts of Statistics.*
London: H.M.S.O.; Admissions from *Reports on the Work of the Prison Department.*
London: H.M.S.O.

In the light of the foregoing, it may seem somewhat surprising that prison populations have increased as fast as they have. Undoubtedly, the major reason for this state of affairs lies in the failure of incarceration rates for "young offenders" (those between 17 and 21) to fall at anything approaching the rate of their adult counterparts. Between 1958 and 1972, the proportion of young offenders being sentenced to prison or Borstal only fell very slightly, from 218 per 1,000 convicted of indictable offenses to 211 per 1,000 (or by only about 3 percent compared with the 50 percent fall among adults). In absolute numbers, while 6,548 17 to 21 year olds were sentenced to prison in 1960, 15,337 received a prison term in 1971.[62]

Such a situation was bound to provoke the concern of the managers of the criminal justice apparatus. Low-level judicial functionaries in the system were clearly exercising their discretion in ways which threatened to produce "a tremendous escalation in costs" if not checked by "some radical action."[63] Already, severe overcrowding of custodial facilities for the young offender had virtually forced an administrative policy of shorter terms and earlier and earlier release (these being to some extent a matter of administrative rather than judicial discretion for this age group). Even allowing for this, however, official forecasts were for the number of young offenders in custody to rise from approximately 7,500 in 1972 to 17,000 by 1980 (an increase of over 125 percent), requiring an additional annual expenditure for maintenance of some £30 million (at 1972 prices), as well as a massive capital investment program to build new prisons. Faced with "social and financial costs which, if present trends are allowed to continue, could reach alarming proportions . . .," an official inquiry, the so-called Younger Committee, was swiftly established.[64]

An examination of its final report suggests that the still nascent English tendencies towards community corrections will be greatly strengthened in years to come. Citing "the constant emphasis in modern thinking and writing upon the potentially damaging effects of custody, even under an enlightened regime" as tending "to undermine confidence in what can be achieved within a custodial system," the Committee concludes "that new ways must be found of controlling as many young adult offenders as possible without committing them to custody and of bringing constructive influences to bear on them while they continue to live and work in the community." Explicitly on the grounds of its usefulness as "a means of promoting the use, and the acceptance by the public, of non-custodial measures . . . ," they suggest a new form of stepped-up probation supervision "for many offenders who are not at present dealt with in the community." And in this way, they hope to secure "a major switch from custody to supervision in the community."[65]

As I suggested at the beginning of this chapter, the question of how far the decarceration of criminals and delinquents has gone is by no means an easy one to answer. Indeed, as we have now seen, there *is* no one answer to this question. Rather, one must conclude that "community-based corrections" have obviously been implemented to quite varying degrees, both intra- and internationally, and, notwithstanding the extravagant rhetoric of decarceration's devotees, perhaps rarely threaten to produce the penitentiary's imminent demise. Nevertheless, the ideological hegemony of this approach is already secure, and its practical impact in many areas is substantial—and only likely to grow in the future.

1. Rothman 1973.

2. Alper 1973: vii-viii; also Schulberg 1973: 39. In Paul Rock's apt phrase, the community here assumes the guise of "a secular Lourdes providing inexpensive redemption" (Personal communication from Rock).

3. *Task Force Report: Corrections:* 1967: 28. For official rhetoric on community treatment. see pages 7–11.

4. Alper 1973: viii.

5. Rothman 1971: xix.

6. Pettibone 1973: 3.

7. Gouldner 1968; for a splendid example of this, see Miller 1973.

8. Foster 1973: 33.

9. Foster 1973: 33. There is a clear reliance here on a primitive version of Stevenson's emotive theory of ethics, which asserts that the connotational force of words often determines the issue of moral disputes: There are "boo" words and "hurrah" words. But "community," as we shall see, can remain an hurrah word only because its concrete referents remain unknown (or at least undiscussed) in the decarceration literature. (For suggesting the relevance of Stevenson's work, I am once more indebted to Paul Rock.) Let us for the moment content ourselves with asking: "Why, if the community is so therapeutic, the offender got into trouble in the first place?" (Greenberg 1975: 4–5).

10. Alper 1973: vii.

11. One sometimes feels that the apologists for decarceration, with their romantic attachment to a curiously shadowy and ill-defined notion of "community," view modern society as, at least potentially, a collection of organic villages; and share with Polsky (1973: 59) "the hope that a hundred or a thousand different Waldens will spring up."

12. Vorenberg and Vorenberg 1973: 165.

13. Vorenberg and Vorenberg 1973: 154.

14. La Fave 1964: Vorenberg and Vorenberg 1973: Cicourel 1968.

15. Cressey 1973: 124.

16. See Vorenberg and Vorenberg 1973: 161.

17. Greenberg 1975: 1.

18. Advisory Council of Judges 1963: 363.

19. Council of Judges 1972: 344. Cf. National Advisory Commission 1973..

20. Younger Report 1974: v.

21. Hood 1974: 390.

22. See Vorenberg and Vorenberg 1973: 163 ff.

23. Cressey 1973: 124.

24. Glaser 1973: 99.

25. Task Force Report: Corrections 1967: 175, my emphasis.

26. Smith 1971.

27. Vorenberg and Vorenberg 1973: 152.

28. See Doleschal 1972; Greenberg 1975; Vera Institute of Justice 1972; Vorenberg and Vorenberg 1973.

29. See Nimmer n. d.; Harlow 1970; Georgia Law Review 1972; De Grazia 1972. The policy of decreasing the historical reliance on institutional modes of handling problem populations extends well beyond the groups we shall consider in this book. For example, among dependent and neglected children, the proportion in residential institutions has fallen from 38.0 percent in 1958 to only 22.9 percent in 1969 (Koshel 1973: 18). Efforts are under way to accelerate this trend. One such program adopted in New York City in 1971 involved the development of "a system of incentive payments for increasing desired

exits from foster care" which paid private agencies $400 for each child returned home after a year in foster care, and gave incentive payments of $1,000 for each hard-to-place child adopted (Sugarman in Fanshell and Shinn 1972: Preface).

30. Blumstein and Cohen 1973.

31. One might also note that "despite an increasing crime rate, state and federal institutions received seventy-nine thousand prisoners in 1970, as compared with over ninety-three thousand in 1961" (Cressey 1973: 124). The recent slight reversal of the long-term trend downward can almost certainly be attributed to the extraordinary short-run sensitivity of the prison population to fluctuations in the level of employment. A recent paper by Robinson, Smith and Wolf (1974) demonstrates that the correlation between the unemployment rate and changes in prison admissions is 0.91 for the federal and 0.86 for the state prison system (both figures significant at the .001 level).

32. Florida Parole and Probation Commission Report 1974: 21.

33. Empey 1973: 36.

34. Task Force Report: Corrections 1967: 45.

35. Task Force Report: Corrections 1967: 42, 40.

36. Gula 1973: 9.

37. For one discussion, see Vorenberg and Vorenberg 1973: 166–172.

38. The reader is cautioned that although information on both programs is relatively plentiful, the overwhelming bulk of it is written by those committed professionally and/or intellectually to the decarceration movement. Special vigilance must therefore be exercised to distinguish rhetoric from reality, "promise" from performance. A *critical* reading of the sources, always important, is nowhere more so than here.

39. Coates, Miller, and Ohlin 1973: 128.

40. Bakal 1973: 155–157.

41. Bakal 1973: 157.

42. Bakal 1973: 151.

43. Miller, cited in Bakal 1973: 172.

44. Bakal 1973: 159–167.

45. Bakal 1973: 158–161.

46. Bakal 1973: 161. Trying to gloss over these somewhat unsavory reasons for haste, other observers seeking to present the program in the best possible light have resorted to quasi-Freudian justifications for the strategy adopted. As they put it "gradual withdrawal of youth [from reformatories] creates an environment in which both staff and youth act out their anxieties about their changing situation — leading to runaways and other serious disturbances" (Coates, Miller, and Ohlin 1973: 127).

47. Bakal 1973: 158–159, 166.

48. Miller 1973: 7.

49. Bakal 1973: 161.

50. Bakal 1973: 175.

51. Bakal 1973: 161–163. This privatization of social control, with the state contracting with private, profit-making individuals and organizations to dispose of problem populations more cheaply than it otherwise could has obvious parallels with the transitional control apparatus characteristic of the eighteenth century. Then, however, the transition was toward rather than away from a form of segregative control based on institutionalization. See the analysis in Chapter Two above.

Other states have sought to emulate Massachusetts' success in closing juvenile institutions. Both Illinois and Pennsylvania have employed Jerome Miller to help them to do so. However, his very visibility and consequent notoriety have hampered efforts to make use of his experience in this fashion. Almost immediately following the closure of the Massachusetts reform schools, Miller left to head the Illinois Family and Children Services [sic]. Within a short period, however, largely as a result of an antidecarceration campaign led by unions for state employees whose jobs his plans threatened, he was forced to leave (although eight of Illinois' twenty reform schools were closed). Currently he is director of community based programs in Pennsylvania, trying once more to replicate his achievements in Massachusetts.

52. Smith 1971: 7–11.

53. Vorenberg and Vorenberg 1973: 162; Smith 1971: 8.

54. For documentation of the remarkable extent to which the political "success" of decarceration is unrelated to its practical success (in terms of its alleged goals at least), see the discussion in Chapter Six.

55. Smith 1971: 25, 31.

56. Smith 1971: 24.

57. As a result, "other states have rapidly copied this program, to a greater or lesser extent, despite the complexity of its methods for determining subsidies and for appraising advances in probation services. Where subsidy programs have been adopted, probation has generally increased markedly and the population of state correctional institutions has declined" (Glaser 1973: 104).

58. Smith 1971: 49–50. However, a recent study of California's institutionalization of juvenile delinquents in the post 1965 period shows that, while the previous upward spiral in the total number of days youth spend in correctional institutions has been all but arrested (a departure from historical precedent), overall it has not fallen. For even as admissions to state institutions have been "drastically reduced . . . there have been notable increases in county sources of institutionalization . . ." which have almost counterbalanced this decline (Lerman 1975: 152ff.). Unfortunately, Lerman's study appeared too late to be fully incorporated into the analysis presented here, but it provides a sobering re-examination of both the Community Treatment and the Probation Subsidy Programs. Notwithstanding official claims of success, he clearly shows how self-serving modifications made by correctional bureaucrats have severely undermined efforts to secure these programs' major goals.

59. Flynn 1973: 80.

60. Younger Report 1974: 38.

61. From 8.5 percent in 1968, it has risen to 28.6 percent by 1971 (West 1973: 56). Innovative approaches have also been adopted to divert juvenile delinquents away from the courts and detention homes. For example, in 1968, the Metropolitan (London) Police set up Juvenile Bureaux and designed a program to substitute a police warning or "caution" for juvenile court proceedings in selected cases. By 1970, 39 percent of juveniles committing offenses were being dealt with in this fashion (Vorenberg and Vorenberg 1973: 157).

62. Younger Report 1974: 38. Again, this casts considerable doubt on the notion that the decline in prison admissions as a proportion of convictions is not real but the product of changing recording practices associated with the 1968 Theft Act. For it is difficult to see why the changes that Act introduced would have produced a sharply declining rate of imprisonment for adults and an almost static one for offenders between 17 and 21.

63. Hood 1974: 389.

64. See Younger Report 1974: 38–39.

65. Younger Report 1974: 5–6, 13, 23. For critiques of this proposal, see Hood 1974; Hawkins 1974; Steer 1974. Once again, as in Massachusetts, public relations' considerations are accorded major significance, reflecting in part the presence within the criminal justice system of a large number of semi-independent decision makers who must be persuaded and cajoled, rather than forced, to adopt the new official policy.

CHAPTER FOUR

The demise of the asylum: decarcerating the mad

> *Whilst in ordinary life every shopkeeper is very well able to distinguish between what someone professes to be and what he really is, our historians have not yet won even this trivial insight. They take every epoch at its word and believe that everything it says and imagines about itself is true.*
>
> KARL MARX and FREDERICK ENGELS
> *The German Ideology**

As we shall see in this chapter, the most striking manifestation of the contemporary movement away from an institutionally based system of segregative control is clearly to be found in that segment of the social control apparatus concerned with the management of the mad. The magnitude and consistency of the changes which have already occurred in this sector have made forecasts of the death of the mental hospital a commonplace, and a plausible commonplace at that. Books such as Lafave and Greenberg's *La Fin de L'Asile* (The End of the Asylum), and Stotland and Kobler's *Life and Death of a Mental Hospital* have recorded the demise of individual institutions; and the mental health bureaucracy has sponsored conferences designed to explore the system-wide implications of the closing of state mental hospitals.[1] A policy of decarcerating the mentally ill is already at an advanced stage of implementation in both England and the United States.

Placed in its proper historical context, the transformation which has been wrought over the past two decades appears little short of astonishing. For it runs counter to a persistent century-and-a-half-old trend in precisely the opposite direction. From the creation of the first publicly

*Copyright © by International Publishers Co., Inc., New York, 1974.

supported asylums in the early nineteenth century, a pattern of consistent year-by-year increases in the number of inmates confined in mental hospitals swiftly established itself. Thereafter it persisted right through the nineteenth century and the first half of the twentieth. Virtually the only exceptions to this spectacular rise in the numbers incarcerated in asylums occurred in periods during and immediately following the two World Wars. Otherwise, there appeared to be a remarkably consistent tendency to underestimate the demand for asylum accommodation, no matter how careful the previous efforts to gauge the local requirements had been. Moreover, as additional facilities were built to meet the apparent excess demand, so they, too, swiftly became filled to capacity, prompting repetitions of the original cycle for as long as money was forthcoming for additional buildings.[2]

In England, where, taken as a whole, the asylum system developed more rapidly than in the United States, the number of people officially identified as insane grew from 21,000 (a rate of 12.66 per 10,000 people) in 1845 — when provision of asylums at public expense became compulsory — to 95,600 (30.30 per 10,000) by the end of the century. As Table 4-1 shows, paralleling these figures for insanity as a whole, the number of patients confined in public lunatic asylums rose from 7,140 in 1850 to 119,659 in 1930. And ultimately, by 1954, the year when the English mental hospital population finally peaked, the number of patients resident in mental hospitals had grown to 148,000, a rate of 33.45 per 10,000 people. By the latter date many of the hospitals themselves, "Victorian barracks" inherited from the nineteenth century, were in an

TABLE 4-1
Total Patients in Public Asylums in England and Wales, 1850–1930 and Rate/10,000 People

Year	Patients	Rate/10,000
1850	7,140	4.03
1860	15,845	7.96
1870	27,109	12.05
1880	40,088	15.73
1890	52,937	18.34
1900	74,004	23.05
1910	97,580	27.49
1920	93,648	24.84
1930	119,659	30.14

SOURCES: *Annual Reports of the Lunacy Commissioners* (1850–1910); *Annual Reports of the Board of Control* (1920–1930). London: H.M.S.O.

advanced state of physical decay and decrepitude. Consequently, it was widely assumed that a massive capital investment program would shortly be required, both to rebuild and replace the most rundown portions of the existing physical plant, and to relieve the overcrowding then, as in the past, endemic in the system — a program which, as one of the ministers responsible for mental health conceded, would involve "not a question of a few million pounds . . . [but] a question of thousands of millions over many years."[3]

Over the same period, the United States experienced a similarly remorseless increase, although the timing of the most rapid rise was somewhat different here. As the insane remained the responsibility of the separate states, and no national inspectorate comparable with the English Lunacy Commissioners was ever created, data on the size of the system as a whole are fragmentary, particularly in the early years. But between 1850 and 1870, for example, the official count of "lunatics and idiots" rose from 31,397 to 42,864;[4] and by 1890 the 120 public and 40 private asylums in the United States contained a total of 91,152 patients.[5] In the present century (with the minor exception of the period 1942–1943, which saw a 0.3 percent decrease in the number of patients), mental hospital populations have continued to rise steadily. Prior to 1955, "the public mental hospital population had quadrupled during the previous half century, whereas the general population had only doubled . . .";[6] and during the last decade of this period, the increase averaged 2.1 percent a year. The consequences were predictable. To cite simply the two largest states: The New York State system in 1955 was (officially) short of 23,000 beds, and suffered from an overcrowding of some 33 percent; while the California system, faced with a similarly massive postwar rise in its mental hospital population, had purchased in 1947 two surplus army facilities (provisional wooden structures) to serve as "temporary" state hospitals — yet despite redesignating these as permanent hospitals, the system likewise confronted serious over-crowding.[7] As in England, a sizeable hospital building program seemed imminent.

Instead, since the mid-1950s, both countries have witnessed an abrupt reversal of the historical trend. Dating from 1954 in England and 1955 in the United States, the number of patients resident in mental hospitals in each country has decreased in each and every year (see Tables 4-2 and 4-3 below); and there has emerged in both countries an explicit commitment to a policy, which has gathered momentum over the past two decades, of "treating" the mentally disordered in the community. Initially, doubts were expressed in some quarters about the significance of the decline in numbers and the likelihood of its long-term persistence. For example, expectations about the further extension of the movement towards deinstitutionalization were criticized for being based on "the arbitrary application of a not very sophisticated formula" which simply estimated future mental hospital populations by projecting forward a very recent and perhaps temporary trend that contradicted all previous trends.[8] But such questioning seems to have disappeared, as the fall has continued uninterruptedly (and in some places even at an accelerated pace) for two decades now. In its place, we have seen an increasingly confident projection of recent trends to their logical limits, typified by the 1961 forecast by the British Minister of Health that he expected "the acute population of mental hospitals to drop by half in the next fifteen years and the long-stay population ultimately to dwindle to zero."[9]

Curiously enough, while the numbers resident in mental hospitals have fallen dramatically over the past two decades, this fall has been accompanied by a steep *rise* in the overall admission rates, which only recently have shown signs of leveling off. Between 1955 and 1968, admissions to mental hospitals in England and Wales rose from 78,586 to 170,527; and although admissions dipped to 162,864 in 1970, this was still more than twice the number admitted in 1955. The rise in admissions has been equally steady and of similar magnitude in the United States. While approximately 185,000 were admitted to mental hospitals in 1956, by 1970 the figure was 393,000 (although, once more, there has since been a slight decline to 377,020 in 1973). Statistically speaking, therefore, the decline in mental hospital populations reflects a policy of greatly accelerated discharge.

There is a strange historical parallel here. The establishment of the asylum system in the first place, particularly in the United States, was accompanied by extravagant claims about the institution's presumed ability to cure. During the era of the "cult of curability,"[10] superintendents of the newly established institutions engaged in a bizarre competitive struggle to achieve the highest cure rates—a contest which eventually led to claims to be able to cure 100 percent of one's patients! If the asylum system thus had its roots in one sort of statistical version of cutthroat competition, its imminent demise seems to have provoked another—only this time, the hospitals, racing to discharge 100 percent of their intake within three months, seem largely unconcerned with labeling their output as cured.

TABLE 4–2
Resident Population in State and County Mental Hospitals
in the U.S.A., 1950–1974

Year	Number Resident	Year	Number Resident
1950	512,500	1963	504,600
1951	520,300	1964	490,400
1952	532,000	1965	475,200
1953	545,000	1966	452,100
1954	554,000	1967	426,000
1955	558,900	1968	400,700
1956	551,400	1969	370,000
1957	548,600	1970	339,000
1958	545,200	1971	309,000
1959	541,900	1972	276,000
1960	535,500	1973	255,000
1961	527,500	1974	215,600
1962	515,600		

SOURCES: N.I.M.H.: *Trends in Resident Patients, State and County Mental Hospitals 1950–1968*, Rockville, Maryland. N.I.M.H. *Statistical Note No. 114*, Rockville, Maryland. (All figures rounded.)

As Table 4–2 shows, mental hospital populations in the United States are now well under half their 1955 levels, having declined over a twenty-year period (1955–1974) by more than sixty percent. The initially moderate yearly decline has accelerated markedly in recent years, with almost half the recorded fall (154,400 out of a total of 343,300) taking place since 1969. Moreover, even these figures tend to mask the magnitude of the change which has taken place. If the size of the mental hospital population relative to the total population had remained constant (and historically the tendency was for it to rise faster than the population as a whole), then starting with 1955 as a base year, mental hospitals would have contained 715,000 people by 1974—the actual total, of course, being half a million less than this "expected value."

With only very few exceptions, the policy of effecting a dramatic departure from traditional state-hospital based psychiatric care has clearly been national in scope—although it has been carried much further in some states than in others. Recent research has demonstrated that "of the state hospital patients admitted with 'major' psychiatric disorders (organic brain syndrome, schizophrenia, other neuroses [sic], and mental retardation) a surprisingly large percentage (about 60%) were, during the period 1969–73, either referred to outpatient clinics or discontinued without any referral. Another 10 percent were referred to nursing homes or homes for the aged."[11]

In some cases, the break with the past has been dramatically sudden, with transfers and ward closures sometimes ordered literally overnight:[12] In Wisconsin, for example, new legislation authorizing an 80 percent reduction of psychiatric beds in the 35 county hospitals produced a 77 percent decline in inpatient population during fiscal year 1974.[13] And in New York State, a 1968 memorandum from the Deputy Commissioner of Mental Hygiene ordering the implementation of a more selective admissions policy was followed by a fall in the state hospital cases from 78,020 in 1968 to 47,739 in 1971, and to 34,000 by 1973, a decline of some 64 percent in five years.[14] In a few states, the cutback in patient population is now almost complete: Thus in California the inpatient census fell from 50,000 in 1955 to 22,000 by 1967, and to only 7,000 by 1973.[15] Announcing that so far as the state government was concerned, "twenty-four hour hospitalization is the least acceptable form of treatment. Locally provided outpatient care is the most acceptable . . . ,"[16] the Reagan administration unveiled a plan to phase out the remaining state hospitals before the end of the decade. And on a national basis, recent estimates have suggested that the population of state hospitals will be no more than 100,000 by 1980, or less than a fifth of what it was in 1955.[17]

Forward planning in England is premised on what amounts to, in some respects, an even more far-reaching transformation of the system there. A recent (1971) Department of Health and Social Security internal memorandum, "Hospital Services for the Mentally Ill," anticipates *the complete abolition of the mental hospital system.* Within fifteen to twenty years . . . all provision will be in District General Hospitals . . . ," with inpatient provision on a minimal basis—about 26,000 places, or 0.5 inpatient beds per 1000 of the general population.[18] A parallel decline is foreseen in the population of institutions for the mentally subnormal. During the 1960s the number of inmates in such places had remained relatively constant at about 60,000 people; the 1971 White Paper on "Better Services for the Mentally Handicapped"—an ironic title in the circumstances—proposes a reduction to a little more than half this many. The existence of "considerable waiting lists [for admission to the institutions] and the increase of life expectancy among the sub-normal themselves" are conceded, but are to be coped with by expanding the role played by "community treatment."[19]

Lest one is inclined to doubt the reliability of the forecasts involved here, one may compare these plans with an earlier, fifteen-year predic-

TABLE 4-3
Resident Population of Mental Hospitals
in England and Wales, 1951-1970

Year	Number Resident	Year	Number Resident
1951	143,200	1961	135,400
1952	144,600	1962	133,800
1953	146,600	1963	127,600
1954	148,100	1964	126,500
1955	146,900	1965	123,600
1956	145,600	1966	121,600
1957	143,200	1967	118,900
1958	142,800	1968	116,400
1959	139,100	1969	105,600
1960	136,200	1970	103,300

SOURCES: E.M. Brooke. "Factors in the Demand for Psychiatric Beds." *The Lancet* (December 8, 1962): 1211, by permission (for 1951-1960). Figures supplied by the Department of Health and Social Security (for 1961-1970). All figures rounded. London: H.M.S.O.

tion covering the years 1961-1975, whose accuracy many were at the time inclined to question. Between 1954 and 1960, as Table 4-3 shows, the residential mental hospital population had fallen by roughly 8 percent, from 148,080 to 136,162. Welcoming this trend, the 1961 report embodying government plans for the hospital service as a whole used it as a basis for predicting "that in fifteen years' time there may well be needed not more than half as many places in hospitals for mental illness as there are today. Expressed in numerical terms, this would be a redundancy of no fewer than 75,000 beds. Even so, . . . if we are to have the courage of our ambitions, we ought to pitch the estimate lower still, as low as we dare, perhaps lower."[20] The author of the report proved to be an excellent prophet: The White Paper had indicated a target of 1.8 beds per thousand people to be reached by 1976; and by 1971 the rate was already almost that low—approximately 2.0 beds per 1,000. As Enoch Powell had urged at the very outset of the process, when he spoke of setting "the torch to the funeral pyre," successive governments of differing political complexions were indeed "erring on the side of ruthlessness . . ."; and as a result, mental hospitals appeared to be "doomed institutions."[21]

With the English government proclaiming that the days of the large mental hospital were numbered, prospects of substantial outlays to improve or even maintain these structures were obviously slim. Immediately following the official announcement of the policy of winding down the mental hospitals, in a clear indication of the practical impact of the new approach, Regional Hospital Boards were instructed ". . . to ensure that no more money than is necessary is spent on the upgrading or reconditioning of mental hospitals which in ten or fifteen years are not going to be required . . . ; for the large, isolated and unsatisfactory buildings, closure will nearly always be the right answer."[22] A decade of such policies naturally produced a further deterioration in the already squalid conditions of many mental hospitals; as well as a series of associated scandals which could be (and were) used as further evidence of the necessity of phasing out the "irredeemably flawed" institutional system.[23]

Meanwhile, in the United States, the continuing fall in the numbers of patients to be housed provided most state governments with plausible reasons for abandoning expensive schemes of capital investment designed to extend and/or renovate their existing mental hospital systems.[24] By the early 1970s, a number of states were not only not adding to or renovating their existing hospitals, they had actually begun to shut some of them down. (Cf. Table 4–4). And more recently, a number of others have given notice of anticipated closures.[25] Nevertheless, the number of hospitals eliminated and slated for elimination does not come close to matching the size of the decline in inpatient population. The number of patients, after all, has fallen by more than 50 percent, while only 14 of the more than 300 state hospitals have been closed; and most states indicate that they have no present plans to add to this total.[26] In a very few states (Florida, Georgia, Mississippi, and Virginia) this policy reflects the fact that, contrary to national trends, their inpatient populations have not fallen very far, if at all. But most states more nearly resemble Arkansas, which has seen the patient census in its two state hospitals fall 90 percent, from 5,000 in 1957 to 450 in 1974, and yet still insists (for public consumption at least) that it does not plan to close either one.

Although a number of factors have contributed to this paradoxical state of affairs, the single most important element has undoubtedly been the need for careful handling of the potentially explosive issue of employee redundancies and layoffs. Unlike psychiatrists and other "professional" staff, who can be bought off with substitute careers in "community psychiatry" or displaced into positions where they serve higher status clients, ward attendants are acutely threatened with loss of their livelihood by state hospital closures. Coming from social backgrounds

TABLE 4–4
Closures of State Mental Hospitals in the United States

State	Number Closed	Year Closed
California	1	1970
	3	1972
Illinois	1	1973
Kentucky	1	1971
Massachusetts	1	1973
Minnesota	1	1971
	1	1972
New York	1	1972
Oklahoma	1	1970
	1	1971
Washington	1	1973
Wisconsin	1	1973
Total	14	1973

SOURCE: M. Greenblatt. "Historical Forces Affecting the Closing of State Mental Hospitals." *Where is My Home?* Mimeographed: Scottsdale, Arizona: N.T.I.S. 1974: 4.

which often closely resemble those of their erstwhile "clients," the patients, ward orderlies usually possess little in the way of formal education and training or transferable skills; and even such experience as they do possess is relatively limited in its applicability to other alternative occupations. (This problem has been compounded by the fact that one alternative sector of the labor market where their "skills" might have been of service—as wardens in prisons and juvenile detention centers—is itself, as we have seen, in a state of contraction.) In consequence, "the psychiatric technician probably has very limited labor market potential outside the state hospital system at payscales comparable to those in state hospitals."[27]

State employee unions do, however, possess considerable influence in state legislatures, an influence accentuated in this instance because most state hospitals are located in relatively isolated rural areas, where closure threatens not merely the livelihood of the hospital workers but the economic viability of the area as a whole. The California experience

is instructive in this regard. The state government here made a particularly determined effort to implement a policy of relying on noninstitutional controls and to shut down "superfluous" institutions. By January
1973, four state hospitals had already been closed, and in that month
the Reagan administration announced plans to close all remaining state
hospitals by 1977 (with the exception of two wings to be kept open for
criminal offenders); and to shut down all hospitals for the mentally
retarded by 1981.[28] By way of response, this provoked a carefully
orchestrated campaign on the part of the California State Employees'
Association, involving intensive lobbying of the state legislature and
clever use of the mass media to highlight the least salubrious aspects
of the decarceration process. This had the desired effect. The legislature
was persuaded to pass a bill making future hospital closures conditional
on its prior approval; and when Reagan vetoed this measure, his veto
was overridden—the first time a gubernatorial veto had been overridden
in California in twenty-eight years.[29] Since then, other states, too, have
reported abandoning or postponing hospital closures in the wake of
organized resistance from employee unions—opposition which can
prove politically troublesome not least because it often relies on the
technique of creating "moral panics" in the surrounding communities
to which patients are being released.[30]

The situation is, however, clearly an unstable and temporary one.
Although civil service unions obviously possess considerable influence in
many state legislatures, this influence has its limits. The irrationality of
a policy that sustains a whole network of vast and unwieldy institutions,
each of which once contained several thousand inmates and all of which
taken together now cope with only a few hundred, is obvious. It
represents a contradiction which in the long run is too blatant to sur-
vive.[31] Ultimately, as Greenblatt suggests, one must "look forward either
to a major metamorphosis in the functions of these hospitals or to
further total shutdowns."[32]

Since the mid-1950s, then, there have been dramatic changes in the
state's handling of the problems posed by the mentally ill. As with the
control of the criminal and the delinquent, segregative techniques in
their traditional form are steadily losing ground to newer "community-
based" alternatives. In the face of an accelerating decline in its
in-patient census, and under increasing attack because of its alleged
negative impact on those it "treats," the mental hospital appears to be
destined for the scrap-heap. Few seem inclined to mourn its passing;
and for the most part there is little inclination to question conventional

accounts of the reasons for its fall from grace. It is these accounts which we must now consider.

1. See the N.I.M.H. sponsored "Where is My Home?", 1974.

2. For a discussion and attempted explanation of this pattern, See Scull 1974: Ch. 9.

3. Cited in Jones 1972: 291; See also Chief Medical Officer's Report 1959: 129: Tooth and Brooke 1961: 710.

4. Wilkins 1872: 55.

5. Mitchell 1894: 4.

6. Joint Commission 1961: 7.

7. Swazey 1974: 222; Weiner 1974: 87.

8. Rehin and Martin 1963: 20; Jones and Sidebotham 1962: 10–21.

9. Cited in Hoenig and Hamilton 1969: 2. See also Stewart et al. 1968; Hecker 1970.

10. Deutsch 1949.

11. Mulhearn 1974: 153.

12. Chase 1973.

13. N.I.M.H. Statistical Note #114: 15.

14. Reich and Siegal 1973: 42.

15. Chase 1973: 18.

16. California State Governor's Budget 1972–1973: 862.

17. See Mulhearn 1974: 153; Horizon House 1975: 3. The massive outflow of people produced in the wake of the run-down and even the closure of state hospitals has created a sizeable market for private entrepreneurs offering "care" for ex-patients in the community, a development some states concede they are actively encouraging (see Indiana Department of Health 1975: 130). There has even emerged whole chains of "convalescent hospitals" and halfway houses run on a profit making basis. For example, one major chain known as "Beverly Enterprises," which began with three convalescent facilities in 1964, now owns 63 board and care facilities and sanitariums in the United States (38 in California alone), and had net revenues of $79.5 million in 1972 (See Chase 1973: 17).

18. Cited in Jones 1972: 339, my emphasis.

19. Significantly, however, only £10 million of the £40 million budgeted for the mentally subnormal over the next five years is to be allocated to these community services (See Jones 1972: 337–339).

20. Enoch Powell, then Minister of Health, in National Association for Mental Health *Annual Report 1961*.

21. All quotes from Powell in National Association for Mental Health *Annual Report 1961*.

22. 1961 Ministry of Health Circular, cited in Jones 1972: 322.

23. See Jones 1972: Ch. 13, esp. 330.

24. Robertson 1974: 63.

25. The Minnesota Department of Public Welfare, for example, recently indicated that "the State's ten mental institutions have been ranked in order of priority for closure . . . " (in Horizon House 1975: 22). Other states publicly acknowledge similar plans to close down one or more state hospitals.

26. See Horizon House 1975.

27. Weiner 1974: 93.

28. Chase 1973: 17.

29. *Los Angeles Times,* January 29, 1974: p. 16, columns 1–13.

30. By and large, the unions rely on "exemplary tales" of the squalor and misery of the conditions in which ex-patients live (and to which they contribute) and similar stories concerning the violence to which they are prone. (For example, the California union made much play of a case in which a man was released from a state mental hospital and 17 days later killed his wife, three of their five children, and himself.) Such activities are unwelcome because they undermine the plausibility of the official version of the reasons for the introduction of decarceration and because, by promoting the notion that ex-patients pose a threat to the social order and more especially to property values, they threaten to widen opposition to deinstitutionalization. For union opposition, see California State Employees' Association 1972; American Federation of State, County and Municipal Employees 1975. For the unions' influence on state policy, see Horizon House 1975: 22, 67, 68–81.

31. Consider, for example, the Massachusetts Legislature's response to the employee problem created by the shutdown of juvenile detention centers. In an effort to blunt the guards' opposition and to head off the political trouble they might try to make, they were simply kept on the state's payroll after all the inmates had been dispersed, allegedly to maintain the empty buildings! As Greenberg dryly comments: "Legislators are unlikely to continue appropriating money for useless work indefinitely" (Greenberg 1975: 30–31).

32. Greenblatt 1974: 4.

PART TWO

Conventional explanations for decarceration: their limitations and inadequacies

The importance of the developments we have surveyed in the last two chapters is beyond question. With respect to both the "mad" and the "bad," there is a vigorous effort under way to reduce the institution to the place of last rather than first resort, and even to eliminate it entirely. Moreover, this new policy has already had considerable impact. In place of a persistent, at least century-old upward trend in the size of institutionalized populations, the nineteen sixties and seventies have witnessed drastic reductions in the size of most mental hospitals and the closing of several of them; the shutdown of a number of juvenile reformatories (and, in the case of Massachusetts, the virtually total abandonment of institutionalization as a response to delinquency); the expansion of halfway houses for coping with both criminals and mental patients; and the use of parole and, more particularly, probation, on an entirely novel scale and in historically unprecedented ways. The obvious question is why has all this been happening.

As the materials we have examined have demonstrated, with respect to the three crucial "problem populations" we are concerned with, a policy of decarceration has clearly been pursued most rapidly and universally in the handling of the mentally ill. The dramatic and readily visible nature of the change in this segment of the formal social control apparatus has encouraged the "Madness Establishment" (to borrow Chu and Trotter's apt phrase) to develop a more or less standardized explanation of why such a transformation has been and is occurring, an explanation which is at once both relatively carefully elaborated and possessed of considerable surface plausibility. Although varying in the relative significance attributed to one or the other, accounts based on this conventional wisdom lay particular stress on two factors — the advent of psychoactive drugs; and the realization, fueled by a mass of modern social-scientific research, that mental hospitals are fundamentally antitherapeutic institutions having a detrimental impact on their inmate populations.

By contrast, the voluminous literature on community corrections rarely gives this question of origins more than passing notice, being for the most part more concerned to propagandize on behalf of the new approach than to examine (critically or otherwise) the social foundations of this change in penal practices. The points its advocates make in an effort to "sell" their product do, however, suggest an implicit reliance on an account couched (aside from the obviously inapplicable factor of advances in drug therapy) in the same basic terms. Once again there is the reliance on the claim that social science has demonstrated that prisons and detention centers are a costly, brutal, and generally counter-productive method of dealing with lawbreakers; while—measured in terms of recidivism rates—the community approach for less money provides greater (or, if one listens to more cautious salesmen, at least equal) "success" in coping with the criminally deviant. Allegedly, it is also more humane.

We now turn, in Part Two, to a detailed critical examination of these standard accounts of why decarceration is taking place. In the first of two chapters, we shall confine our attention to the case of the mentally ill, focusing on the role played by the expansion of drug therapy in reducing mental hospital populations. From this we shall move to a detailed critique of the second and supposedly more generally influential factor, the recognition of the total insti-tution's shared capacity to dehumanize its inmates. As I trust will be apparent by the end of this discussion, both these accounts turn out to be seriously defective—indeed, ultimately unacceptable—as explanations of the deinstitu-tionalization process.

CHAPTER FIVE

The "technological fix"? Psychoactive drugs and community treatment

The reason of a thing is not to be enquired after, till you are sure the thing itself be so. We commonly are at what's the reason of it? *before we are sure of the thing.*

JOHN SELDEN
Table Talk (1689)

They say miracles are past, and we have our
philosophical persons
To make modern and familiar, things supernatural
and causeless.

WILLIAM SHAKESPEARE
All's Well that Ends Well

The early 1950s marked the beginning of what psychiatrists widely regard as a "revolution" in psychiatric therapy. Of course, psychiatrists are (or ought to be) notorious for proclaiming a revolution on the basis of changes which critical outside inspection shows to be a reaction;[1] but in this instance there appears to be a measure of truth in their contentions. At the very least, one must acknowledge that in this period they were given a new treatment modality which enabled them to engage in a more passable imitation of conventional medical practice. In place of acting as glorified administrators of huge custodial warehouses, and instead of relying on crude empirical devices like shock therapy and even cruder surgical techniques like lobotomy to provide themselves with an all too transparent medical figleaf, psychiatrists in public mental hospitals could now engage in the prescription and administration of the classic symbolic accouterment of the modern medicine man—drugs.

The occasion of this happy transformation was the introduction and marketing of what are variously known as "tranquilizing," "psychoactive," or "ataraxic" drugs. The first, and still the most important of these, was a phenothiazine derivative, chlorpromazine — originally synthesized by the French pharmaceutical company, Rhône Poulenc, in December 1950, and marketed in the United States by Smith, Kline, and French as "Thorazine," and in England by May and Baker as "Largactil." According to the drug companies, the psychiatric applications of chlorpromazine were an instance of scientific serendipity. A less charitable view of evidence available on the development phase in the United States[2] suggests an at times almost frantic search for therapeutic applications with which (a) to convince the Federal Drug Administration to allow marketing of the drug; and (b) to persuade American physicians to prescribe it.

Chlorpromazine originated from research "seeking to produce a phenothiazine derivative with a high degree of central nervous system activity primarily for use as an anesthetic potentiator . . . ," and much of the early testing of the drug was done with this in mind.[3] By 1953, efforts to find a commercial use for the compound had been extended to include attempts to demonstrate its value as an antiemetic, controlling nausea and vomiting; as treatment for itching; as a general sedative; and as a help in cases of dramatic and acute psychosis. A Smith, Kline, and French internal memorandum dated April 8, 1953 indicates that "nausea and vomiting are still felt to be the most appropriate indications on which to conduct rapid clinical testing to try to get marketing clearance by the F.D.A."[4] Reflecting this emphasis, by the end of 1953, only five months before it was to be marketed, chlorpromazine had been tested on only 104 psychiatric patients in the United States.[5] Thirteen months later, it was being given to an estimated *two million* patients in the United States alone; and by 1970, U.S. pharmaceutical manufacturers sold $500 million of "psychotherapeutic agents" — of which phenothiazines accounted for $116,500,000.[6]

Thorazine proved to be a financial bonanza for Smith, Kline, and French. On an initial investment for research and development of only $350,000, the corporation realized massive profits. Within a year of its commercial introduction, thorazine had increased the company's total sales volume by one third; and a major proportion of Smith, Kline, and French's subsequent fiscal growth, from net sales of $53 million in 1953 to $347 million in 1970, was directly or indirectly attributable to this enormously profitable product.[7]

Of course, this explosive growth pattern was no accident. It reflected a huge, sustained, and expensive sales drive on the part of the drug companies, particularly Smith, Kline, and French. In 1954, the latter's regular salesforce — nationwide — for all their product lines amounted to 300 people. When the decision was made to promote the use of thorazine for psychiatric cases, a separate "task force" of fifty men was set up to work full time solely on selling this one drug. Over a seven year period, both state legislatures and state hospital staffs were bombarded with a hail of sophisticated propaganda designed to convince them of the virtues and advantages of the drug as a cheap, effective form of treatment suitable for administration on a mass basis to mental hospital patients.[8]

Not surprisingly, in the circumstances (and given the coincidence in the timing and introduction of thorazine and the reversal of the upward trend in the numbers of mental patients), an explanation of the policy of early release and the consequent decline in mental hospital populations which has enjoyed a considerable measure of popularity in some psychiatric and official circles simply attributes the transformation to the growing use and effectiveness of psychoactive drugs. By 1959, authoritative English sources had concluded that "the modern physical treatments and the new tranquilizing and stimulating drugs . . . explain why with a rising admission rate the number [of mental patients] has now dropped each year since 1955."[9] Two years later, the American Joint Commission on Mental Illness and Health was even more definite: "Tranquillizing drugs have revolutionized the management of psychotic patients in American mental hospitals, and probably deserve primary credit for reversal of the upward spiral of the State hospital in-patient load."[10] Since then, such conclusions have continued to receive support in many quarters. When, for example, a recent British Minister of Health was called on to defend plans to phase out all remaining mental hospitals, he did so by claiming that "the treatment of psychosis, neurosis and schizophrenia have been entirely changed by the drug revolution. People go into hospital with mental disorders and they are cured, and that is why we want to bring this branch of medicine into the scope of the 230 district general hospitals that are planned for England and Wales."[11] In the circumstances, the (U.S.) National Committee on Brain Sciences seemed to be on safe ground in 1975 in deciding that "the introduction of the phenothiazine group of drugs in the treatment of schizophrenia has been the outstanding single practical contribution to psychiatry over the last twenty years."[12]

This account has the twin virtues of simplicity, and of reinforcing the medical model of insanity by suggesting that the advent of psychoactive drugs signals a medical breakthrough in this area paralleling earlier ones allowing the successful treatment of other hitherto intractable chronic diseases. Yet despite its evident appeal, as an explanation it is distinctly flawed. For not only does it tend to exaggerate the therapeutic achievement these drugs represent (as I shall show in some detail in a moment), but as Mechanic indicates, it is empirically inaccurate and inadequate in other ways as well.

Studies of a number of English mental hospitals, for example, "show that new patterns of release were observable prior to drug introduction, and they suggest that the tremendous change which took place is due largely to alterations in administrative policies."[13] The Mapperly Hospital was one of the pioneers in this respect, and here the number of patients declined markedly from 1948 onwards, or several years before the advent of psychoactive drugs. The fall, moreover (from 1,310 patients in 1948 to 1,060 in 1956), was a steady one which proceeded at an unchanged pace even after drugs arrived on the scene.[14] Precisely the same pattern is observable at some mental hospitals in the United States. At the Vermont State Hospital, for example, admissions for "schizophrenia" remained virtually constant between 1947 and 1958; but in the same period the number of discharged schizophrenics rose sharply and steadily year by year, from 30 in 1948 to 120 in 1958.[15]

In the late 1940s and early 1950s, then, well before the new drugs were introduced,

> certain hospitals had already adopted a policy of placing "an emphasis on early discharge, or the avoidance of admission altogether, in order to prevent the accumulation of long-stay institutionalized patients. . . . The pioneers' use of social techniques began in certain hospitals well before the national swing was noticed in 1955, and the underlying statistical trends must have long antedated the change in overall bed occupancy.[16]

English figures on the average length of time an individual inmate could expect to spend in a mental hospital reveal the change quite clearly. Comparing the statistics for 1949 with those for 1953 (the latter being the year before the marketing of chlorpromazine and, therefore, the last year in which the use of ataraxic drugs could not conceivably have influenced the outcome), we find that "the median duration of stay for all male patients discharged in 1953 was 1.87 months, whereas in 1949 it had been 2.14; for women patients the corresponding figures were 1.98 in 1953 as against 2.32 in 1949.[17] What becomes obvious, then (as Aubrey Lewis has suggested), is that national figures on mental hospital populations, when taken by themselves, may be a seriously misleading guide to when the deinstitutionalization process actually began. For they tend to mask the earlier changes at the local level and to obscure the degree to which the fall in overall numbers, when it did come, represented a continuation rather than a departure from pre-existing trends.

Undoubtedly, one of the major supports for the notion that the introduction of psychotropic drugs has been the major factor behind the fall in mental hospital populations is the work of Brill and Patton.[18] In a series of reports on the New York State Hospital system, they attempted to use statistical comparisons of hospital populations over time to specify this relationship, and their work is commonly cited as one of the "definitive research projects [which] . . . confirmed the earlier assessments of the drug's 'revolutionary' impact upon mental hospitals."[19] Curiously enough, in all their papers save the first, published in 1957, even Brill and Patton concede their inability to identify "the drug influence clearly as an isolated factor . . ." and confess that it has become "impossible to identify the specific part played by psychopharmacology. . . ." While continuing to insist on the primacy and "utmost importance" of the use of psychoactive drugs, their account increasingly incorporates, in a vague and ad hoc fashion, references to changes in mental hospital atmospheres, as well as largely unspecified changes in the "social, legal, economic, administrative, and technical forces" which impinge on the mental hospital.[20] Allegedly, only the 1957 study reveals the pure and unalloyed influence of the phenothiazines, and "without the first year's study, it would indeed be difficult to identify the effect of drug therapy among the various influences on the patient population."[21]

Obviously, therefore, any assessment of whether Brill and Patton have established "a direct cause and effect relation" between drug treatment and the fall in mental hospital populations (as is sometimes suggested)[22] must proceed by giving close attention to this first paper, to see whether it does indeed show what they and others have claimed for it. When this is done, however, one's confidence in their findings quickly evaporates. It turns out that their work does not rest on the obvious foundation for a study which claims to examine the relative impact of drug treatment versus lack of drug treatment—namely a comparison of the release rates of patients (preferably randomly) assigned to one or other treatment modality. As they acknowledge: "This paper is not a comparison of the results in two groups of cases, one of which had drug treatment and the other did not. Instead it compares and contrasts the total results of two successive years of work in a mental hospital system." Ultimately, their whole assessment of the impact of drugs comes to rest on the contention that "we know of no other major change in operating conditions which took place between 1954–55 and 1955–56 . . ." which could have produced the observed fall in hospital population.[23]

This is clearly inadequate, and its inadequacy becomes still more patent when one realizes that much of the other data they present appear specifically to contradict their own interpretation of their findings. In the first place, the decline in hospital populations was not confined to categories where drug therapy could have been expected to exert a strong influence. Then again, although subsets of the patient population differed widely in the proportions given drug therapy (ranging from a low of 9% of males with central nervous system lues to 46% among female psychoneurotics, and with 33.9% of women receiving drug therapy compared with only 20.9% of males), "*no quantitative correlation could be shown between the percentage of patients receiving drug therapy in a given hospital or a given category and the amount of improvement in releases.*"[24]

All in all, it seems odd that Brill and Patton's research has received as much attention as it has, and downright perverse to claim it provides "definitive" evidence that drugs caused the fall in hospital populations. The oddness and perversity appear even more pronounced when it turns out that there have been other, in many respects more satisfactory, studies of changes in mental hospital populations (made at the same time as theirs) which failed to show that any relationship whatsoever existed between the introduction of drugs and the fall in resident populations. For example, Epstein and his colleagues undertook an elaborate retrospective study of the impact of drugs on release rates in the state of California. Unlike Brill and Patton, they employed direct comparisons of those treated and not treated with drugs, and of hospitals which employed drugs on a large scale with those that adopted a more conservative stance. In a report on the data collected on white male schizophrenics, they showed that "where a difference is found between the retention rate of ataraxic drug treated patients and those not so treated, the untreated patients consistently show a somewhat lower retention rate." Both within and between hospitals, "the drug treated patients tended to have longer periods of hospitalization. . . . "Furthermore, the hospitals wherein higher percentages of first admission schizophrenic patients are treated with these drugs tend to have somewhat higher retention rates for this group as a whole." The inescapable conclusion was that psychotropic drugs' "usage does not appear to have been associated with the more rapid release rate which has been observed in recent years."[25]

Even if this contradictory evidence had not been uncovered, to rest content with an "explanation" connected simply in terms of pharmacological progress would imply the acceptance of a naively deterministic relationship between technological advances and changes in social control styles and practices, to the neglect of the influence of the social context in determining the uses to which these advances are put. This objection applies with particular force when the dependent variable is the rate at which mental patients are discharged back into the community. For over the years, social scientists have accumulated a mass of data which demonstrates beyond question that there are "too many social correlates of discharge for it to be regarded purely as a clinical phenomenon."[26]

After all, even those who most strenuously defend the idea that drugs are responsible for the current policy of deinstitutionalization do not contend that phenothiazines *cure* their patients—merely that they provide a measure of symptomatic relief.[27] And supposing one accepts this contention for the moment: One must still ask whether, in other contexts, the more subtle and less visible control of patient behavior which the new drugs allegedly offered might not have been used simply to ease internal management problems and decrease the incidence of "overt" blatant physical restraint within the institution, while having little or no effect on discharge patterns.[28] Nor is it easy to see how a simple technological determinism of this sort can account either for the sudden acceleration of the decline in American mental hospitals' populations from the mid-1960s on, when no change of comparable magnitude occurred in England,[29] or (to cite another important aspect of the policy of decarceration) for the conditions of existence endured by the mentally disabled discharged into the "community." Equally seriously, this approach clearly cannot be extended to account for the decarceration of other types of deviants—criminals, juvenile offenders, and so on—groups which have not (at least not yet) been subject to "treatment" with such drugs.[30] Yet (as we have seen in Chapter Three), in these areas, too, the state has been pursuing a policy of deinstitutionalization. Thus, instead of allowing us to see all these developments as a unitary phenomenon, concentration on the "technological fix" leads us in the direction of a series of unconnected, ad hoc explanations of developments in each of these sectors.

But there remains a still more damaging objection which proponents of the pharmacological explanation have been forced to finesse: namely, a growing volume of evidence which suggests that claims about the therapeutic effectiveness of so-called "antipsychotic" medication — mainly the phenothiazines — have been greatly exaggerated. For example, a recent double-blind study[31] of young male schizophrenics by Rappaport and Associates was able to demonstrate only a short-term beneficial effect of chlorpromazine treatment. Moreover, besides its ephemerality, this improvement was observable only during the period between hospitalization and discharge, that is while patients were institutionalized. Compared with patients given a placebo, those assigned to chlorpromazine treatment during their hospital stay proved significantly more susceptible to deterioration once they left the hospital. Indeed, a history of drug treatment was associated with an *increased* likelihood of rehospitalization upon release, a finding directly contrary to the one claims for phenothiazine's effectiveness would lead us to predict.[32] In general those patients randomly assigned placebos while hospitalized and not taking phenothiazines at follow-up "showed significantly greater clinical improvement and less pathology at follow-up, significantly fewer rehospitalizations and significantly less overall functional disturbance in the community than any other group of patients. . . . Also, significantly fewer patients in the placebo group became worse from discharge to follow-up. . . . In the long run, most patients *not* given phenothiazine do better. . . ."[33]

There can be no question but that the extreme optimism which greeted the advent of psychoactive drugs, and which persisted for a number of years, reflected the weakness and poor design of many of the evaluations made at that time far more than the actual efficacy of the drugs themselves.[34] Remarkably few of the early studies of chlorpromazine's effects met even the minimal criteria of a scientifically acceptable research design. To a limited extent, this reflected the underdevelopment of techniques for controlling experimental bias during the early 1950s, but many early studies failed to use what controls *were* available; and long after a consensus emerged on "the double-blind, placebo controlled method as virtually a *sine qua non* of clinical drug research," tests continued to be conducted, and claims of the drug's "efficacy" supported, on the basis of nonblind and single-blind designs.[35] Lack of methodological rigor was apparent in all aspects of the testing program. Sample sizes were frequently very small — occasionally just a single patient — and sometimes the number of patients treated was not even noted. Reviewing 61 of these early studies, Bryant and his coworkers found that such potential sources of bias "as differential treatment of experimental subjects, previous and concomitant therapy experience, and duration of illness . . ." were seldom considered or controlled for, while long term follow-up studies were entirely absent. "An adequate description of the method used to rate patients' improvement was lacking in many of the reports and reliability of the ratings was, likewise, neglected."[36] Subsequent careful reviews of the relevant literature have, scarcely surprisingly, demonstrated that "uncontrolled studies" of this type "gave a *systematically* more positive evaluation of drug effect than controlled studies.[37]

All of this should not be taken to imply that the administration of such drugs has no behavioral effects. To the contrary, the preponderance (though by no means all) of well-designed, well-conducted studies show that these drugs are better than placebos if given in sufficiently high dosage.[38] There can be no question, for example, that "excessive doses of neuroleptics produce severe reductions of motor activity and a general loss of spontaneity" — that they function, in effect, as "chemical strait-jackets."[39] For lower, more routine, and less flexible dosages, however, the evidence is distinctly more ambiguous and careful studies suggest that positive findings may be more a reflection of setting and expectations than of actual effects of the drug.[40] Undoubtedly, a positive bias is widespread, with most practitioners accepting without question "the effectiveness of continual low-dosage chemotherapy in controlling bizarre behavior in the chronically hospitalized population . . . ,"[41] and the doctors' beliefs being reflected in their behavior.[42]

Yet "major investigations, using standard rating instruments, reveal that fewer than 50 per cent of patients hospitalized for several years improve in response to neuroleptics."[43] Less scrupulously controlled studies, which (as we have seen) generally exaggerate the therapeutic effectiveness of drug treatment, in this instance only confirm the same general pattern. In their review of studies of chlorpromazine usage to treat chronic schizophrenia, Glick and Margolis report that the definition of improvement generally used by these researchers allowed them to count as "improved" patients whom drugs simply rendered less troublesome in a hospital context, but who, it was conceded, were not fit for release.[44] Yet even with these generous criteria of improvement following drug use, the mean rate of improvement in the twelve double-blind studies they reviewed was only 17.5%.[45]

More recently, and even more damagingly, a highly impressive comparative study by Paul and his associates of "hard-core" mental patients randomly assigned to drug or placebo treatment under "triple-blind" conditions[46] discovered "a complete absence of differential effects on patient behavior as a function of drug maintenance versus placebo [use]." Specifically designed to test the effectiveness of psychoactive drugs as actually prescribed in practice, their data "failed to demonstrate any effectiveness at all for continued low dosage maintenance therapy." Indeed, "in the early stages of treatment . . . drugs interfered with improvement."[47] But if phenothiazines are ineffective for substantial portions of the target population, and if in any event the types of maintenance doses generally prescribed are largely ineffective, how can anyone seriously contend that the advent of drug therapy is the main reason for the decline in mental hospital populations (the more so since the drugs are apparently *least* effective with the groups whose release has been *most* crucial to the running down of mental hospital popula-tions—the old, chronic cases)?

Even if most careful studies of the effectiveness of psychoactive drugs were far more uniformly favorable than we have seen, serious diffi-culties would remain for proponents of the idea that the introduction of such drugs is the primary factor in the fall of mental hospital popula-tions. For one thing, most of the studies we now possess consider short-term effects only. Where long-term follow-up studies do demonstrate the existence of a drug effect (and because of "generally faulty research designs" evidence on this point is muddled and contradictory),[48] this effect is generally quite small;[49] and "the difference between those patients treated with drugs and these not treated with drugs decreases over time. . . . As for the quality of the patient's adjustment after he leaves the hospital, the results of drug therapy are even less encouraging: the majority of those who live in the community continue to be unpro-ductive and are often a burden to their families."[50]

Rappaport's research suggests that the typical measures used to record improvement in a hospital context (and in terms of which drugs are often alleged to be efficacious) may simply not tap the kinds of factors important for successful functioning in the outside world. And his finding that patients on chlorpromazine perform significantly better in a hospital setting than do these on a placebo, whereas on the outside this relationship is almost precisely reversed, provides presumptive evidence in support of this position.[51] More generally, the growing body of evidence on "state dependent learning" suggests that much of what is learned under the influence of drugs may not be carried over into behavior in an undrugged state.[52] And this presents yet another serious problem for those who continue to place their faith in phenothiazines as a sort of "magic bullet"—for even if we were to grant their dubious premise, there is reliable evidence that once beyond the reaches of staff supervision, very many ex-patients simply fail to *take* their drugs on a regular basis![53]

At best, therefore, one is left with the conclusion that the introduction of psychotropic drugs may have facilitated the policy of early discharge by reducing the incidence of florid symptoms among at least some of the disturbed, thus easing the problems of managing them in the community; and perhaps also by persuading doctors with an exaggerated idea of the drugs' efficacy of the feasibility of such a policy. But that their arrival can be help primarily responsible for the change is clearly highly implausible.

1. See Scull 1975b.

2. The evidence is presented, though with little in the way of a critical perspective, in Swazey 1974: esp. Chapter 7. Clearly the massive medical-commercial exploitation of new drugs on the basis of flimsy scientific evidence is by no means confined to those used in psychiatry, but rather is an endemic feature of the existing medical-industrial complex. A major role here is undoubtedly played by the ruthless profit seeking of the drug companies, and the convergence of this with the self-interest of the medical profession. The history of the single other most profitable drug introduced by Smith, Kline, and French, the amphetamines, is revealing in this respect. As with Thorazine, when amphetamines were introduced in the 1930s, their uses for a wide range of conditions— as a nasal decongestant, an antidote for depression, and somewhat later, as an appetite depressant—were vigorously promoted by the company and readily accepted by the profession. Five articles in the medical literature were used by Smith, Kline, and French in support of these claims, and just as was later the case with chlorpromazine, these studies were conducted on a very small number of subjects (less than 150) under conditions which rendered them useless as scientific tests of the drug's efficacy. Nevertheless, and despite mounting reports of serious side effects from 1939 on, ranging from addiction to psychosis to death, both the drug companies and the medical profession continue even now to derive enormous revenues (and profits) from substances whose clinical usefulness is doubtful, and whose lethal effects are certain. Only in 1973 did the F.D.A. make even token efforts to restrict amphetamines' use, and so far with only limited effect. As we shall see in this chapter, that the introduction of chlorpromazine marks merely a re-enactment of this history grows steadily more likely (For the amphetamine example, see Grinspoon and Hedblom, 1974; Zinberg 1975).

3. Swazey 1974:9.

4. Cited in Swazey 1974: 179.

5. Swazey 1974: 195.

6. Swazey 1974: 160; U.S. Department of Commerce 1971: 2; also Balter and Levine 1969.

7. Swazey 1974: 161.

8. For details on this campaign, see Swazey 1974: 202 ff.

9. Chief Medical Officer's Report 1959: 128.

10. Joint Commission 1961: 39.

11. Sir Keith Joseph in Hansard, December 7, 1971: 280–81; see also Brill and Patton 1957, 1962; Hecker 1970: 261; Pollack and Taube 1973: 10; Klerman 1974: 87.

12. Cited in Swazey 1974: xi–xii.

13. Mechanic 1969: 61–62; See also Brown 1960; Brown *et. al.* 1966:*passim,* esp. 17; Hoenig and Hamilton 1969: esp. 8 ff.; Wing and Brown 1970.

14. Lewis 1959: 207.

15. See Chittick, Brooks, and Deane 1959.

16. Wing and Brown 1970: 174, 9. Their account suggests that the new drugs' importance lay in facilitating the spread of the new administrative techniques—which leaves unanswered the question of why these techniques were officially supported and fostered. This is a point to which I shall return.

17. Lewis 1959: 207.

18. Britt and Patton 1957, 1959, 1962, 1966.

19. Swazey 1974: 235–236.

20. Brill and Patton 1966: 289. These changes are themselves left unexplained (as well as unspecified), except insofar as they are attributed to the indirect effects of the optimism generated by the advent of drug therapy.

21. Brill and Patton 1959: 499.

22. Swazey 1974: 237.

23. Brill and Patton 1957: 512.

24. Brill and Patton 1957: 513–514, my emphasis. In an effort to explain away this apparently devastating finding, they lamely suggest it "probably" reflects a differential responsiveness to drugs among the various categories of patients. But among its defects, this "explanation" turns out to be a pure tautology—the only evidence of this differential response is the lack of correlation between treatment levels and release.

25. Epstein *et al.* 1962, 42–44. For similar results and conclusions, this time using data from Washington D.C., see Linn 1959. Myers and Bean (1968: 96 ff.), using Connecticut data, found that drug treatment produced discharge rates no greater than those from custodial care with first admissions, while for rehospitalized patients "the discharge rate for drug therapy is lower than for custodial care." As the N.I.M.H. study group (1964: 256) pointed out, the drawback with these studies is that "the patients were not randomly assigned to the drug treatments." But the direct comparison of drug and nondrug cases is markedly superior to the methodology employed by Brill and Patton. And, as Epstein *et al.* (1962:40) point out, their work does demonstrate the relationship between "drug effects and release rate under operational conditions."

26. Brown 1960: 427; see also Greenley 1970, 1972; Wing *et al.* 1959; Watt and Buglass 1966.

27. See Clark 1956: 283: "It is well-known that patients can remain grossly psychotic and yet become passively cooperative, less overactive and destructive, or more docile. Such improvement may be more important to the custodian than the patients."

28. Indeed, the former turns out to be something more than a hypothetical possibility. There is good evidence that "neuroleptics are often used for solving psychological, social, administrative, and other non-medical problems" (Crane 1973: 125). Researchers have consistently found that, particularly with relatively large doses, "the most striking psychiatric responses to CPZ [chlorpromazine] were 'somnolence' and 'psychic indifference' " (Swazey 1974: 146). The relevance of these findings for mental hospital adminis-

trators was made starkly apparent from the outset. In Lehmann and Hanrahan's words: "Patients receiving the drug became lethargic. Manic patients often will not object to bed rest, and patients who present management problems become tractable. Assaultive and interfering behavior ceases almost entirely. The patients under treatment display a lack of spontaneous interest in their environment . . . [and diminished motor activity.]" (Lehmann and Hanrahan 1954: 230). One can understand why early researchers thought chlorpromazine might "produce a veritable medicinal lobotomy" (cited in Swazey 1974: 105). The superintendents proved apt pupils. A dramatic inverse relationship quickly became established between the use of psychotropic drugs and the use of more conventional forms of restraint. (For a vivid illustration of this, see Brill and Patton 1962: 21, figure 2). And as recent research by Crane makes clear, tranquilizers are still being widely used to "tranquilize": "Patients who present serious management problems are most likely to receive large quantities of neuroleptics for long periods of time, although the persistence of severe psychosis would suggest chemotherapy is not effective in such cases" (Crane 1973: 125).

29. See Tables 4–2 and 4–3 in Chapter Four, above. Advocates of the pharmacological explanation themselves failed to see in currently available drug therapies anything which would produce "a massive acceleration of the process of shrinkage" (Brill and Patton 1962: 35).

30. I say "not yet" advisedly. Enthusiasts for psychotropic drugs clearly see this situation as purely temporary. To cite just two examples: Contending that we are "in urgent need of a mass therapy for conduct and personality disorder, social incapacity, economic dependence, unemployability and vagabondage . . . ," Brill and Patton (1966: 294) argue that these problems are reflections of "the large number of psychiatric casualties whose primary and presenting symptoms are those of gross economic and social incapacity . . ."; and thus that "the difficulties of these persons clearly lie in the field of psychopharmacology." Similarly, Klerman (1974: 87–88) has recently suggested that as a direct result of the drug revolution. "much social deviance, previously regarded as legal, is being redefined as mental health; [sic] and it is hoped that psychopharmacologic agents will prove useful in altering behavior deviance such as alcoholism, drug addiction, perhaps even crime and delinquency." For critiques of such notions, see Kittrie 1971; and (more polemically) Szasz 1963, 1965.

31. A "double-blind study" involves setting up an experimental situation so that neither the observers nor the patients are aware of what form of "medication" is being given to any participant — that is, neither side knows whether any particular patient is receiving active medication or an inert (placebo) form.

32. See Rappaport *et al.* n.d.: i, 9, 11.

33. Rappaport *et al.* n.d.: 14, 9, emphasis in the original. Although Rappaport *et al.* provide no evidence on whether their findings apply to groups other than young male schizophrenics, other studies have demonstrated similar findings with other subsets of the mentally ill population.

34. Clark (1956: 282) suggests that psychiatric responses to new somatic treatments follow an "almost predictable sequence. . . . It consists of initial over-enthusiasm, usually based on a small number of preliminary optimistic reports; this is followed by disenchantment as subsequent, more systematic studies fail to verify initial enthusiastic claims. . . ." The subsequent history of psychotropic drugs appears likely to confirm this generalization. In this connection, as Leveton (1958: 233) notes:

> It would not be surprising to find the following excerpt in the most current journal: "The chronic, disturbed, untidy classes constitute a large percentage of cases treated . . . — those who were the most difficult to care for, who had failed to respond to other forms of therapy. Patients showing marked habit deterioration such as soiling,

wetting, and destructiveness, became more cleanly, less destructive, and better able to care for themselves. . . . [There is] the conservation of energy of the nurses and other employees, which can consequently be directed into productive fields of activity." This was written in 1925; the drug was sodium bromide.

35. Glick and Margolis 1962: 1087. For recognition of the importance of this type of experimental design, see Leveton 1958; Clark 1956; Sainz *et al.* 1957.

36. Bryant *et al.* 1956: 2–7, cited in Swazey 1974: 234–235. A simultaneous and more extensive review, by Bennett, of 962 papers dealing with the use of chlorpromazine in psychiatric hospitals found that "only ten papers mentioned controlled studies" Bennett 1956: 19.

37. Davis 1965: 552; Foulds 1958; Fox 1961; Glick and Margolis 1962.

38. Davis 1965: 553. Granted that "most [but not all] of these studies which did not show a therapeutic effect used only very small fixed doses." But this is precisely what the maintenance regime which most hospital patients and ex-patients are placed on is likely to consist of!

39. Crane 1973: 126. For further evidence that the primary effect of psychotropic drugs, given in sufficient dosage, is one of blunting the affect, see the references cited in footnote 28 above. According to one of the most widely accepted medical texts on pharmacology: "All the phenothiazines used in psychiatry diminish spontaneous motor activity in every species of animal studied, including man. In high doses, varying with the individual compound, they tend to produce cataleptic effects so that bodies and limbs of animals may be molded into various postures and remain immobile for long periods of time. Indifference to environmental stimuli and consequent taming are easily seen . . ." (Goodman and Gilman 1969: 158–159). The attractions of these drugs as management devices are thus easily seen, and are not disputed here.

40. Evidence on dosage given to hospital patients or ex-patients is hard to obtain. Where it does exist, it suggests a frightening picture of medical irresponsibility, with drugs being routinely and massively prescribed as management devices, without regard in many cases to either recommended maximum dosages or to the known long-term adverse effects of phenothiazine medication. To consider the first of these: A recent General Accounting Office Report on the use of "psychotherapeutic drugs" in Veterans' Administration mental hospitals found that 10% of the patients in the hospitals they visited were taking more than the recommended daily maximum dosage of phenothiazines.

> In some wards more than 40 percent of the patients were receiving dosages in excess
> of the recommended maximums. . . . Numerous research studies . . . have concluded
> that little evidence exists to support the simultaneous use of more than one psycho-
> therapeutic drug on the same patient—a practice commonly referred to as poly-
> pharmacy. These studies have also shown that polypharmacy increases the possibility
> of adverse reactions and have suggested that it be avoided if at all possible. At the
> hospitals visited, 2,002 patients, or about 32 percent, were taking more than one
> psychotherapeutic drug. . . . One patient was taking eight different drugs—three
> antipsychotic, two anti-anxiety, one anti-depressant, one sedative, and one anti-
> Parkinson. Three of these drugs were being given in dosage equal to the maximum
> recommended. Another patient was taking seven different drugs. . . . Two of the
> drugs were being given in dosages above the maximum recommended (G.A.O. Report
> 1975: ii, 7, 8).

Yet even low maintenance dosages of these drugs risk serious and often permanent negative consequences for the patient. Shortly after the introduction of ataraxic drugs, and during the height of the aggressive sales campaign designed to boost their use, a few cautious voices expressed doubts about "the presence on the open market of drugs which have not been adequately assayed and which, at their best, may not perform as wished, and at their worst, may cause incalculable physical and mental distress" (Glick and Margolis 1962: 1087; See also Sainz *et al.* 1957: 10). Increasingly, such warnings appear prescient. Through most of the 1960s there continued to be a dearth of long term follow-up studies and a general lack of concern with this issue. For example, the N.I.M.H. Study Group which investigated phenothiazines was content to invoke evidence drawn from a *six week* trial as "attesting to the safety of the active drugs" (N.I.M.H. Study Group 1964: 248). Now, however, evidence is accumulating that neuroleptics give rise to a range of serious side-effects, some of which are dangerously common, and many cases persist for *years* following the withdrawal of medication. Although this subject continues to receive remarkably little attention in the literature, even low maintenance doses have been found to produce these effects (See Crane 1973: esp. 126ff.). Among the effects are: "Parkinson's syndrome" characterized by muscular rigidity, shuffling gait, loss of associated movements and drooling; "dystonia" and "dyskinesia" characterized by uncoordinated spasmodic movements of the body and limbs; "akathisia" characterized by constant pacing, inability to sit still, and chewing and lip movements; and "tardive dyskinesia" characterized by sucking and smacking movements of the lips, rocking and uncontrolled jerky movements of the extremities (See Klein and Davis 1969). Some scientists have concluded that tardive dyskinesia is symptomatic of chronic brain damage. Recent studies show that this condition afflicts 15–25% of patients in mental hospitals who have received long term phenothiazine treatment (Klein and Davis 1969: 100). For a discussion of the effects of set and expectation in biasing clinical evaluation, and evidence of a similar lack of concern with negative side effects in psychoactive drugs used to treat "problem children," see Srouffe and Stewart 1973; see also Schrag and Divorky 1975.

41. Paul *et al.* 1972: 106. It is remarkable "how dependent the medical community has become on chemical agents . . . Physicians and nurses who must deal directly with hospitalized patients are firmly convinced that most patients would become unmanageable if the use of drugs were discontinued. Those employed in non-institutional mental health centers fear that they may be forced to give up programs responsible for keeping patients in the community" Crane 1973: 128, 127.

42. Lenz et al. (1971) report that 87% of a sample of hardcore long-term patients were being given such drugs; Crane (1973) gives a figure of 85% of "hospitalized schizophrenics"; Brill and Patton (1966) report that over 70% of New York State mental patients were being so treated in 1966.

43. Crane 1973: 125.

44. The definition of "moderate improvement" used by Blair and Brady was typical:

Patients who still suffer from serious psychiatric symptoms such as delusions and hallucinations, although these are diminished in intensity and severity. Their behavior has improved and their social conduct is satisfactory, but they have a limited capacity to adjust themselves to any environment other than that to which they are accustomed. They are allowed the freedom of the hospital grounds on their own. They are capable of simple manual and occupational tasks under some supervision. They require a moderate degree of support from the nursing staff (Blair and Brady 1958: 625).

45. Glick and Margolis 1962: 1088–1089. (The range of improvement, however, varied from a low of 5% to a high of 78%, suggesting dramatic differences in the methods or competance of evaluation.) In one of the few relatively well-designed early English studies of chlorpromazine's effects, Elkes and Elkes (1954) reached essentially the same conclusion: "Few of these chronic psychotic patients showed improvement which enabled them to become more useful members of mental hospital society. Others become less difficult nursing problems. Three were considered fit for parole [out of a total of 27], but none were thought fit for discharge. The relief afforded by chlorpromazine thus appears to be primarily symptomatic."

46. That is, these directly carrying out the experiment were not even aware that it was designed to measure the effectiveness of drug treatment.

47. Paul *et al.* 1972: 106–111.

48. See Gittleman *et al.* 1965.

49. E.g., in a recent eight year follow up study, Engelhardt *et al.* (1960, 1963, 1964, 1967) conclude that chlorpromazine does significantly better than placebo in preventing rehospitalization; but the difference is comparatively slight–on the order of ten percent.

50. Crane 1973: 125.

51. Rappaport *et al.* n.d.: esp. 8, 16.

52. See Hartledge 1965; Srouffe and Stewart 1973.

53. See Mason *et al.* 1963; Hare and Wilcox 1967.

CHAPTER SIX

Social science and social policy:
the critique of the total institution

In a colossal refuge for the insane, a patient may be said to lose his individuality and to become a member of a machine so put together, as to move with precise regularity and invariable routine; a triumph of skill adapted to show how such unpromising materials as crazy men and women may be drilled into order and guided by rule, but not an apparatus designed to restore their pristine condition and their independent self-governing existence. In all cases admitting of recovery, or of material amelioration, a gigantic asylum is a gigantic evil, and figuratively speaking, a manufactory of chronic insanity.

JOHN ARLIDGE
On the State of Lunacy . . . (1859)

I

Perhaps partly in response to the criticism that serious account must be taken of social factors, and partly reflecting doubts emerging on other grounds about the plausibility or sufficiency of the pharmaceutical explanation, others have sought to attribute the decline in mental hospital populations to the growing disenchantment during the 1950s and 1960s with the adequacy of such institutions as a response to mental illness. In this view, a decisive factor underlying the shift away from the mental hospital was the superior understanding achieved in this period of the effects of these institutions on new inmates. As Hoenig and Hamilton put it: "The policy of avoiding long-term hospitalization derives its main justification from the belief that it will protect the patient from institutionalization."[1] A spate of social scientific research in the 1950s and 1960s (the most famous example of which was Goffman's *Asylums*[2]) was devoted to the elucidation of the baneful effects of institutionalization. All this research had shown, purportedly for the first time, that the defects in existing mental hospitals were not simply the consequence of administrative lapses or the lack of adequate funds, but rather that they reflected fundamental and irremediable flaws in the basic structure of such places — flaws so serious as to call into question their therapeutic usefulness — or rather, to suggest that they were fundamentally antitherapeutic.

The consensus was clear. Presented most persuasively by Goffman, it was that the crucial factor in forming a mental hospital patient was not his "illness," but his institution; that his reactions and adjustments, pathological as they might seem to an outsider, were the product of the ill effects of his environment rather than of intrapsychic forces; and, indeed, that they closely resembled those of inmates in other types of "total institutions," a term that came to encapsulate this whole line of argument. The mental hospital, it now appeared, far from sheltering and helping to restore the disturbed to sanity, performed "a disabling custodial function." The work of men like Duncan Macmillan and T.P. Rees, British pioneers of the concept of the open hospital, had demonstrated "beyond question that much of the aggressive, disturbed, suicidal, and regressive behaviour of the mentally ill is not necessarily or inherently a part of the illness as such but is very largely an artificial by-product of the way of life imposed on them [by hospitalization]."[3] Major American psychiatrists expressed fears that "the patients are infantile . . . because we infantilize them."[4] Studies of institutions as diverse as research hospitals closely associated with major medical schools,[5] expensive, exclusive, and well-staffed private facilities,[6] and undermanned and underfinanced state hospitals,[7] all revealed a depressingly familiar picture. To the researchers, the very "similarity of these problems strongly suggests that many of the serious problems of the state hospital are inherent in the nature of mental institutionalization rather than simply in the financial difficulties of the state hospitals."[8] Apparently, "life in such a community tended inexorably to attenuation of the spirit, a shrinking of capacity, and slowing of the rhythms of interaction, a kind of atrophy."[9]

The conclusion was inescapable. Mental hospitals "are probably themselves obstacles in the development of an effective plan of treatment for the mentally ill."[10] Policy recommendations followed naturally: "The time has come when we should ask ourselves seriously whether the interests of the mentally ill are best served by providing more psychiatric beds, building bigger and better mental hospitals. Perhaps we should concentrate our efforts on treating the patients within the community of which they form a part and teach that community to tolerate and accept their idiosyncracies."[11] After all, considering what current research had shown, surely "the worst home is better than the best mental hospital. . . ."[12] And given that "the hospital as a form of treatment for the severely ill psychiatric patient is always expensive and inefficient, frequently anti-therapeutic, and never the treatment of choice . . . ,"[13] one could not help thinking that "in the long run the abandonment of the state hospitals might be one of the greatest humanitarian reforms and the greatest financial economy ever achieved."[14]

The logic of this critique, with suitable modifications, was easily extended to include a more general assault on the institution as the primary locus of social control for other types of deviance. Particularly over the past decade and a half, prisons (and their junior counterparts, the reformatories) have come under mounting attack. To use Gary Wills' words, the prison ought now to be seen as a classic "failed experiment," possibly

> [the most] disastrous survivor of the Enlightment still grasping at a death-like life. [In] our culture's human sewer, clogged and unworkable with human waste . . . , the criminal is sequestered with other criminals, in conditions exacerbating the lowest drives of lonely and stranded men, men deprived of loved ones, of dignifying work, of pacifying amenities. . . . Smuggling, bullying, theft, drug traffic, homosexual menace, are ways of life. Guards, themselves brutalized by the experience of prison, have to ignore most of the crimes inflicted on inmates, even when they do not connive at them, or incite them. [As a result,] prisons teach crime, instill crime, inure men to it, trap men in it as a way of life.[15]

Wills' language may be more vivid and his prose more brilliant and forceful than most social scientists can muster, but his conclusions differ little, if at all, from theirs.[16] Drawing on the early work of Sykes and Clemmer[17] on the "pains of imprisonment" and the process of "prisonization," and emphasizing Goffman's dramaturgical portrait of the total institution's shared capacity for dehumanization, the latter have likewise despaired of incarceration: Almost by definition, imprisonment weakens ties to conventional institutions and disrupts family life. At best, the artificial "prison community" would be ill-suited to teach law-abiding behavior. But it is almost never at its best. And in view of its recurrent brutalizing, depraving features, the stigma that comes with it, and its contribution to the acquisition of criminal skills and attitudes, it is, practically speaking, about the worst solution that could be devised to the problem of what to do with the criminal and the delinquent.

In place of the traditional stress on the need for institutionalization, there has developed an increasingly elaborate attempt to convince the public, and, more importantly, the policy makers, of "the value and safety of community care"[18] and community corrections. As we have seen, in some circles, "community treatment" has come to be elevated into a new therapeutic panacea. Supported by ever larger injections of federal funds in the United States, community psychiatrists became an increasingly important segment of the psychiatric profession as a whole. Particularly during the nineteen sixties, "an influential group of community psychiatrists, clinical psychologists, and other professionals were being listened to increasingly at the state and federal levels."[19] In parallel fashion, careers and reputations were being made in the emerging field of "community corrections." In combination, it is suggested, such discoveries and the propaganda of those professionally committed to them, both logically implied and naturally produced a change in social policy.

No one familiar with the climate of contemporary liberal intellectual opinion can avoid recognizing the depths of current pessimism here concerning the value of institutional responses to all forms of deviance, or the degree to which decarceration has been elevated, in such circles, to the status of a new "humanitarian" myth, comparable only with the similar myth which attended the birth of the asylum. But in general, social policy proves only mildly susceptible to the shifting intellectual fads and fashions of the day.

The question remains as to why this one at least appears to have had so profound an impact. Granted that the advocates of the community approach vigorously proselytized on behalf of their cause, yet why were they listened to—particularly when their proposals ran counter to the deeply entrenched interests of institutional psychiatry and the correctional establishment, long powerful interest groups in the political arena?

The conventional answer to these questions has three basic elements: (1) the emergence of a renewed concern on the part of the state for inmates' social and therapeutic rights, a concern which has unavoidably led to efforts to save prisoners, mental patients, and others from the destruction of their essential humanity with which they are threatened by the corrupting effects of the institution; (2) the therapeutic or rehabilitative promise of community care, a factor whose appeal has been bolstered by the favorable outcome of early efforts in this direction; and (3), more particularly in the case of the mentally disturbed, an alleged increasing tolerance on the part of the community towards its errant members.[20]

Each of these arguments, though, is seriously defective. It is all very well to assert that "the higher level of tolerance for deviance in the post-World War II period has raised the prospect that the mentally ill and retarded could be returned to families and retained in residential neighborhoods."[21] But where this increased tolerance comes from is not explained; nor is evidence offered to demonstrate its existence — unless, of course, it is a mere tautology (such people have been returned to the community, which shows that the community must be more tolerant than it once was; therefore increased tolerance must account for the return of the insane — and perhaps other deviants — to the community.) And the issue is still more complicated than is suggested by asking why or whether a changed tolerance for deviant behavior has developed. There is also the question of whether this change is an independent (as the Wolperts would have it) or a dependent variable; whether it helped to produce the change of policy, or was itself the product of the changed policy.

What evidence we do have bearing on this issue suggests that the latter is the more plausible causal sequence. With respect to the mentally ill, it quite clearly became official policy in this period to discourage the admission or re-admission of patients who in an earlier era would have been taken without question, and whom relatives or neighbors actively sought to have institutionalized.[22] Similarly, as we have seen in Chapter Three, officials of the criminal justice system have demonstrated a steadily rising reluctance to incarcerate even serious adult and juvenile offenders, despite the demonstrable political unpopularity of these policies. The vociferous community protests which usually accompany "community treatment" programs or decisions to release criminals under minimal supervision onto the streets are scarcely the reaction one would expect from those becoming more "tolerant" of the presence of deviance.

In view of what we know of the circumstances surrounding the return of the mentally ill to the community, the claim that this change was motivated either by concern for the patients' rights, or because of the therapeutic benefits likely to ensue, seems still more unlikely. In the first place, "the massive release of patients to facilities in residential neighborhoods" *preceded* "substantial data collection and analysis" on the likely effects of decarceration. In fact, even now we lack "substantiation that community care is advantageous for clients."[23] Put bluntly, "data have not been generated by the mental health sector nor by the evaluators of their programs or by those who fund the care system . . . for determining what kinds of facilities are most beneficial or where those facilities should be sited." Furthermore, "the hospital release trend is independent of [the availability of] community after-care facilities";[24] and for at least one important class of ex-patients, discharge under such circumstances, far from being therapeutic, has been positively fatal: "Mortality rates for elderly patients increase dramatically upon release. . . ."[25]

The deinstitutionalization of the criminal and the delinquent exhibits many of the same features, and prompts essentially the same conclusions.[26] In this area as well, there remains massive official ignorance of decarceration's likely effects on crime rates and rehabilitation. Even those attempting to put the best possible face on the shift away from incarceration are forced to concede that "there is not a wealth of sound evidence upon which to justify the current effort to deinstitutionalize correctional programs."[27] Indeed, "it is striking that the emphasis on early diversion of offenders has grown with so little data as to its effects on crime, on the operation of the criminal justice system, and on the quality of treatment afforded."[28]

Among the remarkably few efforts to develop empirical support for the preference for community programs was the study conducted by the California Adult Authority of its Community Treatment Program for juveniles, which involved the comparison of matched samples of juveniles sentenced to a youth prison and to community treatment. Because of its rarity, and because its findings apparently lent strong support to the decarceration cause, this study continues to be widely cited, as if it provided definitive support for the superiority of the community approach. In fact, it does nothing of the kind. Later independent evaluation of the program's results indicated that the favorable conclusions reflected manipulations of the data which stopped just short of outright falsification. The basis of the claim that community treatment was superior rested on the evidence that recommittal for parole violation was much lower for the experimentals than for the controls (33 percent versus 55 percent). But when known *offenses*, rather than parole violations, were examined, it turned out that the experimentals had substantially *more* known violations than the controls. The former appeared to have done better only because "the noticed offenses were reacted to differently by the experimental and control organizations."[29] Or, to put it less euphemistically, "the recidivism rates were arranged in such a way as to make the experimentals appear favorable. . . . In the light of these facts the C.T.P. gives little support to the thesis that probation is superior to institutionalization for reducing recidivism."[30]

By contrast with a more recent study of the closing of Massachusetts juvenile reformatories, however, the evaluation of the Community Treatment Program appears almost a model of analytic rigor. The Massachusetts study relies on three basic measures of effectiveness, all of which are worse than useless (unless, that is, one shares with the authors a prior commitment to "demonstrating" the desirability of community treatment). In the first place, questionnaires were administered to measure attitudes of the released youth and others who had taken part in the release process, a procedure exhibiting a naiveté about the problems of response bias which almost passes belief. In the circumstances, no one but a sociologist could be surprised to learn that "in general the [delinquent] youth responses are rather favorable."[31] A favorable evaluation was further guaranteed by the second measure of "success" employed: "Because the major objective of the conference was to remove youth from institutions, we may for this purpose classify any placement which removed the youth from an institutional lifestyle as a successful placement."[32] And finally, the superiority of a noninstitutional approach was allegedly demonstrated by comparing (poorly measured) recidivism rates of juveniles placed in different settings (institutions, foster homes, own homes, etc.). But juveniles were obviously not assigned randomly to each of these modalities; quite the contrary, it was explicitly acknowledged elsewhere in the same evaluation that an effort was made to tailor the type of placement decided on to the circumstances of the individual case.[33] To then proceed to use higher recidivism rates in institutional settings to argue for the superiority of community treatment is at best astonishingly careless.[34]

Not only has evaluation been routinely slapdash and frequently nonexistent, but very often "community treatment" has been no more than a slogan with little or no cognitive content.[35] In other words, the "treatment" in the community which allegedly replaces the penalty of confinement is present in name only. We have already seen, in Chapter Three, how Massachusetts abruptly closed all its juvenile institutions, without bothering to wait to provide community alternatives as a replacement. More generally, the massive expansion of the population on probation and parole has not been accompanied by extensions in the degree and scope of outside supervision. Excepting certain cosmetic (and small-scale) programs designed to "sell" decarceration to judges and other members of the criminal justice system, the standard probation officer's workload remains "far too great to permit adequate investigation for assessment or control purposes, let alone for appreciable assistance."[36] In consequence, "nearly everywhere, probation and parole supervision is negligible if not meaningless."[37] These problems are only further compounded when, as is usually the case, halfway houses and the like are located in the most decayed and deteriorated parts of cities.

Again, the situation with respect to the mentally ill is basically comparable. Overall, there has been no adequate licensing supervision or inspection of board and care facilities for released mental patients; and no effort has been made to avoid their "ghettoization" in the poorest, least desirable of neighborhoods.[38] And "in the absence of adequate after-care and rehabilitation services, the term 'community care' [remained] . . . merely an inflated catch-phrase which concealed morbidity in the patients and distress in the relatives."[39] As a natural consequence, "one form of confinement has been replaced by another, and the former patients are just as insulated from community attention and care as they were in the state hospital."[40] As far back as 1961, the Joint Commission on Mental Illness and Health, itself engaged in promoting the notion of decarceration, was forced to concede that "generally little attention is given to the psychological and social needs of these patients."[41] Over the past fourteen years the situation has not changed, and, to judge from the continuing official inaction, this does not greatly concern the authorities.

Recent research has shown that it remains true that

> for the long-term hospitalized patient, the move is usually into a boarding home facility . . . where little effort is directed towards social and vocational rehabilitation. [In practice,] it is only an illusion that patients who are placed in boarding or family-care homes are "in the community." . . . These facilities are for the most part like small long-term state hospital wards isolated from the community. One is overcome by the depressing atmosphere, not because of the physical appearance of the boarding home, but because of the passivity, isolation and inactivity of the residents.[42]

A paper by Epstein and Simon graphically illustrates the effects of this neglect. Table 6–1 presents their findings concerning two groups of geriatric patients. Group A represents the control group not subject to diversion and institutionalized at one-year follow-up; Group B, a group diverted to "community alternatives" and institutionalized at follow-up.

TABLE 6-1

Activity Scale Items—Institutionalized Patients

Item	Percent Group A	Percent Group B
Toileting		
No incontinence or rare accidents	70	48
Incontinent	30	52
Bathing		
No help needed	38	7
Takes no part	38	61
Grooming		
Cares for skin, hair, nails	33	16
Takes no care	46	71
Dressing		
Without assistance	52	20
Does not dress	35	55
Money Use		
Makes purchases or is able	32	5
Cannot handle money	60	89
Money Availability		
Has	37	14
Has none	47	86

SOURCE: Adapted from Epstein, L.J. and Simon, A. "Alternatives to State Hospitalization for the Geriatric Mentally Ill." *American Journal of Psychiatry* 124 (1968), 959. Copyright 1968, The American Psychiatric Association. Reprinted by permission.

At follow-up, 83 percent of Group A were in state mental hospitals and 17 percent in nursing and boarding homes; whereas 96 percent of Group B were in boarding homes, and only 4 percent were in state hospitals. The differences between the two are obvious and startling: "Fewer of the [Group A, hospitalized] patients were incontinent, fewer took no part in bathing, more were able to bathe without help, fewer took no responsibility for their grooming, more dressed without assistance, fewer failed to dress and remained in hospital gowns, and more had money available and were capable of making occasional purchases."[43] Looking at precisely the deleterious effects commonly attributed to hospitalization, it is apparent that by every measure the so-called community facilities are markedly inferior. The picture is a grim one, and scarcely what one would gather from reading the liberal rhetoric on decarceration.

II

If the claimed virtues of the community are thus largely without substance, what of the institution? As we have seen, a crucial element in the move towards a noninstitutional response to deviance has been the purported "discovery" by social scientists in the 1950s and 1960s of the institutional syndrome — the notion that confinement in an asylum may amplify and even produce disturbance; that in the "moral career of the mental patient" the institution may be more important than the illness; that the prison is the nursery and breeding ground of crime. Supposedly, what had formerly been held to be the natural products of an unfolding intra-individual pathology or character deficiency were finally, and for the first time, seen as in large part the reflection of a "natural" response to a grossly deforming environment.[44] But as I shall now try to show, only a narrow and a historical view of contemporary developments gives such arguments even a surface plausibility.

With due deference to the claims of sociologists convinced that understanding of society waits on advances in their peculiar discipline, recognition of the baneful effects of these conditions emerged early in the history of the asylum and took sophisticated forms. Indeed, the resemblances between these early criticisms and the "discoveries" of modern social science are simply extraordinary. Contrary to the sedulously promoted myth that the asylum was a therapeutic institution, nineteenth century critics, both English and American, insisted that it was a prison, likely to intensify rather than reduce the pathology of its inmates. They possessed a clear perception of the sources of this problem. The monotony and artificiality of asylum life were themselves the source of profound disturbances in adaptation, systematically unfitting patients for the return to the outside world, and promoting the type of adaptation Goffman was later to dub "colonization." Furthermore, the asylum in large part manufactured the very human materials which "justified" its existence. Its peculiar routines and deprivations produced behavior interpreted as pathological by outsiders; and the behavior was then used, in *Catch 22* fashion, to justify those very routines and deprivations. Such problems, as we shall now see in more detail, were perceived as structural and not as the product of bad intentions or the scarcity of resources; since they were an inescapable concomitant of the institutional solution, they could be eliminated only by shifting to a system of community care.

Criticism along these lines ran counter to the dominant orthodoxy of the period. By no means was it confined to a criticism of mental hospitals. Indeed, there was explicit recognition of the general applicability of the critique of incarceration. Total institutions of all sorts, and particularly those taking members of a single sex, were seen as

> unnatural, unfavorable to the growth of social virtues and graces, and injurious to the moral nature in greater or less degree. . . . The degree to which they are injurious to the inmates depends of course upon the extent to which the practice of congregating them together and isolating them from the world, is carried; but there is no escape from certain evil consequences. Nunneries, monasteries, armies, navies, boarding schools, in short every establishment of the kind, if its secret history were known, would probably show this. . . .[45]

There can be no question, though, that the most plausible and elaborate version of this position was articulated with respect to the mental hospital. (This, incidentally, is also true of the modern literature on this subject.) Accordingly, I shall for the most part concentrate on an analysis of this material, noting from time to time how similar criticisms were made of other types of incarcerating establishments.

The emergence of a system of state-run asylums had been in part the product of the vigorous proselytization of an increasingly elaborate institutional ideology by reformers and the still nascent psychiatric profession; and in turn the state's commitment to this solution had encouraged and promoted the further refinement of such ideological rationalizations. Early in the century, the weight of "informed" opinion embraced an extreme therapeutic optimism, as advocates of the asylum sought to convert others to the merits of their proposed solution to the problems of insanity. On the one hand, they provided an elaborate account, resting on remarkably little empirical investigation or documentation, of the gross unsuitability of the family and community as arenas for the treatment of the insane, and of the need to insulate the insane from the pressures of the world. On the other, they promoted the notion of the asylum as providing a forgiving environment in which humane care on a large scale was possible, in and through which a substantial proportion of lunatics could be restored to sanity.[46] Reality soon turned out to be brutally different.[47] By the last third of the nineteenth century, public asylums had become mammoth institutions in which the conditions of the patient's existence departed further and further from those in the outside world, for his return to which his incarceration was still ostensibly preparing him. Dominated by routine, their individuality smothered, the inmates endured the highly organized monotony characteristic of existence in these huge custodial warehouses. The asylum had become, as it remained through the middle of the twentieth century, a museum for the collection and exhibition of the varied specimens making up the refuse of a capitalist society.[48] And while the rhetoric of rehabilitation remained, the ideological defense of its existence came increasingly to rest on the functionality of incarcerating such difficult and troublesome elements of society.

Even in the early stages of the lunacy reform movement, when the asylum was pictured in terms reminiscent of a romantic idyll, in England, at least, a few isolated figures refused to bend to the weight of professional and informed opinion, and raised their voices against the tendency to incarcerate all those labeled as mad.[49] Before long, however, the arguments of its proponents ignored and their suggestions rejected, the anti-institutional position went into temporary eclipse. For a quarter of a century, roughly between 1840 and 1865, the supporters of the asylum solution reigned supreme and virtually unchallenged in both England and America; and the new class of asylum administrators, in the process of consolidating its professional identity, continued to rely heavily on the elaborate account of the advantages of this approach developed in the course of the reform movement.

But as reported cure rates relentlessly dwindled, leading many to extreme therapeutic pessimism, and as the asylum came less and less to resemble the ideal the first generation of reformers had sought to institute, so, almost simultaneously in the two countries, the anti-asylum position once more gained adherents and at least a measure of respectability. Some of these critics had themselves been leading proponents of the asylum's virtues in the early years of the reform process, and they now recoiled in horror from the monster they had helped to produce. A few of these were laymen, the most famous being Samuel Gridley Howe. Others had acted as asylum superintendents, and so had a more intimate acquaintance with the deficiencies of asylum treatment.[50] The other major group of critics, often of a younger generation, were representatives of an emerging medical speciality which sought to compete with the asylum superintendents for the more affluent, and perhaps less serious, cases of mental disturbance. In England, these were a number of well-known physicians with an upperclass clientele who for diverse reasons had developed an interest in the problems of psychological medicine (men such as Clark, Maudsley, Granville, and Arlidge); in the United States, they consisted primarily of the rapidly organizing profession of neurology (Hammond, Mitchell, Spitzka, Beard), which in some instances at least drew adherents from the ranks of assistant asylum superintendents who had either taken their superiors' curative rhetoric seriously or else had grown impatient with the normal slow bureaucratic advancement governing a career in institutional psychiatry.[51] Most generally, the asylums' (and asylum superintendents') most articulate and outspoken detractors were those who were unwilling to accept the retreat from earlier ideals, and who insisted that if the existence of asylums could not be justified on the grounds that they were curative institutions, then their existence could scarcely be justified at all.

All of these people had come to view the asylum as an unmitigated disaster. By now, the operations of the system had revealed the basic accuracy of the earlier criticisms by men like Hill and Conolly, and had provided a wealth of factual detail with which to flesh out the analysis they had made. Consequently, the work of the second generation of critics was usually both analytically penetrating and empirically well documented. (Indeed, it is difficult to see how, in its essentials, and with respect to either its intellectual cogency or its empirical support, the modern critique elaborated by Goffman and his coworkers is substantially superior.)

Trying to account for their own disillusionment, these men sought to remind the public that, at the outset of the reform process, the proponents of moral treatment had insisted that "the grand object to be kept in view when providing for the accommodation of the insane, is to assimilate their condition and the circumstances surrounding them as closely as possible to those of ordinary life . . . yet we may say of the 'ward system' that it is about as wide a departure from those conditions as can well be conceived."[52] Any effort to change this state of affairs necessarily involved the absurd and self-contradictory endeavor to eliminate the institutional aspects of the institution. The magnitude of the difficulty was perhaps expressed most clearly in one of the parallel critiques of the juvenile reformatory. As the Massachusetts State Board of Charities put it:

> We may as well try to imitate within a house sunshine and rain, and clouds and dews, and all the shifting scenes of nature, as imitate, in a reformatory, the ever varying influences of family and social life, with its trials and temptations, its defeats and triumphs, which are so potent to fashion character. We may as well try to teach by precept, or upon a stage, the graces and affections and virtues which grow out of close and long-continued family relations, as teach them in a great household made up of hundreds (or even scores) of children of the same class, the same age, the same sex,

and, worse than all, of the same vicious habits. We have, at best, a make-believe society, a make-believe family, and, too often, a make-believe virtue; while what boys need is a real family, real society, real life, even if its virtue is not patent and approved of men. . . .[53]

The logical and empirical absurdity of the task had not prevented many from trying to achieve this impossibility, but, not surprisingly, the critics thought, all of these trials had proved a demonstrable failure.[54]

To put it in its bluntest terms, "the inmates of an . . . asylum are in point of fact in a prison . . . ,"[55] and the atmosphere of the prison was such that it was likely to amplify rather than reduce their disturbance.[56] The deadening routine of asylum existence was a factor here: Surely "the want of society, the absence of all amusement and employment, both of body and mind, must tend to *increase* rather than relieve the morbid irritation of the brain."[57] Even a few asylum superintendents, acquainted at first hand with the "idle monotony" of their inmates' existence, complained that it produced "dull and dormant minds, dozing for years in silence and stupidity."[58] Outside critics were still more emphatic. As they pointed out: "To the medical officer these are not so many *individuals*, having particular characteristics and particular bodily dispositions, with which he is thoroughly acquainted, but they are apt to become so many lunatics, whom he has to inspect as he goes on his round of the establishment, as he inspects the baths and the beds."[59] Convinced of the pernicious effects of incarceration, S. Weir Mitchell complained that "in the sadness . . . of the wards . . . , the insane, who have lost even the memory of hope, sit in rows, too dull to know despair, watched by attendants; silent, grewsome [sic] machines which eat and sleep, sleep and eat."[60] Those who felt inclined to protest the proposition that asylums were "monstrous evils . . . , [the men] who advocate and defend the present asylum system . . . should not forget that there is one point of view from which they who organize, superintend, and act, regard the system, and that there is another point of view from which those who are organized, superintended, and suffer, view it."[61] For the visitor, who lacked the peculiar blindness induced by a position as superintendent of such an institution, few things could be more depressing than "the sight of so many patients in the prime of life sitting or lying about, moping idly and listlessly in the debilitating atmosphere of the wards, and sinking gradually into a torpor, like that of living corpses. . . ."[62]

Who would want to share the monotonous wretchedness in which the unhappy patients spend their days, "debarred from home, from the

sight of friends, from the society of their families . . . , shut out from
even a hope of any change that *might* be beneficial to them . . . ," confined in "a monastery of the mad?"[63] Indeed, "what would be the
consequence, if we were to take a sane person, who had been accustomed
to enjoy society and . . . were to lock him up in a small house with a
keeper for his only associate, and no place for exercise but a miserable
garden? We should certainly not look for any improvement in his moral
and intellectual condition. Can we reasonably expect that *a treatment
which would be injurious to a sane mind could tend to restore a deranged
one?*"[64] Small wonder that "asylum life is deadly to the insane."[65]

Other institutions for the deviant had similarly deleterious effects,
since incarceration for these groups too was "*not founded on a good and
sound principle.*"[66] "The larger a community of infirm or defective
persons is, the more they act upon each other; the more salient become
the peculiarities flowing out of their infirmity; the more they become
like each other and the more unlike ordinary persons — hence the less
fitted for ordinary society."[67] The blind and the mute provided graphic
proof of this thesis. Their behavior often exhibits

> morbid tendencies. . . . Now these are lessened, and their morbid effects
> corrected in each individual, by intimate intercourse with persons of sound
> and normal condition — that is, by general society; while *they are strengthened
> by associating closely and persistently with others having the like infir-
> mity.* . . . Guided by this principle, we should, in providing for the instruction
> and training of these persons, have the association among them as little as
> possible, and counteract its tendencies by encouraging association and
> intimacy with common society. They should be kept together no more closely
> and no longer than is necessary for their special instruction; and there should
> be no attempts to build up permanent asylums for them, or to favor the
> establishment of communities composed wholly, or mainly, of persons subject
> to a common infirmity.[68]

Collection of delinquents under a single roof was likewise "unnecessary and undesirable." As the blind need contact with the normal to
prevent accentuation and ossification of their "differentness," so too
"the young need the constant presence, the influence and example of
their elders. Nature mingles them in due proportion in common families and in general society, and any wide departure from this proportion
is unfavorable to the best moral growth." The foolishness of the contrary
policy was patent. To attempt to make use of instruments of segregative
control as engines of reformation was to ignore the obvious, that human
beings "need not only teaching and preaching, not merely instruction

and precept, but they need even more than these, good example and the opportunity of imitating it. They need to *exercise* their moral powers, to struggle with temptation and overcome it, rather than to be removed from it. . . ."[69] In our endeavor "to cure vice by the social ostracism of the vicious . . . ," we "gather them together and keep them in close and corrupting contact."[70] Under these conditions, which could almost have been designed to spread criminality like an infection, "*the longer [a child] is in an asylum, the less likely he is to do well in outside life.*"[71] Not only that, but the inmates of a reformatory "*must be publicly exhibited*; they must become known to a large number of persons as belonging to a vicious class; they will get a character as such, and *it will stick to them through life,*" hampering, if not entirely obstructing, their efforts to reintegrate themselves into the community. "But more and worse than all this," taught that they are vicious, depraved, beyond redemption, "they would learn to consider themselves as such!"—a transformation of image and identity which renders the whole process almost irreversible.[72]

To return once more to the case of the insane, it was apparent that for those who had to endure it, "the effect of living constantly among mad men or women is a loss of all sensibility and self-respect or care; or, not infrequently, a perverse pleasure in adding to the confusion and diversifying the eccentricity of those about them." Such a pathological environment thus encouraged the very behavior which was then used to justify its existence: "Paroxysms of violence alternate with fits of sullenness; both are considered further proofs of the hopelessness of the case." The peculiar routines of the asylum are quite unlike those of the outside world, and yet some of the inmates manage to adjust to them. By a cruel irony, those who manage this transition most effectively at the same time destroy their ability to function in the outside world: "After many hopeless years, such patients become so much accustomed to the routines of the house, as to be mere children; and are content to remain there, as they commonly do, until they die."[73] Equally pathetic were the "numerous examples . . . in which it was evident that although the patients were not yet sufficiently recovered to be restored to their families without superintendence, [yet] a continued residence in the asylum was gradually destroying body and mind."[74]

Such problems sprang neither from any want of good intentions nor from the lack of adequate resources to do the job properly. Rather, the whole structure rested on the misguided premise that the asylum could ever, under any circumstances, be an apparatus for cure. In "enlightened" states like Massachusetts, those charged with inspecting the state hospital system were able to "speak unhesitatingly in terms of general commendation respecting the condition and management of the public Hospitals"; and yet still conclude that reliance on them should be decreased, if not eliminated.[75] Following an extensive survey of asylums in the London metropolitan area, Granville came to the same conclusion. One could no longer doubt that "the management of asylums generally is now certainly as honest, and, I believe, as earnest and intelligent as possible. The faults in the present system are rather incidental to the system itself than to the manner in which it is worked."[76] Both Parliament and public must somehow be educated out of the "stereotyped prejudice that a lunatic is a lunatic and an asylum is the best place for him . . . ,"[77] and be brought to see that "future progress in the improvement of the treatment of the insane lies in the direction of lessening the sequestration and increasing the liberty of them."[78]

The advocates of decarceration and community care realized that their recommendations ran counter to the dominant convictions of the day. As the American neurologist Hammond put it: "It is the commonly received opinion among physicians and the public generally that as soon as possible after an individual becomes insane, he or she must at once be placed under the restraint of a lunatic asylum. . . ."[79] This was a situation for which both English and American critics (in a sense rightly) held asylum superintendents mostly responsible. But "these views are erroneous . . ." and must be refuted.[80] For it had become clear, to these men at least, that

> the curative influences of asylums have been vastly over-rated, and that those of isolated treatment in domestic care have been greatly under-valued. . . . It has long been the accepted doctrine among psychiatrists that insanity can only be treated curatively in asylums. . . . A wider knowledge of insanity . . . would have taught them that a very considerable number of cases of insanity run a short course and recover in domestic life with no great amount of treatment, and that perhaps not of a very scientific kind.[81]

And it was not just curable cases which did not belong in the asylum: *No* individual "should ever be confined in a lunatic hospital if he can have proper care and control out of it,"[82] a doctrine which made plain that, of the current denizens of the asylum, "large numbers are needlessly detained."[83] "Instead of acting on the general principle of confining the insane in asylums, and making the particular exceptions, we ought to act on the general principle of depriving no one of his liberty, and of then making the necessary exceptions which will undoubtedly be necessary in the cases of insane persons, as in the cases of criminals."[84] Such a policy would bring the release of large numbers of "chronic and incurably insane persons neither dangerous to themselves or others . . . [who] might very well be at large . . . ," and probably would be, were it not that "the world has grown to the fashion of thinking that madmen are to be sequestrated in asylums, and cannot now . . . conceive the possibility of a different state of things."[85]

The same approach should be adopted with respect to groups like the delinquent: As Howe put it, with all the force he could command, "VICIOUSLY DISPOSED YOUTH SHOULD NOT BE BROUGHT TOGETHER BUT PUT FAR ASUNDER." After all, "it is hard work to make straight a single crooked stick — harder yet a bundle of them if *taken together*."[86] If only the public could be taught the error of their ways, then not only would deviants benefit by being spared the unpleasantness and corrupting effects of institutional existence; but, in addition, a community-based response held out the prospect of a major and continuing improvement in their handling and in the moral tone of community life as a whole. For in order that "the work may be done well, it must be done by the people themselves, directly, and in the spirit of Him who taught that the poor ye shall always have *with* you — that is, near you, in your hearts and affections, within your sight and knowledge; and not thrust far away from you and always shut up by themselves in almshouses or reformatories, that they may be kept at the cheapest rate by such a cold abstraction as the State government."[87]

Yet despite the elaborateness and intellectual force of these accounts of the superiority of community care, and despite the social prominence of many of the advocates of decarceration, their efforts had no substantial impact. At least they were spared the fate of their predecessors — men like Conolly and Hill — whose criticisms were by and large simply ignored (though like the latter, their case never drew an intellectually adequate response from their opponents); but in terms of practical results they fared no better. On the contrary, in a truly ironic fashion they may have helped to intensify the very conditions they were complaining of.

For when the pressure for eliminating the institutional aspects of asylums was at its height, the defenders of segregative control evolved a scheme which, by briefly promoting the illusion that it represented an approach towards community care, served to disarm the less perspicacious critics, while leaving intact the essential structure of the existing system. This was the so-called cottage plan. Rather than congregating the inmates of an asylum into a single central facility, this system involved distributing them into a number of discrete buildings or cottages, which were originally supposed to simulate a community of families in the outside world. Bemis, the superintendent of the Worcester State Hospital in Massachusetts, was an early enthusiast in behalf of this arrangement, seeing it as at least a closer approximation to a normal existence, and perhaps as ultimately paving the way to a more complete form of decarceration. The scheme, he thought, had a number of advantages from the patients' perspective. "Though not in their own homes [the ideal solution] they have a home, live in a family and are members of a society, useless it may be, but still they are identified as part of a community."[88]

In the end, Massachusetts rejected the Bemis plan, though for a time it had seemed to stand a chance of adoption.[89] However, an outwardly similar plan (at least, it *called* itself a cottage plan) was adopted soon afterwards at Kankakee in Illinois. Here the new system was shown to be a simple and cheap method of increasing the number of lunatics who could be crowded into a single institution, and thus it was more economical than the old congregate system[90] — a factor which doubtless accounts for its rapid adoption elsewhere.[91] In the process, it became a grotesque parody of its original form, with individual "cottages" containing up to several hundred inmates apiece. In Hurd's words: "The result of this method of construction has been practically to remove all restrictions as to the number of insane patients to be cared for in any one hospital, and we now have hospitals of patients and employees of 3,000, 4,000 and even higher."[92]

During the nineteenth century, the one place where, even for a brief period, a policy of community care appeared to stand some prospect of being introduced was the state of Massachusetts. Quite apart from the modest scheme suggested by Bemis, which I have already referred to, a more radical plan of deinstitutionalization was seriously considered in some official circles during the late 1860s. Howe exerted great influence on the Board of State Charities (the body charged with general oversight and administrative review of state activities in the area of insanity and its control), and under his persuasion the Board swiftly became highly critical of the existing, asylum-based policy.[93] In its place, they advocated that insanity be dealt with "by consecrating a multitude of private houses to the cure and care of the [insane] poor, instead of thrusting them away from us and immuring them in habitations which we ourselves avoid and teach our children to avoid as the worst into which men can fall." To continue "building up more hospitals or aggregating the insane in masses" was to perpetuate a policy which had already proved to be disastrous, and the state ought rather to consider a community-based system resembling the one successfully employed for centuries at Gheel in Belgium.[94]

But the Board of State Charities lacked the power to implement its own proposals—and in any event, even *its* commitment to the new approach proved short-lived. Battered by a variety of pressure groups opposed to its proposals, the Board was forced in its 1870 Report to issue a retraction. The policy which a year before had been so desirable and well-tried was now dismissed as impractical and utopian, contrary to the best interests of both the insane and the community. Disingenuously and almost humiliatingly, the Board denied that it had ever recommended the policy it had in fact been zealously advocating over the previous three years. Apparently, all they had *really* meant to suggest by their earnest and detailed discussions of the possibility of eliminating the asylum was the desirability of boarding out some few (very few) cases of chronic insanity in the community.[95]

If the Board of State Charities, nominally in charge of the system, could not withstand the pressures to adhere to the traditional system, an apostate asylum superintendent could scarcely hope to do so—and when Bemis persisted in recommending his version of the cottage approach, an excuse was found to force his resignation.[96] Everywhere the advocates of decarceration had failed. Their policy had to wait nearly a century for adoption—by which time the earlier generations of critics were largely forgotten, and the approach was hailed as a blending of modern social science, humanitarianism, and therapeutic advances.

1. Hoenig and Hamilton 1969: 245.

2. But see also, among others, Stanton and Schwartz 1954; Greenblatt *et al.* 1955; Belknap 1956; Rees 1957; Hunt 1957; Caudill 1958; Wing 1962; Barton 1965.

3. Hunt 1957: 13–21. One British psychiatrist, Russell Barton (1965), gave this iatrogenic phenomenon the status of a new psychiatric label all its own—"institutional neurosis."

4. F. C. Redlich, in the preface to Caudill 1958: xi.

5. See Barrabee 1951.

6. Stanton and Schwartz 1954.

7. Belknap 1956.

8. Belknap 1956: 232.

9. A. D. Miller 1974: 54.

10. Belknap 1956: xi.

11. Rees 1957: 527.

12. Cumming and Cumming 1957: 55.

13. Mendel 1974: 18.

14. Belknap 1956:212. There is a delightful historical irony here: Nineteenth-century lunacy reformers in both England and America used precisely these two potential benefits, humanitarianism and economy, as their major arguments for *building* an asylum system. See Scull 1974; Grob 1973; Deutsch 1949.

15. Wills 1975:3, 8. Reprinted with permission from *The New York Review of Books*. Copyright © Nyrev, Inc.

16. See Cressey 1973; Bakal 1973; National Advisory Commission 1973.

17. Sykes 1958; Clemmer 1938.

18. Hunt 1957: 21 *et passim*.

19. Wolpert and Wolpert 1974: 73.

20. Wolpert and Wolpert 1976. Particularly with respect to criminals and delinquents, where "humanitarian" considerations obviously have less political appeal, there is also a more or less overt recourse to a fourth factor which should and has stimulated the move towards a community-based approach — the cost savings that may thus be realized. Generally, however, cost savings are pictured as a more or less fortuitous (if fortunate!) side effect of policy decisions actually taken on these other grounds, rather than as a centrally important independent variable. Furthermore, little or no effort is made to specify why the state has only recently begun to exploit the financial savings apparently available all along through deinstitutionalization; or to explain why cost factors suddenly become so salient as to override other considerations. We shall delay further consideration of these issues until Chapter Eight.

21. Wolpert and Wolpert 1976.

22. See Brown *et al.* 1966, chs. 3 and 5, esp. 51ff., for case histories of individuals exhibiting grossly disturbed behavior whose hospitalization was repeatedly resisted by the authorities even when requested by relatives experiencing severe difficulties in coping. See also *New York Times*, March 18, 1974:1, 17; Reich and Siegal 1973.

23. Wolpert and Wolpert 1974: 14-19. Compare the revealing remark by one of the leading bureaucrats in the field: "After five and one-half years in community mental health, I still do not know of any proof I could provide you as to why community care is better than hospital care" (Ahmed 1974: 169).

24. Wolpert and Wolpert 1974: 19-25. For recent criticism of New York State for announcing the restriction of the hospitalization of geriatric and chronic schizophrenics without making alternative provision for such persons, see *Psychiatric News*, Oct. 4, 1972:1; Reich and Siegal 1973; for England, cf. M.I.N.D. 1971.

25. Wolpert and Wolpert 1976. Marlowe (1974:116), for example, found that closing one California state mental hospital meant that "two to three times as many patients died as could have been expected to die in the absence of relocation."

26. Even on the face of it, the idea that the state apparatus has suddenly become suffused with concern for the rights of the criminal has a distinctly implausible air about it — particularly when one recalls that decarceration of criminals was carried furthest in Reagan's California, where the very notion of prisoners' rights was anathema.

27. Empey 1973:37.

28. Vorenberg and Vorenberg 1973: 181.

29. Lerman 1968: 57.

30. Robison and Smith 1971: 69–70. See also Ward 1973: esp. 193, 199–200.

31. Coates, Miller, and Ohlin 1973: 138.

32. Coates, Miller, and Ohlin 1973: 141. Sic! Further comment seems redundant.

33. Coates, Miller, and Ohlin 1973: 134–135.

34. Incidentally, and perhaps even more devastatingly, the use of recidivism rates as the major measure of the "success" of community treatment has gone largely unexamined by decarceration's advocates, although there is good evidence that it is a grossly unsatisfactory index (see American Friends' Service Committee 1971: 41ff.; Greenberg 1975). For example, "penalties may affect crime rates by deterring or incapacitating potential offenders, as well as by rehabilitating them. Thus far the impact of community alternatives for imprisonment on *crime rates* (instead of recidivism rates) has not been assessed" (Greenberg 1975: 8, emphasis in the original).

35. Koshel 1973: 4.

36. Glaser 1973: 99.

37. Clark 1970: 237.

38. For California, see Lamb and Goertzel 1971; Silberstein 1969; Chase 1973; for New York and Michigan, see *New York Times* Jan. 21, 1974, p. 31, March 22, 1974, p. 40, March 24, 1974, pp. 1, 17; for Canada, Stewart *et al.* 1968. For England, see Wing 1971: 189: "None of the publications of the Department of Health and Social Services has dealt in detail with the alternative residential and occupational facilities which would seem to be necessary. No one can be in any doubt that many patients who used to become long-stay still develop chronic handicaps, and the present community services do not provide adequately for them."

39. Brown *et al.* 1966: 10.

40. Wolpert and Wolpert 1974: 61.

41. Joint Commission 1961: 184.

42. Lamb and Goertzel 1971: 29–31.

43. Epstein and Simon 1968: 960.

44. See Brown *et al.* 1966; Wing and Brown 1970. Compare the claim of the British Younger Commission that the introduction of Borstal for young offenders in 1895 and the confident reliance on incarceration thereafter was a reflection of the fact that "there had been no research to cast doubt on the success of treatment or to point to the damaging effects that institutional life could have" Younger Report 1974: 48.

45. Howe 1854: 20.

46. Perhaps the best single synthesis of this pro-asylum ideology is Browne 1837. For discussion of the development and decline of analogous rehabilitative ideologies in other institutional settings (reformatories, prisons, etc.) see Rothman 1971.

47. See Scull 1974, esp. Ch. 6; Grob 1966; Rothman 1971.

48. See Scull 1974, Chs. 7 and 9. For similar conclusions about the juvenile reformatory, see Mennel 1973: esp. 199ff.

49. See Hill 1814; Reid 1816; Conolly 1830; Anon. 1839.

50. In England, these included John Charles Bucknill and Lockhart Robertson, former superintendents of the Devon and Sussex County Asylums respectively. American

examples include Tilden, of the California State Asylum, and Bemis of the Worcester State Hospital in Massachusetts. Significantly, by the time they began to criticize asylums in public, both Bucknill and Robertson had achieved sufficient eminence in the field of psychological medicine to escape the constraints of the role as a salaried employee in a public asylum system. Bemis, who had not, sought to wean his asylum board away from its exclusive dependence on the institution, and even, as we shall see, enjoyed a temporary success in this regard. Within a short time, however, the board was forced to abandon its new scheme as utopian, and with it to abandon Bemis. Shortly thereafter, the latter resigned his position and retreated into private practice. For a fuller account, see Grob 1966: 209–213.

51. E.g., James Kiernan. Despite the element of generational conflict, a much more important structural similarity between the English and American representatives of this group was their elite status in the medical profession, reflected in an orientation towards the values of world science uncharacteristic of the more traditional psychiatric practitioners of the period. For a brief sketch of American neurology in the late nineteenth century stressing this point, see Rosenberg 1968: 248ff.

52. Arlidge 1859: 201.

53. Massachusetts State Board of Charities Annual Report 1866.

54. See Clark 1869: 90–100.

55. Anon. 1839: 16; also Massachusetts State Board of Charities Vol. IV, 1867: xxxviii-ix.

56. See Howe 1871; Sanbourne 1891: 294–296. Maudsley went further: "Indeed, I cannot help feeling, from my experience, that one effect of asylums is to make some permanent lunatics" (Maudsley 1871: 432).

57. Anon. 1839: 41.

58. Hartford Retreat Annual Report Vol. 41, 1865: 22–23.

59. Maudsley 1871: 431.

60. Mitchell 1894: 19.

61. Maudsley 1871: 427.

62. Massachusetts State Board of Charities Vol. IV, 1867: xl.

63. Conolly 1830: 39; Mitchell 1894: 17.

64. Anon. 1839: 39, emphasis in the original.

65. Mitchell 1894: 14–15.

66. Howe 1909 Vol. II: 512ff., 518ff., emphasis in the original.

67. Draft of unpublished article by Howe on the education of handicapped children, cited in Mennel 1973: 42; see also Brace 1872: 235–236.

68. Massachusetts Board of State Charities Annual Report 1866, emphasis in the original.

69. 1854: 15, 20: 23, emphasis in the original.

70. Howe 1909, Vol. II: 530.

71. Brace 1872: 235–236, emphasis in the original.

72. Howe 1854: 21, emphasis in the original.

73. Conolly 1830: 21–22. See also Maudsley 1871: 427: "I am not ignorant, however, of the fact that there are some chronic lunatics who have been in asylums for so many years that it would be no kindness to remove them—who have indeed so grown to the habit of their lives that it would be cruel to make any change; but I hold that to be no

argument for subjecting anyone else to the same treatment in order to bring about the same result."

74. Conolly 1830: 20; also Sanbourne 1891: 303.

75. "The principal evils and disadvantages of these establishments grow mainly out of the very nature of their organization and material arrangements." Massachusetts Board of State Charities Vol. V, 1868: xxxvii.

76. House of Commons Select Committee 1877: 397.

77. Bucknill 1880: x.

78. Maudsley, cited in Clark 1869: 98–99.

79. Hammond 1879: 1; also Massachusetts Board of State Charities Vol. IV, 1867: lvii.

80. Hammond 1879: 2.

81. Bucknill 1880: 114.

82. Bemis in Worcester State Hospital Annual Report Vol. 37, 1869: 75.

83. Edinburgh Review 1870: 225; also Sanbourne 1891: 300.

84. Maudsley 1871: 424–425.

85. Maudsley 1867: 424; also House of Commons Select Committee 1877: 53–55, evidence of Lockhart Robertson; and Jarvis, cited in Clark 1869: 101.

86. Howe 1854: 17–20, emphasis in the original.

87. Howe, cited in Sanbourne 1891: 295. For reasons which were never clearly articulated, there was little enthusiasm in this period for extending the benefits of "community corrections" to the adult criminal. It was conceded by the critics that the logic of their position inevitably led one to have "no faith in the reformatory machinery of penal institutions for adults." Yet evil as imprisonment undoubtedly was, "it may under certain circumstances be a necessary one" (Howe 1854: 17). This "necessity" was never spelled out, but it seems reasonable to conclude that a number of factors may have contributed to this perception. Prominent among them is the fact that, unlike the insane or the delinquent, criminals could not readily be pictured as "unfortunate" or "misguided"; and as men who had maturely "chosen" a life of crime, they were less obviously promising candidates for rehabilitation. In addition, their fate was more directly and consciously designed as an example to deter others. All of which tended to militate against proposals to eliminate, in large part, the punitive element in the response toward them. In this respect, it is perhaps worth noting that even in the midst of contemporary moves towards decarceration, community alternatives for adult offenders remain somewhat underdeveloped. And most of the arguments advanced currently in favor of dealing with the criminal in the community have an obviously derivative air.

88. Bemis, cited in Grob 1966: 213. In a letter to the Governor of Massachusetts, Howe had earlier proposed a similar scheme for juvenile delinquents: "My wish is that we may be enabled to *hire* small farms, and without altering the buildings at all, or having anything marked and peculiar about them, to colonize our boys in them under the care of plain substantial farmers, and their *wives and families*. . . . This is the next best thing to distributing the boys, and paying for their care and keep among the households of the state." Howe to Governor Andrew, Dec. 21, 1862, reprinted in Howe 1909, Vol. II: 513.

89. See Grob 1966: 217 ff.

90. See the account by its first superintendent, Dr. Richard Dewey, in Hurd 1916, Vol. 2: 222–252. Throughout, in his ingenuous fashion, Dewey stresses how desirable the new

system is, not because it produces more cures, or a more pleasant environment for the inmates, but because it's more *economical.*

91. Massachusetts *did* adopt it the second time around, as did Ohio, Indiana, Dakota, New York (at Ogdensburg and Islip), and St. Elizabeth's in Washington, D.C. (Hurd 1916, Vol. 2: 247).

92. Hurd 1916, Vol. 1: 401. A precisely analogous fate befell critics of the juvenile reformatory. Here, too, starting with the Massachusetts State Reform School for Girls at Lancaster (1855) and the Ohio State Reform Farm for Boys at Lancaster (1857), a "cottage" or so-called family plan became popular. The resemblances between family and plan were purely verbal: In Ohio, for example, the plan began "with forty boys to each family" [sic!] (Hawes 1971: 85). Once again, the cottage system served "to facilitate efficient categorization and storage of social rejects" (Mennel 1973: 199). On the origins of the cottage system in this context, see Mennel 1973: esp. 52ff.; and on its fate, 199 ff.

93. For example: "Men differing in age, from boyhood to threescore; differing in race, in religion, in culture, in tastes, in habits, in capacities, in desires, are all brought within the same enclosures, and by night at least, shut up in the same four walls; subjected to the same general discipline; the same diet; the same dull routine of lying down; getting up; eating; walking; in a word, to the same dreary monotony of life. . . . This disadvantage cannot be overcome; and the evil consequences flowing out of it cannot be evaded, in establishments having the material unity of ours." Massachusetts State Board of Charities Vol. 4, 1867: xxxviii.

94. Massachusetts State Board of Charities, Vol. 4, 1867: xliii, lvi; also Vol. V, 1868 and Vol. VI, 1869, *passim*.

95. Massachusetts State Board of Charities, Vol. VII, 1870: esp. xl–xlii; see also Grob 1966: 221ff.

96. Grob 1966: 216ff. Leading asylum superintendents could not disguise their relief at his defeat. Isaac Ray wrote, "I am glad the coup de grace has been delivered at his preposterous cottage scheme, for I feared, at one time, it would be adopted." Kirkbride concurred: "The fact that Worcester has given up the scheme is an indication that Brother Bemis is no longer there, and also, of returning reason among these good people." (Ray to John Sawyer, February 15, 1873; Kirkbride to Earle, March 3, 1873. Both cited in Grob 1973: 334–335.)

PART THREE

Social control and welfare capitalism

So far I have shown that decarceration has been taking place on an increasing scale and has been adopted as the most desirable way of dealing with a wide range of deviance in both England and America. By placing the move away from segregative control in its historical context, I have suggested the underlying significance of this change in social control styles and practices. And I have striven to illustrate the defects and inadequacies which vitiate conventional accounts of the sources of the drive to deinstitutionalize the deviant. There remains, however, the obvious requirement of providing a more satisfactory explanation of this policy change. It is to this that I now turn; seeking at the same time to provide a practical demonstration of my contention in the first chapter of this book—namely, that the interrelationships between deviance and social control must necessarily be studied from a historically informed, macro-sociological perspective if we are to gain a theoretically adequate grasp of these phenomena.

CHAPTER SEVEN

Structural sources of the failure of the nineteenth century decarceration movement

In death as in life, the poor are treated in an utterly unfeeling way. They are flung into the earth like the carcasses of dead animals.

FREDERICK ENGELS
The Condition of the Working Class in England

One more word about giving instruction as to what the world ought to be. Philosophy in any case always comes on the scene too late to give it. As the thought of the world it appears only when the actuality is already there cut and dried . . . when philosophy paints its gray in gray, then has a shape of life grown old. By philosophy's gray in gray it cannot be rejuvenated but only understood. The owl of Minerva spreads its wings only with the falling of dusk.

G .F. HEGEL
The Philosophy of Right

The immediate question raised by the materials discussed in the previous chapter is, of course, why one group of critics of the institutional approach to the management of deviance was successful: while the other, employing almost identical arguments and possessed of considerable political influence and skill, was not. After all, as we have just seen, in its essentials, and with respect to either its intellectual cogency or its empirical support, the modern critique elaborated by Goffman and his followers is neither more developed nor, in any other relevant respect, substantially superior to its predecessor. (Furthermore, the respectability and social standing of the nineteenth century critics were if anything more securely established than those of their modern counterparts.) By the time both parts of this question have been answered, I hope we shall be brought, finally, to a more satisfactory understanding of the structural forces underlying the contemporary adoption of decarceration as official state policy.

This chapter, then, begins the concluding section of my argument by examining the failure of nineteenth century efforts to institute a system of community deviance management. At the outset, one may note that the radically different fate of two sets of arguments which seem formally to be substantially "the same" suggests that the acceptance and application of the "findings" of social science are dependent not so much on the intrinsic merits of the propositions being advanced but rather on the receptivity of the audience to which they are addressed. I shall advance the contention that this receptivity in its turn reflects the context within which decisions are being made; and that it is the presence of structural impediments (or imperatives) to the adoption of the policy which is the key to understanding the failure (or success) of deinstitutionalization.

For the most part, as Chapter Six has shown, the nineteenth century critique of institutional forms of social control was focused on the lunatic asylum. It was here that the critics' arguments were advanced in their most developed and compelling form; and it was here that the empirical evidence documenting the malign influence of institutions was most abundant. Moreover, the image of deviance and its control which dominated and legitimized the treatment of the insane—the therapeutic model—was framed in such a way as to imply that the well-being of the deviant was a legitimate object of concern. The lunatic, after all, was "sick," and to an important extent was not responsible for his situation. Hence, his control was "treatment," not "punishment," and was allegedly undertaken "for his own good." In such a context, suggestions that the treatment administered actually tended to harm him, and that an alternative policy provided a better approach to management and cure, could be advanced in a relatively straightforward fashion and apparently stood some chance of being implemented.

By contrast, control of adult criminals and, to a somewhat lesser extent, of juvenile delinquents, was dominated by a rational-legal approach, in which "it was assumed that deviance was the natural product of unbridled self-interest, and legal controls were necessary to maintain social harmony and guarantee individual rights."[1] Such deviants were pictured as "offenders" who ought to receive retribution for acts they had responsibly chosen to perform. In a control system premised on the notion that prisoners deserved (and ought to get) punishment, the infliction of certain sorts of pain and privation was viewed as "an eminently reasonable response."[2] Thus, when prisoners suffered deprivations, their own depravity was ample justification for such treatment. And if prisons and reformatories were unpleasant places, that was what they were intended to be—indeed, had to be, if they were to deter others. As for the prisoner's tendency to recidivate, for most people, that too was viewed as more the product of his innate criminality than of any secondary influence the penitentiary might have exercised or failed to exercise.[3]

All of this suggests that in understanding the failure of the nineteenth century decarceration movement, our attention ought primarily to be concentrated on discovering the reasons for that failure in the arena where the movement apparently stood most chance of success—the treatment of the mentally ill. When we do this, it becomes apparent that there were a number of elements which contributed to the lack of elite receptivity in this period to the notion of a community-based system for coping with the mentally disturbed. Even in the early part of the nineteenth century, English critics had difficulty rendering their arguments against the asylum plausible, partly because of the considerable basic legitimacy with which tradition had already endowed it: a legitimacy which was naturally all the stronger forty or fifty years later. Moreover, institutions whose humane and charitable design had been persistently stressed over the years were not readily susceptible to charges that they damaged and dehumanized their patients. By the latter part of the nineteenth century, the critics faced a further problem, in that the kinds of spectacular, obvious abuse and maltreatment of patients which earlier reformers had been able to demonstrate and utilize in order to rouse a largely indifferent public to a concern with the treatment of lunatics had by and large disappeared.[4] Complaints about the dullness and destructiveness of routine simply did not possess the same impact as allegations of the chaining, flogging, rape, and murder of inmates.

Then again, as the advocates of decarceration sometimes recognized, the sheer scale of investment of public money in the asylum solution over the previous fifty years created a kind of institutional inertia. As the *Edinburgh Review* reluctantly conceded: "The amount of capital sunk in the costly palaces of the insane is becoming a growing impediment. So much money sunk creates a conservatism in their builders . . . which resists change."[5] (And it was not just the money: by now, both the authorities and the psychiatric profession had a considerable intellectual and emotional investment in the asylum solution.)

A further obstacle to securing the release of the insane from asylums (men like Henry Maudsley wrongly thought it was the only serious one) "lies in the public ignorance, the unreasonable fear, and the selfish avoidance of insanity."[6] The asylum's critics were inclined to deride these fears,[7] but they were real enough. There could be "no doubt [that] in the eyes of the public these establishments are the necessary places of detention of troops of violent madmen, too dangerous to be allowed outside the walls."[8] If pressed, an educated minority might concede that "some, no doubt, may be at liberty without much, if any, risk to others. . . ." But the qualification came swiftly: "Yet their number is comparatively few—much fewer, certainly, than is generally supposed. . . . The Bellinghams, the Hatfields, the McNaughtons and the Oxfords, whose deeds of violence have given them a historical notoriety, belonged to the class of 'mild and manageable' lunatics, who may safely be allowed to enjoy all the privileges and immunities of the sane!"[9] The asylum critics argued that a closer acquaintance with the inside of an asylum would be enough to quiet all these fears. For although

> the visitor to an asylum enters the wards with the expectation of meeting violent maniacs . . . , he has not taken many steps . . . before the illusion begins to vanish; he may even ask, "Where are the mad people?" as he sees nothing but groups of patients seated around the fire, or lolling about in a dreary sort of way, perfectly quiet, and only curious about the curiosity of the stranger. This is the class of people who form at least 90% of the inhabitants of our asylums. . . .[10]

But the point was that most people were never likely to see the inside of an asylum.

By removing the insane from the community and sequestering them behind the walls of an institution, the possibility of ordinary people misperceiving and exaggerating the most common features of mental disturbance was greatly exacerbated. Lacking the corrective provided by close daily contact with such deviants, the public were likely indeed to view crazy people as a threat and a menace. The cases they were most likely to hear about were these of violent mania, since mild cases scarcely merited attention in the mass media. And after all, why else were lunatics locked up in the first place, unless it was because it was not safe to leave them at large?

As one might expect, the radical critique of the value of asylum treatment resoundingly failed to attract many coverts from the ranks of the asylum doctors. To the contrary, the profession provided one of the most powerful sources of opposition to the decarceration movement. Those advocating the closing of asylums saw this as an expression of simple self-interest: "It will be much to the credit of this body if the majority cordially assent to this experiment. It will be strange if some do not earnestly oppose it."[11] For "vested interests are growing up which warp the minds of the medical superintendents, as any great or radical change in the treatment of the insane would, they imagine, endanger their present position."[12]

One can well see how medical superintendents, who under such proposals would retain only the most violent and objectionable class of patients, and who were informed that their efforts had little or nothing to do with whether or not their patients recovered,[13] might "imagine" that their position was threatened—or might conclude, with Pliny Earle, that were the reformers to have their way, the superintendent's "office would seen degenerate, in general estimation, to that of 'Keeper.'"[14] Their opponents, however, displayed a misplaced confidence that "against this common sense will continually rise and say: The aggregation of persons in morbid condition of mind is the rotten stone in your foundation. The principle is false, and most of your daily work is to counteract the evils flowing from it. It should be followed no further than is absolutely necessary."[15]

Common sense might say so; but the public clearly did not, being already inclined to be sceptical of such "utopian" and "impractical" schemes. As a precaution, however, the superintendents produced more arguments and "evidence" to reinforce the conviction that to release lunatics back into the community would be a policy fraught with all sorts of undesirable consequences.[16] Such lobbying was particularly intense in, though by no means restricted to, those few cases where a policy of deinstitutionalization appeared to stand some chance of adoption, most notably in Massachusetts.[17] The best professional opinion could always be cited to support the contention that "the dangers incident to insane persons being at large are much greater than is commonly supposed."[18] The community could expect crime to increase, because investigation of clinical records had shown that, in many instances, crime and insanity were inseparably linked.[19] Lives as well as property would be in danger, for the mentally disturbed were liable to commit acts of sudden and unprovoked violence—and "it is worthy of note, too, that many of these acts, even those of peculiar atrocity, are often committed by individuals who, with all their obvious mental infirmity, had previously been regarded as perfectly harmless."[20]

In addition to the undoubted dangers of these kinds, leaving the insane outside the asylum walls would permit them to reproduce promiscuously, thereby augmenting the already worrying increase in insanity.[21] Furthermore, even if a particular lunatic when left at large remained docile and peaceable, and chaste into the bargain, the malign influence of his mere presence was sufficient to threaten the mental integrity of all normal people with whom he had contact. If asylum doctors were to be believed: "No insane person is *harmless*, in the only true sense of the term; he is ever doing mischief in mind and body and may at any moment add physical violence to the sinister mental influence he is perpetually exerting on himself and these with whom he is associated."[22] For this reason, Isaac Ray warned, "the poor sufferer cannot receive the ministry of near relatives, without endangering the mental integrity of those who offer them."[23]

As if all this were not sufficient to account for the failure of the early movement to deinstitutionalize the insane, the very basis of the critics' case rested on a fundamental misreading of the public's concerns. The central element of their critique was that asylums were a therapeutic disaster. And one may grant that for those who still saw cure as the primary issue, the fact that asylums were "more almshouses than hospitals"[24] was a condemnation of the entire system. But to those who were already convinced of the value of a custodial operation (and most of the influential classes in both societies, as well as the asylum superintendents, now felt this way), such complaints were quite simply an irrelevance.[25]

For all the criticisms which could be made of them, asylums were still a convenient way of getting rid of inconvenient people. The community was used, by now, to disposing of the derelict and troublesome in this fashion, placing them where, as one physician put it, "they are for the most harmless because they are kept out of harm's way."[26] In various ways, the functionality of custody for widely differing segments of society operated to sustain a system which had apparently failed; and to help to ensure that critiques of institutionalization would appeal to only a very limited audience. Asylums' earlier association with social reform gave a lingering humanitarian gloss to the huge, cheap, and avowedly custodial dumps where the refuse of the community was now collected together. Meanwhile, medical control of these institutions, and the rhetoric about cure that went with that control, provided a further legitimation of the custodial warehousing of these, the most difficult and troublesome elements of the disreputable poor. Working people had little alternative but to make use of the asylum as a way of ridding themselves of what, in the context of nineteenth century working class existence, was undoubtedly an intolerable burden: the caring for their sick, aged, decrepit, or otherwise incapacitated relatives. From the upper classes' perspective, the existence of asylums to "treat" the insane at public expense could be invoked as a practical demonstration of their own humanitarian concern for the less fortunate.

Far from asylums having been "altruistic institutions . . . detached from the social structures that perpetuate poverty,"[27] they were clearly important elements in sustaining these structures. For at this period, the influential classes in both England and America were all but unanimous in their unwillingness to insulate the population as a whole from the twin spurs of poverty and unemployment. Under the conditions characteristic of early industrial capitalism, relief threatened to undermine radically the whole notion of a labor market. It interfered with labor mobility. It encouraged the retention of "a vast inert mass of redundant labor" in rural areas, where the demand for labor was subject to wide seasonal fluctuations.[28] It distorted the operations of the labor market, not least by creating cost differentials between one town and one region and another. And the guarantee of subsistence had a pernicious effect on labor productivity and discipline. On the ideological level, this determination to restrict relief was at once reflected and strengthened by the hegemony of classical liberalism. The latter's insistence that every man was to be free to pursue his fortune and at the same time was to be held responsible for his own success or failure, coupled with its dogmatic certainty that interference with the dictates of the free market could only be counterproductive in the long run (a proposition which could even be "proved" theoretically), rendered the whole notion of social protectionism an anathema.[29]

Hence came the stress on the principle of "less eligibility" (enforced in large part through the discipline of institutions like workhouses and asylums); and the abhorrence of payments to individuals in the community (so-called "outdoor relief") as the two central elements in dealing with the problems of extreme incapacity of one sort or another.[30] For despite the ferocity of their ideological proclamations,[31] as a practical political matter, the upper classes were aware of the impossibility of adhering rigidly to the dictates of the market. But although "the residuum of paupers could not, admittedly, be left actually to starve,"[32] the pressures of the market place must be interfered with as little as possible. Here, an institutionally based system allowed the maintenance of conditions of relief which ensured that no one with any conceivable alternatives would seek public aid. In such a context, the asylum played its part, removing from lower-class families the impossible burdens imposed by those incapable of providing for their own subsistence, and thus ensuring that a potent source of discontent could be neutralized without having to alter society's basic structural arrangements.

Consider, for a moment, what an alternative policy of managing the insane in the community would have involved. Keeping lunatics "on the outside" would have entailed making provision for relatively generous pension or welfare payments to allow for their support. But at the least this would have raised the possibility that the living standards of families with an insane member would have been raised above those of the working class generally. Moreover, under this system, the insane alone would have been beneficiaries of something approximating a modern social welfare system, while their sane brethren were being subjected to the rigors of a Poor Law based on the principle of less eligibility. Such an approach would clearly have been administratively unworkable, especially given the labile nature of lunacy itself,[33] and the consequent ever present possibility that given sufficient incentive (or rather desperation), the poorer classes would resort to feigning insanity. These obstacles presented an absolute barrier to the development of a plausible alternative, community-based response to the problem of insanity—in fact none of the critics of the asylum was ever able to suggest even the basis of such a program: a *sine qua non* of their objections receiving serious consideration.

One final, and more general, point: The rejection of anything resembling a modern system of social protection or welfare and the use of institutional forms of social control were intimately connected in yet another way. For an important implication of the highly restrictive welfare policies characteristic of the United States and England until well into the twentieth century was that asylums, workhouses, and the like (as well as the more overtly coercive and punitive extensions of the control apparatus—prisons and reformatories) represented one of the few costs of production which were "socialized"—that is, taken over by the state rather than by the private sector. On the one hand, this meant that expenditures on segregative controls were highly visible, which was one source of the constant pressure to economize and keep costs in such institutions to a bare minimum.[34] But on the other hand, the relatively limited degree to which the state apparatus absorbed the costs of production meant that the fiscal pressures from this source on the state were relatively slight; so that the expenses of a segregative control apparatus thought necessary on other grounds were more readily absorbed.

As capitalism developed further, however, so the demands on the poor-law system changed, from instilling discipline and industriousness in a period of abundant unskilled human labor, to maintaining the capacity and willingness to work of an increasingly valuable resource. To an ever-increasing extent, the "workers' physical strength and good will had become important assets. Social insurance became one of the means of investing in human capital."[35] Although slowed in varying degrees by the persisting appeal of classical liberal ideology, both societies began to construct the basic elements of the modern welfare state.[36] In the next chapter, I shall argue that this development, coupled with a virtually simultaneous and massive expansion of the role of the state in other sectors of English and American society, decisively transformed the social context within which the social control apparatus was embedded; and that the ramifications of these changes account in large part for the move towards "community treatment" for the deviant.

1. Spitzer, forthcoming: 41. See also Ch. 2 in Spitzer for a discussion of different "images of deviance" and their implications.

2. Spitzer, forthcoming: 41. Such beliefs still persist in many quarters, and even now, "legislative and executive sensitivity to these sentiments imposes fairly sharp restraints on the use of alternatives perceived by the general public as too lenient for the adult offender . . ." (Greenberg 1975: 29–30). I suggest that it is only under extraordinary circumstances that concerns with deterrence and with visiting retribution on those guilty of violating the criminal law will lose their normal centrality in policies directed at the control of the criminal.

3. The Massachusetts State Board of Charities expressed the common prejudice when it blamed the prevalence of crime and delinquency on the existence of "inherited organic imperfection—vitiated constitution or *poor stock*" (Second Annual Report, 1864). In the late nineteenth century, the most popular "scientific" support for these attitudes was the Lombrosian notion of the "born criminal"—an atavism or reversion to a more primitive pre-social type of man, whose biology was his destiny. Lombroso's conclusions were given wide currency in popularized form in both England and America. (See, for example, Fletcher 1891; Weir 1894; Ellis 1900; Henderson 1901; also Wolfgang 1960.) When they began to lose their scientific respectability, the same pessimistic conclusions about the criminal and delinquent classes found a new justification in the emerging "science" of eugenics. Drawing on Mendelian genetics, men like Galton provided an authoritative gloss for the notion that attributes like criminality were biologically transmitted from generation to generation without regard to the social environment. (See Haller 1964; Higham 1955; Fink 1962.) All of these ideas not merely protected the prison and reformatory from charges of failure, but provided an unassailable argument for the incarceration of the morally delinquent; this being one of the only sure ways of ensuring that they did not procreate.

To us, there seems to be an obvious contradiction between a legal system based on the concept of *mens rea* and a view of criminality as biologically determined. If these men perceived the contradiction, however, they seem to have preferred to ignore it. For general discussions of perceptions of criminals and delinquents in this period, see Platt 1969: Ch. 2; Mennel 1973: Ch. 3.

4. Although anti-asylum forces made vigorous enough use of such cases of this sort as they could still uncover; see Eaton 1881: 265–266: "The last investigation of the New York asylum for insane convicts disclosed facts that would disgrace Turkey; filth, vermin, contagious disease, food hardly less fatal than starvation itself; two pistol balls in the body of one inmate, fired by his superintendent; a lunatic shackled and handcuffed night and day for two months; but no records of medicine, of treatment, of punishment, or of diet!"

5. *Edinburgh Review* 1870: 231. The same was true, of course, of prisons and reform schools, "great piles of brick and mortar . . . so strongly built and richly endowed, that they cannot be got rid of easily" (Howe 1909, Vol. II: 520).

6. Maudsley, cited in House of Commons Select Committee Report, 1877: 55. Compare one of his modern counterparts: "It should not be forgotten that one of the reasons the general public in England and America are so ready to part with their money for the building of mental hospitals, is their fear of the mentally ill and their desire to have them put away even at a price." (Rees 1957: 527).

7. See House of Commons Select Committee Report 1877: 55.

8. *Edinburgh Review* 1870: 224.

9. *North American Review* Vol. 82, 1856: 93.

10. *Edinburgh Review* 1870: 224.

11. Massachusetts State Board of Charities Vol. IV, 1867: lvii.

12. *Edinburgh Review* 1870: 231.

13. Bucknill 1880: 114.

14. Cited in Massachusetts Board of State Charities Vol. IX, 1872: 83.

15. Massachusetts Board of State Charities Vol. IV, 1867: lviii.

16. Those in charge of reformatories for juvenile delinquents employed similar tactics to discredit the efforts to promote the use of noninstitutional alternatives for *their* clients. Such proposals were attacked as "dangerously permissive." Delinquents were, after all, a threat to the moral and physical integrity of the community. Schemes to leave them at large were well-meaning but foolish: "Shall we take these children as they are brought to us, thieves, liars, profane swearers, licentious, polluted in body and soul, and put them in your families in that condition?" Second Convention of Managers and Superintendents of Houses of Refuge and Schools of Reform, *Proceedings*, 1859: 29. For a general discussion of opposition to deinstitutionalization on the part of reform school superintendents, see Mennel 1973: 46ff.

17. The opposition here was led by Pliny Earle, superintendent of the Northampton State Hospital (see his annual reports for 1871 and 1872; also Massachusetts State Board of Charities Vol. IX, 1872: esp. 84–85). His efforts were vigorously supported by other well-known institutional psychiatrists; see, for example, Isaac Ray: "I read your report with an unusual degree of interest, especially your observations concerning the family and cottage methods of caring for the insane. These projects I regard as the offspring of that class of men to be found in every community whose only chance of achieving notoriety is to find fault with everybody else and who suppose they magnify themselves by depreciating others." Ray to Earle, Feb. 18, 1872, Pliny Earle Papers, at the American Antiquarian Society.

18. Kirkbride 1880: 26.

19. E.g., see Leavesden Asylum Annual Report 1876: 2.

20. Kirkbride 1880: 27.

21. See House of Commons Select Committee 1877, evidence of Dr. J.C. Browne.

22. Granville 1877 Vol. 2: 194, emphasis in the original.

23. Ray 1863: 174.

24. Bucknill 1880: 123.

25. See Scull 1974: 440–459; and Rothman 1971: 269–287.

26. Hanwell Asylum Annual Report Vol. 25: 36.

27. Herbert Gans, in Preface to Greer 1972: xi.

28. Polanyi 1944, Chs. 7 and 8; Hobsbawm 1968: 99–100, 104–105.

29. See Rimlinger 1971, esp. Ch. 3.

30. This abhorrence of outdoor relief enjoyed an extraordinarily long ideological hegemony. Even such groups as the aged were not exempt from its effects. In England the opposition to such relief policies was undoubtedly bolstered by memories of the disastrous impact of the Speenhamland system during the late eighteenth and early nineteenth centuries. This "system" involved the systematic provision of aid in wages on an outdoor basis to supplement the income of workers otherwise unable to earn sufficient to provide for their own or their families' subsistence. Not only was this approach utterly incompatible with a wage labor system (without which capitalism could scarcely function); but it also served to pauperize, demoralize, and degrade the masses and "eventually ruined the people it was [allegedly] designed to succor" (Polanyi 1944: 81). The lesson thus learned concerning the evils of outdoor relief was not soon forgotten by liberal economists. It was spread widely in the United States through the "Social Darwinist" doctrines of Herbert Spencer (See Hofstadter 1944). As late as 1913, Dicey criticized a highly restricted state old-age pension plan, passed in England in 1908, as "in essence nothing but a new form of outdoor relief for the poor . . ."; and into the 1920s and 1930s, orthodox liberal economists continued to believe, with Von Mises, "that as long as unemployment benefit is paid, unemployment must exist" (both cited in Polanyi 1944: 283).

31. For example, see Spencer (1868: 353–354):

> The well-being of existing humanity, and the unfolding of it into this ultimate perfection, are both secured by the same benificent, though severe discipline, to which animate nature at large is subject: a discipline which is pitiless in working out of good: a felicity pursuing law which never swerves for the avoidance of partial and temporary suffering. The poverty of the incapable, the distress which comes upon the imprudent, the starvation of the idle, and those shoulderings aside of the weak by the strong, which leaves so many "in shallows and miseries," are the decrees of a large, far-seeing benevolence. It seems hard that an unskillfulness which with all his efforts he cannot overcome, should entail hunger upon the artisan. It seems hard that a labourer incapacitated by sickness from competing with his stronger fellows, should have to bear the resulting privations. It seems hard that widows and orphans should be left to struggle for life or death. Nevertheless, when regarded not separately, but in connection with the interests of universal humanity, these harsh fatalities are seen to be full of the highest benificence—the same beneficence which brings to early graves the children of diseased parents, and singles out the low-spirited, the intemperate, and debilitated as the victims of an epidemic."

32. Hobsbawm 1968: 88.

33. See Scull 1974: Ch. 9.

34. See Scull 1974: Ch. 7.

38. Rimlinger 1971: 10.

36. Rimlinger 1971, Chs. 5 and 6.

CHAPTER EIGHT

"Success" in the twentieth century: welfare capitalism and the changing exigencies of domestic pacification and control

"Oh," replied Mr. Pickwick, looking down a dark and filthy staircase, which appeared to lead to a range of damp and gloomy stone vaults, beneath the ground, "and those, I suppose are the little cellars where the prisoners keep their small quantities of coals. Unpleasant places to have to go down to: but very convenient, I dare say."

"Yes, I shouldn't wonder if they was convenient," replied the gentleman," seeing that a few people live there, pretty snug. That's the Fair, that is."

"My friend," said Mr. Pickwick," you don't really mean to say that human beings live down in those wretched dungeons?"

"Don't I?" replied Roker, with indignant astonishment: "why shouldn't I?"

"Live! Live down there!" exclaimed Mr. Pickwick.

"Live down there! Yes, and die down there, too, wery often!" replied Mr. Roker; "and what of that? Who's got to say anything agin it? Live down there! Yes, and a wery good place it is to live in, ain't it?"

CHARLES DICKENS
Pickwick Papers

It is not well to sneer at political economy in its relations to the insane poor. Whether we think it right or not, the question of cost has determined and will continue to determine their fate for weal or woe.

GEORGE COOK
The American Journal of Insanity, 1866

In this chapter we turn, finally, to the task of providing an alternative account of the reasons for the "success" of the contemporary decarceration movement. A proper grasp of the sources of this change will be shown to rest on an understanding of the internal dynamics of the development of capitalist societies. Or, to put it another way, the attempt to manage an increasing proportion of the "deviant" within the community (or rather a geographically and socially limited sector of the community), will be seen to be a response to the changing exigencies of domestic pacification and control under welfare capitalism.

To summarize my thesis briefly at the outset, I shall argue that with the coming of the welfare state, segregative modes of social control became, in relative terms, far more costly and difficult to justify. This is particularly clear in the case of the group we have given most attention to, the mentally disturbed, who were formerly confined in "monasteries of the mad." As we have just seen, until well into the twentieth century, there had been little or no alternative to keeping the chronically disabled cases of insanity in the asylum; for although the overwhelming majority were harmless, they could not provide for their own subsistence, and no alternative sources of support were available to sustain them in the outside world. However, with the advent of a wide range of welfare programs providing just such support, the opportunity cost of neglecting community care in favor of asylum treatment — inevitably far more costly than the most generous scheme of welfare payments — rose sharply.[1] Simultaneously, the increasing socialization of production costs by the state, something which has been taking place at an increasing pace during and since the Second World War, and of which modern welfare measures are merely one very important example, produced a growing fiscal crisis, as state expenditures continuously threatened to outrun available revenue.[2] In combination, a focus on the interplay of these factors enables us to resolve what at first sight is a paradox — namely the emergence and persistence of efforts to curtail expenditures for control of "problem populations" at a time when general expenditures on welfare items were expanding rapidly. For it is precisely the expansion of the one which made both possible and desirable the contraction of the other.

Noninstitutional approaches are less immediately palatable when, instead of "sick" people, their object is criminals and delinquents. Incarceration, after all, has come to be virtually synonymous with punishment over the past century and a half; and the notion that law-breakers deserve to suffer (i.e., be imprisoned) for their offenses is a belief not easily abandoned. However, as the fiscal pressures on the state have intensified during the 1960s and 1970s, so noninstitutional techniques for coping with the criminal and the delinquent have come to exert an ever-greater fascination for criminal justice planners and policy makers. Diversionary programs enjoy a mounting popularity as traditional convictions as to the value of imprisonment for purposes of retribution and deterrence not so coincidentally lose their long-standing hold — on policy makers, if not on the public at large.

In what follows, I shall begin discussing the reasons for the proliferation of state functions in advanced capitalist countries, paying particular attention to the growth of the welfare state. I shall then move to a consideration of how this qualitative transformation in the scope of state activity is connected with the abandonment or modification of segregative forms of social control. Finally, following this general discussion of the decarceration process, I shall endeavor to demonstrate on a concrete descriptive level how fiscal considerations have been reflected in the process of deinstitutionalization.

At the outset of any discussion of the welfare state, it is, of course, essential to distinguish analytically the concrete historical *origins* of particular welfare measures and of the welfare system as a whole "from the on-going *function* they play within [a] particular social formation. . . ."[3] Clearly, the advent of the welfare state reflected in some measure a lessened resistance to such legislation on the part of a capitalist class increasingly led to confront the implications of the fact that, in an advanced economy, "human faculties are as important a means of production as any other kind of capital."[4] Equally, however, the historical genesis of the welfare state is also the product of political struggles on the part of increasingly organized labor movements. To this extent, welfare measures represent "social concessions" made under the threat of, or in anticipation of popular discontent and struggle.[5] More specifically, "the greater security enjoyed by many during wartime, despite the absolute fall in living standards, . . . [and] the political necessity for capitalist states to avoid a return to slumps of the interwar scale, and their ability to implement this by means of Keynesian policies . . . made demands for extended state intervention in the field of welfare irresistible. . . ."[6] The post-war growth in the relative strength of the labor movement, substantially a reflection of the largely successful pursuit of full-employment policies during this period, has produced a consolidation and extension of these earlier gains.

Social polarization and the more acute forms of class conflict have thus been minimized by the working classes' ability to extract a whole series of economic and social reforms; reforms which have modified but not destroyed the underlying character of the capitalist political and economic system. Indeed, such compromises on the part of the state apparatus vis-à-vis the dominated classes have to a significant extent served to strengthen the system as a whole; even while, as Gough points out, they have necessarily involved the sacrifice of "the short-term and even long-term *economic* interests of particular sections of capital."[7] All this is in keeping with the historical role of state intervention under capitalism. For throughout the development of this type of social formation, the quasi-autonomous state apparatus has served to modify the inherently self-destructive tendencies of a pure market system,[8] at first through welfare measures which helped to ensure the adequate reproduction and maintenance of labor power, but increasingly also through efforts to improve the *quality* of that labor power.

In functional terms, that is, social welfare has increasingly come to occupy a dual role in capitalist states. On the one hand, a substantial proportion of welfare expenditure—for health, housing, education, and the like—represents a form of social investment, directly or indirectly raising the productivity of a given amount of labor. The scope of such investment reflects the accelerating replacement of "raw" labor power by skilled, technical labor power. Technological advance has meant that "the quality of labor power must necessarily be raised in all capitalist economies to match the increased sophistication of production and its attendant social processes . . . and this has . . . necessitated the intervention of the state."[9] On the other hand, outlays on social welfare represent "social expenses," that is, services required to maintain social harmony.[10] They have bought the allegiance of skilled workers to the system at what was initially a relatively modest cost. But perhaps more importantly in this regard, welfare payments at a level close to subsistence have increasingly been required to cope with the problems posed by the growing class of economically redundant and superfluous people.

For the obverse of the growing demand for highly skilled and "internally motivated" forms of wage labor is a contracting market for unskilled workers, who come to form an almost permanent surplus population at the margins of the economy. Technological progress creates "a constant stream of underemployed, unemployed, prematurely used up, obsolete, or unemployable individuals."[11] The "classical unemployed" formed what Marx called an industrial reserve army, ". . . that belongs to capital quite as absolutely as if the latter had bred it at its own cost,"[12] and which served to regulate (and depress) the level of wages. More and more this ceases to be true, for "raw labor power does not compete with technical labor power, in the context of capital intensive technology."[13] And yet, "at the same time, the greater volume of surplus makes it possible to support growing numbers of these people, however miserably. . . . Thus a new class is generated, consisting mainly of those who have lost even their competitive link to the labor market," and who constitute "a permanent welfare class."[14]

All this has formed part of a process whereby, in all advanced capitalist societies (and particularly since 1945), there has been a prolonged expansion of government expenditures, as the state moves to take on "a qualitatively expanded role . . . in capitalist social formations."[15] Especially notable, apart from the rising outlays on social services which we have just discussed, has been the growing expenditure on such things as aid to private industry, and items designed to improve the economic infrastructure (e.g., roads, education, government supported research and development.) The budgetary impact of all this activity has been startling. Even if one leaves aside the other components of state spending, in the United Kingdom, the social services have swallowed a proportion of the Gross National Product which has risen from 10.9 percent in 1937 to 24.9 percent by 1973; and an essentially similar pattern has been observable in the United States, where such outlays have risen from 9 percent of the Gross National Product in 1955 to 15 percent in 1969.[16]

A number of factors besides real improvements in services have contributed to the upward pressure on state budgets in this period. The United States and England, like other developed economies in the capitalist world system, have found that the costs of state services (especially social services) rise faster than the average price level, everywhere forcing an ever higher expenditure merely to maintain the same services in real terms. Undoubtedly this reflects the fact that on the average productivity rises less fast in the state than in the private sector of the economy; which in turn reflects the relative predominance of low productivity, labor-intensive services in the state sector. Then too, in addition to the technical difficulties associated with *any* effort to raise productivity in service occupations, the situation "is undoubtedly exacerbated in the case of state services by the absence of competitive pressure to reduce costs."[17] Furthermore, it is clear that "the size of income maintenance expenditures has been heavily influenced by the growing proportion of aged in Britain and America . . .,"[18] and, indeed, by the general "tendency of the dependent population to expand as a proportion of the total."[19]

Turning to the question of the impact of all this on the social control apparatus, and considering first the case of the mentally ill, in the post-World War II period, state mental hospitals have experienced acute budgetary strains under the impact of severe cost inflation and two more specific related factors. The widespread unionization of state employees and the associated "advent of the eight-hour day and forty hour week in state institutions . . . virtually doubled unit costs. . . .[20] On top of this, a number of class action suits on behalf of hospital inmates were brought during the 1960s and 1970s (in the United States at least). Decisions such as Wyatt v. Stickney (1972) attempted to lay down minimum standards of treatment, while others sought to eliminate "institutional peonage," the employment of unpaid patient labor to reduce institutional costs. To the extent that they are implemented, these decisions unquestionably "force upon the states huge expenditures . . .";[21] but they will obviously have no force if institutions can be emptied and closed instead.[22]

In such circumstances, the continuation of an increasingly costly social control policy which, in terms of effectiveness, possesses few advantages over an apparently much cheaper alternative becomes ever more difficult to justify; and the attractiveness of that alternative to governments under ever greater budgetary pressures, whatever the political difficulties in the way of its realization, becomes steadily harder to resist. In the words of those who have served as bureaucratic managers of the system: "Rising costs more than any other factor have made it obvious that support of state hospitals is politically unfeasible . . . ; this is the principal factor behind the present push to get rid of state hospitals."[23] To put it bluntly: "In a sense our backs are to the wall; it's *phase out* before we go *bankrupt*."[24]

To the extent that psychoactive drugs have played a role in the adoption of a policy of decarceration (and, as I have shown in Chapter Five, their significance in this respect is usually greatly exaggerated), I would suggest that it is the existence of these structural pressures which in large measure accounts for their being used in this way, rather than simply to ease the problems of internal management in asylums. Similarly, the impact of these pressures explains the differential susceptibility of the relevant audiences to the substantially identical criticisms of the asylum put forward in the 1860s and 1870s, and again in the 1950s and 1960s. The arguments had not changed, but the structural context in which they were advanced clearly had. Their contemporary reappearance allowed governments to save money while simultaneously giving their policy a humanitarian gloss. And to take the argument a step further, it is the intensity and extent of such pressures which account for the persistence of this policy despite public resistance to it, and despite the accumulation of evidence that in terms of its *ostensible* goals, community care is substantially a failure.

As states realized that decarceration was feasible, they began to maneuver to obtain the cost savings it offered. Some of the largest savings immediately realizable came from the cancellation of planned new construction, and decisions to do this were widespread.[25] In the

United States, large savings for hard-pressed local governments were also available where patients could be discharged from state hospitals (where they were provided for at state expense) to private, profit-making "convalescent homes"—not just because provision in such places was less costly, but also because changes in the social security laws in the late 1950s made it possible for these people to collect social security (and thus be supported at federal expense) so long as they were not in psychiatric institutions.[26] A number of states followed California's lead in providing financial inducements to counties to avoid sending patients to state hospitals for in-patient care.[27] In England, ministerial calls for "ruthless" cutbacks in the number of psychiatric beds were coupled with plans which included virtually no provision for increased community care. The plans promised major cost savings, and as a consequence, drew extensive support from right-wing political figures.[28]

For reasons we have already discussed, the pace of expansion of state expenditures on "social services" in both countries increases markedly during the 1960s and 1970s. As it does so, the incentives to accelerate the movement toward deinstitutionalization likewise intensify. And it is precisely in this period that the momentum of the drive to shut down institutions and minimize incarceration gathered its greatest force. The range of devices used to divert potential inmates away from institutions was further expanded, and those already in existence were applied with greater urgency and effect. Welfare regulations were changed to make aid to mental patients discharged into the community more readily available.[29] Screening projects were set up to encourage the placement of potential admissions, particularly geriatric cases, in non-hospital settings.[30] Involuntary commitment was made far more difficult in some jurisdictions, also helping to reduce hospital intakes.[31] Perhaps most elaborate and effective of all was the system devised by the state of California in the Lanterman-Petris-Short Act (1967).[32] Under this approach, counties were, in effect, bribed not to use state hospitals—a scheme which led to a further acceleration in the decline of state hospital populations, allowed the closure of four state hospitals within a five year period, and produced substantial cost savings for the state.[33]

Once the drive for control of soaring costs is seen as the primary factor underlying the move towards decarceration, both these and a number of other aspects of this change which formerly appeared either fortuitous or inexplicable become readily comprehensible. For one thing, this perspective allows us to see the spread of the policy of deinstitutionalization to the criminal justice sector, and the rise of efforts to decarcerate criminals and delinquents, as part of a single, unitary phenomenon. At first, movement in this direction was tentative, small-scale, and experimental. But by the late 1960s, as the pressure to alleviate the upward spiral in relief costs mounts: as the magnitude of the capital expenditure otherwise required for new prisons and reformatories becomes apparent; and as the size of the savings community approaches can produce on current outlays is documented; so there begins a rapid expansion of programs designed to divert the criminal and the delinquent away from the institution.[34]

Then again, ever since segregative control became the dominant mode of managing deviance, the public has shown consistently little desire or inclination to have officially labeled serious deviants returned to their midst.[35] Studies made in the earlier phases of the decarceration movement indicated a continuing attitude of hostility, fear, and intolerance towards the mentally ill,[36] and the presence and strength of these feelings have been amply documented by subsequent reactions, as efforts have continued to return the mentally ill to the community. Residents have fought hard to ensure that if the mental patients *are* released, they are not released into *their* neighborhoods, a favorite tactic in this battle being the enactment of restrictive zoning ordinances.[37] Similar measures have frequently been employed to exclude such "undesirable" elements as criminals and addicts; and a recent study of the diversion of juvenile delinquents likewise concluded that "the actual establishment of group homes in local communities is often vehemently resisted by residents."[38]

These resistance strategies have naturally been most successfully employed by middle and upper class communities. Even those who have devoted their well-paid "expertise" to developing public relations techniques for the "neutralization of community resistance to group homes" have been forced to concede that these community homes have the best chance of being established in transient neighborhoods, "or where the local residents are not particularly capable of organized opposition." And they confess there are but "few strategies with potential for gaining access to a community that has the ability to organize itself in opposition or in support of issues."[39] In any event, on cost grounds, there has been little pressure to place ex-mental patients or other types of deviants in such "respectable" settings. Instead, decarceration has produced

> the growing ghettoization of the returning ex-patients along with other dependent groups in the population; the growing succession of inner-city land use to institutions providing services to the dependent and needy . . . , the forced immobility of the chronically disabled within deteriorated urban

> neighborhoods . . . , areas where land-use deterioration has proceeded to
> such a point that the land market is substantially unaffected by the intro-
> duction of community services and their clients. . . .[40]

(Of course, in such areas there is also an absence of organized community
opposition to the presence of these people.)[41] As if they are industrial
wastes which can without risk be left to decompose in some well-
contained dump, these problem populations have increasingly been
dealt with by a resort to their ecological separation and isolation in
areas where they are by and large no longer visible, and where they may
be safely left to prey on one another.[42]

But in many places, the sheer numbers involved have led to spillovers
into "residential," usually working- or lower-middle-class communities.
The opposition this has aroused has been further stimulated by complaints over the scope of "aftercare" facilities provided (or rather not
provided). If the program for decarcerating the mentally ill was to live
up to rhetorical claims about its being undertaken for the ex-patients'
welfare, these aftercare facilities would have had to be extensively
present; but this would have been extremely costly,[43] and if the program
was to realize financial savings they had to be substantially absent. They
are absent.[44] Thus, "the actual transfer of patients had tended to favor
the preferred re-assignment according to economy goals. For patients
who have been 'dumped' by hospitals prematurely, both therapeutic
and civil rights have been violated, as well as the rights of the recipient
communities."[45] Governments have consistently made the most of the
opportunity to secure "a major retrenchment in the psychiatric services
program, made possible by a rapidly declining hospital population. The
professional administrators were unable to convince . . . the government
of the necessity to greatly expand community services and to redeploy
staff and resources from institutional to community services."[46]

In the burgeoning field of community corrections, the situation is
essentially no different. In 1972, for example, when Massachusetts
abruptly and virtually overnight closed down all juvenile reform schools
in the state, not even token efforts had been made to develop an
infrastructure capable of providing community supervision or control
over those released.[47] As for adult criminals, the most authoritative
national survey in recent years of the corrections field pointed out that
"the United States spends only 20 percent of its corrections budget and
allocates only 15 percent of its total staff to service the 67 percent of
offenders in the corrections workload who are under community

supervision . . ."—with the result that 67 percent of felons and 76 percent of misdemeanants were dealt with in case loads of over 100 per staff member.[48] Six years later, following major efforts to accelerate the diversion of criminals away from prison, the situation was essentially unchanged, perhaps worse, with the average probation officer's workload "far too great to permit adequate investigation for assessment or control purposes, let alone for appreciable assistance."[49]

It is quite clear, of course, that from the point of view of state expenditures, incarcerating problem populations of all descriptions in state institutions is extraordinarily costly, usually (though not universally) far more so than a deliberate policy of coping with them in the "community." This is particularly obvious when, as has unquestionably been the case with the contemporary decarceration movement, the rhetoric of promoting rehabilitation through community treatment is taken no more seriously than similar hyperbolic talk about treatment in the institution. Under such conditions, there emerge quite startling discrepancies in comparative costs on a per capita basis. This holds true whether one looks at the case of dependent and neglected children,[50] criminals,[51] juvenile delinquents,[52] or mental patients.[53]

One must grant, however, that reality is more complicated than this simple comparison might suggest. In the first place, the cost savings theoretically available from deinstitutionalization may not always be realized. For example, a re-examination of data on the Community Treatment and Probation Subsidy Programs in California indicates that much of the savings expected (and claimed) to result from such programs has not in fact materialized—although statistical juggling and administrative sleight of hand have concealed this from both the state government and most academic researchers. Among other factors, this cost overrun reflects the fact that declines in the number of commitments to institutions have been offset by increases in the average length of time served. Likewise, the Community Treatment Program has been modified so as to increase substantially the number of months probationers are subject to intensive supervision in the community, thus necessitating a sizable expansion in the number of probation officers. Such an outcome can be easily understood. For a policy of emptying prisons and reformatories clearly threatens the organizational interests of the correctional bureaucracy. Yet it is that very bureaucracy which is charged with implementing the new policy. Since it retains discretionary powers (as with length of stay or of probationary supervision), it may be expected to try to manipulate those powers to ensure organizational survival.[54] Ultimately, if decarceration is to realize its full potential for reducing state expenditures, such groups must either be bought off or circumvented.

Even where such problems are brought under control, obstacles remain. In the short run, at least, many of the costs of a mental hospital or prison system are fixed and unchangeable, regardless of the number of inmates occupying the institutions. As a consequence, a sizable fraction of the savings potentially available from decarceration may not be immediately realizable, being postponed until the number of those incarcerated falls far enough to allow the state to close institutions and thereby eliminate fixed costs. But on the other hand, to the extent that the adoption of diversionary policies obviates the need for massive expansion of the physical capacity of the existing institutional system (as has indubitably been the case with both asylums and prisons), decarceration provides a direct and immediate source of relief to the state's fiscal crisis whose importance is obvious, even while its dimensions are extraordinarily difficult to estimate with any precision.[55]

For example on the capital budget side, by the mid-1950s much of the existing physical plant of the mental hospital systems in both England and America, largely an inheritance from the nineteenth century, were rapidly approaching a degree of decay and decrepitude which would have made replacement mandatory.[56] Moreover, annual admissions were already displaying a persistent tendency to rise markedly from one year to the next, a trend which, as Table 8–1 shows, grew still more prominent over the next decade and a half. If the proportion of admissions becoming chronic long-stay cases had remained at or close to its historic levels, substantial new construction would obviously have been called for. Instead, as retention rates fell sharply, mental hospitals were pictured as "dying" institutions on which it was naturally foolish to spend any more by way of renovation—and capital expenditure on them was reduced to a minimum.[57]

With respect to current expenditures, adequate data on the savings thus produced unfortunately do not exist. Such data as we do possess are highly fragmentary and incomplete.[58] One useful indicator, however, is provided by the information presented in Table 8–2. As these figures show, state expenditure on mental hospitals, excluding capital items, as a proportion of state expenditures has consistently fallen since the mid-1950s, paralleling the fall in patient numbers. In many states the decline has been steep and dramatic: between 1955 and 1974, from 5.26% to

TABLE 8-1
First Admissions to (U.S.) State and County
Mental Hospitals, 1950-1968*

Year	Admissions	Year	Admissions
1950	114,054	1960	140,015
1951	112,979	1961	146,393
1952	118,213	1962	129,698*
1953	123,854	1963	131,997
1954	121,430	1964	138,932
1955	122,284	1965	144,090
1956	123,539	1966	162,486
1957	128,124	1967	164,219
1958	137,280	1968	175,637
1959	137,795		

SOURCES: U.S. Department of Health, Education and Welfare: Public Health Service: Patients in Mental Institutions, Part II State and County Mental Hospitals 1950-1965. Washington, D.C.: Government Printing Office. N.I.M.H. *Statistical Note No. 14.* Rockville, Maryland: N.I.M.H.

*Note: Figures for 1962 and all subsequent years were artificially deflated by changes in recording practices introduced at the end of 1961.

only 1.79% in Illinois; from 5.86% to 2.40% in Massachusetts; and from 7.04% to 3.20% in New York. And overall, the proportion of state expenditures absorbed by the mental hospital sector has almost halved over the same period. These drastic reductions are all the more remarkable since they have been achieved in the face of a series of developments which appeared to threaten equally drastic *increases* in the proportion of state revenues absorbed by mental hospitals. We have already discussed a number of these: the general tendency of productivity to rise less fast in the state sector; the unionization of hospital workers and the advent of the forty hour work week; the "right to treatment decisions" by the courts; and rising admissions rates. The productivity factor alone in other spheres of state activity has meant that "the cost index of state services has risen faster than the average price level and a greater level of expenditure is required just to maintain the level of services in real terms."[59] In all the circumstances, merely to have held state hospital costs down to a constant proportion of state budgets would clearly have been out of the question without vigorous attempts to divert potential patients away from the hospital, so as to at least slow the rate at which admissions were rising and to continue efforts to shorten the stay of these who did end up as hospital inmates. Table 8-3 provides

TABLE 8-2

Expenditures on Mental Hospitals as a Percentage of General State Expenditures, 1955–1974 (Selected States and Nationally)

	California	Illinois	Indiana	Massachusetts	Michigan	New York	Washington	All States
1955	2.57	5.26	3.53	5.86	2.73	7.04	1.79	3.38
1956	2.56	5.03	2.98	5.28	2.67	7.80	1.88	3.32
1957	2.60	4.48	3.29	4.93	2.63	7.41	2.00	3.25
1958	2.60	4.02	3.58	5.60	2.72	6.88	1.92	3.25
1959	2.43	4.00	3.38	5.36	2.61	6.66	1.91	3.09
1960	2.42	3.88	3.24	5.18	2.50	5.92	1.98	2.98
1961	2.36	4.01	3.06	5.67	2.34	5.73	2.15	2.99
1962	2.29	3.82	3.09	5.69	2.34	3.85	1.85	2.91
1963	2.23	3.79	3.02	5.13	2.34	5.37	1.64	2.79
1964	2.11	3.56	2.72	4.88	2.36	5.14	1.62	2.70
1965	1.97	4.08	2.65	4.65	2.37	5.45	1.61	2.68
1966	1.83	3.92	2.65	4.49	2.14	4.85	1.50	2.53
1967	1.72	4.12	2.51	4.18	2.08	4.69	1.50	2.46
1968	1.49	3.40	2.56	3.92	2.07	4.41	1.40	2.37
1969	1.34	3.10	2.51	3.49	1.99	4.12	1.49	2.29
1970	1.24	2.68	2.43	3.43	1.91	4.07	1.28	2.20
1971	1.10	2.45	2.23	3.16	1.92	3.74	1.18	2.03
1972	1.00	2.26	2.12	2.93	1.79	3.06	1.07	1.90
1973	0.93	2.07	2.08	2.51	1.69	3.04	1.04	1.90
1974	0.86	1.79	2.05	2.40	1.61	3.20	0.90	1.87
% change 1955–1974	67	66	42	59	41	55	50	45

SOURCE: U.S. Bureau of the Census: State Finances. Washington D.C.: U.S. Commerce Department.

NOTE: The above figures are calculated on the basis of current expenditures. Capital items are excluded.

TABLE 8-3

Average Duration of Hospitalization at State Mental Hospitals
in California (in Days) 1966-1967—1969-1970

Hospital	1966–1967	1967–1968	1968–1969	1969–1970
Agnews	135.9	111.0	96.5	18.0
Mendocino	108.7	88.0	72.2	8.0
Napa	150.6	135.1	108.3	61.0
Dewitt	104.1	96.9	80.3	24.0
Camarillo	145.2	123.5	128.1	18.0
Metropolitan	122.6	108.9	81.7	14.0

SOURCE: ENKI Research Institute. *A Study of California's New Mental Health Law.*
Chatsworth, California: 1972, by permission.

evidence of just how far the latter approach has gone in certain
jurisdictions.[60]

The promise of such cost savings largely explains the curious political
alliance which has fostered and supported decarceration.[61] Social
policies which allegedly benefit the poorest and most desperate segments
of the community do not ordinarily arouse particular enthusiasm
among the so-called fiscal conservatives. The goal of returning mental
patients to the community is clearly an exception, for in addition to the
liberal adherents one might expect, it has attracted prominent, sometimes decisive, support from their ranks.[62] Similarly, conservatives are
ordinarily in the forefront of demands that retribution be heaped on the
heads of those (lower-class) elements who violate the law. Yet
diversionary programs, which have the effect of sparing the criminal
classes the pains of imprisonment, have been pursued most vigorously
and "effectively" in California, under the conservative administration
of Ronald Reagan. This congruence of opinion between what are the
two poles of "legitimate" political discourse has helped to render
decarceration politically irresistible, since it has reduced the possibility
of the movement's central premises being subjected to political scrutiny,
and has lent the whole enterprise the character of self-evidence. (This
broad political base also helps to account for the consistency with which
the policy has been pursued over time, and in places as disparate
politically as New York or Massachusetts and Reagan's California.)

The drive for financial savings has been evident in all phases of the
program. Confining our attention simply to the case of the mentally ill,
one consequence of this policy has been ineffectual complaints from
individuals who take seriously the rhetorical concern with the welfare of

those who formerly ended up as "long-stay," that is, life-long, inmates of mental institutions, that the actual implementation of the policy is producing "a relatively good service for the acutely ill . . . side by side with a second class service, or no service at all, for the chronic patient."[63] But this is clearly the most desirable approach on cost-effectiveness grounds — to concentrate one's efforts on those one has some prospect of restoring to the workforce and to self-sufficiency, and to abandon the rest to the cheapest alternative one can find.

One group for whom restoration in these terms is by definition a hopeless goal is the aged, particularly those past the official retirement age.[64] And despite the growing proportion of elderly people in the populations of both England and America, largely successful efforts have been made to prevent this being reflected in a parallel accumulation of the aged in mental hospitals. Restrictive admissions policies have been adopted, whose effect has been substantially to exclude the hopeless aged. For example: "In New York State a selective admission policy was introduced in 1968," aimed at diverting as many of the aged as possible to general hospitals, or to "foster homes for the aged." Within a year, this policy had effected a 42 percent reduction in the numbers of aged persons admitted into mental hospitals.[65] More generally, in the United States between 1955 and 1968, while the number of admissions (all ages less those over 65) *rose* more than 55 percent, from 89,144 to 138,474, admissions of those over 65 *fell* by almost 20 percent, from 33,140 to 26,594.[66]

Moving from admissions to length of stay, a similar policy has been pursued to clear elderly long-stay patients out of the mental hospitals into less expensive alternative situations. In the United States, the overall size of the resident mental hospital population fell by a relatively constant amount each year from 1955 to 1964 (1.2% per annum); but since 1964, there has been "an accelerated rate of discharge from year to year."[67] By 1970, for example, the rate was 9 percent a year. During this period, "discharge of the elderly patients has involved considerable transfer from the state hospital facilities to community nursing and convalescent homes."[68] A substantial proportion "of the acceleration of the population decrease in the State and county mental hospitals in the 1960s was undoubtedly due to the placement of long-term chronic patients into nursing homes"; and it now seems "fairly certain that the entire range of purely *psychiatric* facilities cares for less than half of the aged mentally ill."[69]

Most significantly, given our present concerns, N.I.M.H. data reveal that:

> The reductions in the numbers of elderly patients resident in and admitted to inpatient psychiatric services, particularly State mental hospitals, in recent years appear not to have shifted the locus of care to community-based psychiatric facilities (community mental health centers and other out-patient psychiatric services) to any great degree. Instead, they have been accompanied by substantial increases in the number of mentally ill and mentally disturbed residents in nursing and personal care homes."

As Table 8–4 shows, between 1963 and 1969, there was a "near doubling of the number of mentally ill patients resident in those homes . . . from about 222,000 in 1963 to almost 427,000 in 1969 . . .";[70] and by 1972, the number had grown again, to 640,000.[71] More detailed data from the same source provide powerful support for the contention that the driving force behind this transfer has been the cost savings which result. In the first place, "the State mental hospitals which have released large numbers of elderly over the past ten or more years, have failed to play a significant role in the follow-up support of these released patients." More seriously, "there appears to be a disproportionate utilization of homes offering personal (i.e., custodial-type) care only, by those elderly being transferred from mental hospitals,"[72] so that what we seem to be seeing is "the emergence of a new pattern in custodial care for the mentally ill elderly."[73] Even within the larger category of

TABLE 8–4

Number of Patients with Mental Disorders Resident in Mental Hospitals and Nursing Homes in the U.S.A. in 1963 and 1969, Classified by Age

	1963		1969	
	State and County Mental Hospitals	*Nursing Homes*	*State and County Mental Hospitals*	*Nursing Homes*
Total	504,604	221,721	369,929	426,712
Under 65	355,762	34,046	258,549	59,126
65 +	148,842	187,675	111,420	367,586

SOURCE: Adapted from N.I.M.H. *Statistical Note No. 107*, Table 2. Rockville, Maryland: N.I.M.H.

old-age homes, "as the level of provided service [and cost!] declines—
from nursing-care homes to personal care homes—the admissions
coming from mental hospitals as a percent of total admissions to these
homes increases."[74]

As this suggests, one indirect consequence of decarceration has been
a much greater involvement of the private sector in spheres of social
control which were formerly the exclusive province of the state. The
pattern of the socialization of loss and the privatization of profit, already
well-established in the military-industrial complex, is now imprinting
itself on new areas of social existence. Particularly in America, an
effort is under way to transform "social junk"[75] into a commodity from
which various "professionals" and entrepreneurs can extract a profit.
Medicare and the nursing home racket are merely the largest and most
blatant examples of this practice. At the other end of the age spectrum,
for the very young who become dependent and neglected, the system of
"foster care" involves increasingly "heavy reliance upon the purchase by
the public social welfare sector of child care services from private
agencies."[76] In between, there have appeared whole chains of enterprises
seeking to capitalize on this emerging market, ranging from privately
run drug treatment franchises to fair sized corporations sprawled across
several states dealing with derelicts and discharged mental patients.[77]
Largely free of state regulation or even inspection, and lacking the
bureaucratic encrustations of state-run enterprises, such places have
found ways to pare down on the miserable subsistence existence charac-
teristically provided in state institutions.[78] For our present purposes,
what is important about these places is that while, in an obvious sense,
they are the creatures of changes in state policy; yet on another,
admittedly secondary, level they come to provide one of that policy's
political supports and a source of pressure for its further extension.[79]

In this context, the reality that "community care" for many of its
"beneficiaries" frequently involves no more than a transfer from one
institution to another institution or quasi-institutional setting is by no
means confined to the case of the aged insane. Table 8–4 shows that
in 1969 over 59,000 of those under the age of 65 and officially designated
mentally ill were confined in nursing homes of various types. Many
others are in so-called "halfway houses" or ex-welfare hotels.[80] In the
words of a recent report of the situation in Michigan, many such patients
have been dumped "in facilities having fifty or more residents. . . . Large
quasi-institutional settings cannot be expected to provide the anticipated [therapeutic] benefits of community placement."[81] But, of

course, they do provide the benefit of substantial cost savings to the state.

The discharge pattern for the elderly insane closely corresponds to the expanding provision of subsistence level support for them by Federal and local governments, with the most rapid decrease coming in the late 1960s and 1970s following the passage of Medicare.[82] Similarly, the decarceration of other mental hospital inmates has coincided with administrative reorganizations and changes in bureaucratic regulations which have facilitated the granting of the minimal outside support that permits the return of patients "to the community." Finally, the development of diversionary programs for criminals and delinquents has likewise been heavily influenced by the offer of Federal and state financial incentives to those jurisdictions switching to a "community corrections" approach.[83]

One should notice here the effects produced by the more fragmented nature of the United States' political structure, and the differential impact within that structure of the fiscal crisis, felt more acutely at the state and local levels. Welfare has increasingly become a federal responsibility (or at least is federally funded) whereas institutional programs like mental hospitals have remained a State (occasionally a county) responsibility. This situation has greatly magnified the attractions of decarceration for states hard-pressed for money; for with some administrative juggling with "conditions of eligibility" it permits the transfer of costs to a different level of government and thus relieves, temporarily at any rate, some of the local fiscal crisis.[84] Almost certainly, this has had much to do with the much more rapid decline in institutional populations in the United States, as compared with England.

CONCLUSION

In the first chapter of this book I argued for the adoption of an approach to the study of deviance and social control which would be at once both macrosociological and historically informed. In the intervening pages, I have striven to provide an example of the kinds of understanding only this type of approach can provide us with. Viewed in historical perspective, the shift away from a social control apparatus placing heaviest emphasis on segregating deviants into institutions like prisons, asylums, and reformatories is clearly a development of potentially far-reaching significance. Yet it has hitherto remained but little-studied and poorly understood. On the one hand, lacking any kind of historical or structural context, most of the accounts of decarceration which we *do* possess have done little more than reproduce the ideology of the movement's participants. In consequence, the whole enterprise is presented as an essentially beneficent "reform," having its roots in the progress of social scientific understanding and/or improvements in medical technology. We have seen that neither of these "explanations" is satisfactory. On the other hand, some of those who have studied or participated in the implementation of particular variants of the general policy have developed a more jaundiced view of its achievements. But these individual findings have remained fragmentary and unconnected with one another; and in the absence of any theoretical understanding of the decarceration process taken as a whole, these critics have generally been unable to grasp the full significance of their own observations.

It is precisely this broader organizing framework that this book has sought to provide. Placing the decarceration movement in historical context, I have argued that this shift in social control styles and practices must be viewed as dependent upon and a reflection of more extensive and deep-seated changes in the social organization of advanced capitalist societies. In particular, it reflects the structural pressures to curtail sharply the costly system of segregative control once welfare payments, providing a subsistence existence for elements of the surplus population, make available a viable alternative to management in an institution. Such structural pressures are greatly intensified by the fiscal crisis encountered in varying degrees at different levels of the state apparatus; a crisis engendered by advanced capitalism's need to socialize more and more of the costs of production—the welfare system itself being one aspect of this process of socialization of costs. It is the pervasiveness and intensity of these pressures, and their mutually reinforcing character, which account for most of the characteristic features of the new system of community "care and treatment," and which enable us to comprehend the continued adherence to this policy even where it provokes considerable opposition.

In the circumstances, it is scarcely surprising to learn that decarceration in practice has displayed remarkably little resemblance to liberal rhetoric on the subject. Indeed, the primary value of that rhetoric (though far from its authors' intent) seems to have been its usefulness as ideological camouflage, allowing economy to masquerade as benevolence and neglect as tolerance. Clearly a certain proportion of the released inmates are able to blend unobtrusively back into the communities from whence they came. After all, many of those subjected to processing by the official agencies of social control have all along been scarcely distinguishable from their neighbors who were left alone, and presumably they can be expelled from institutions without appreciable additional risk. But for many other ex-inmates and potential inmates, the alternative to the institution has been to be herded into newly emerging "deviant ghettoes," sewers of human misery and what is conventionally defined as social pathology within which (largely hidden from outside inspection or even notice) society's refuse may be repressively tolerated. Many become lost in the interstices of social life, and turn into drifting inhabitants of those traditional resorts of the down and out, Salvation Army hostels, settlement houses, and so on. Others are grist for new, privately-run, profit-oriented mills for the disposal of the unwanted — old-age homes, halfway houses, and the like. And yet more exist by preying on the less agile and wary, whether these be "ordinary" people trapped by poverty and circumstance in the inner city, or their fellow decarcerated deviants.

As Paul Rock has suggested, what seems to be happening here is the development of modes of control analogous in certain respects to the seventeenth century Acts of Settlement.

> Those acts were designed to enforce immobility upon the poor. People were barred from travel, work, or alien residence. As a kind of shadow parish, sanctuaries and bastard sanctuaries housed the criminal, the debtor, the bankrupt, the pauper, and the eccentric in relatively unpoliced and autonomous areas of geographical and social space. [So, too, in the present,] a growing resort to zoning regulation, defensive alliances among residents, the tendency to provide welfare and other provisions in centralized locations, and the economics of housing have worked together to create new sanctuaries. In effect there has been a limited restoration of neo-feudal styles of control. It is unlikely that the new deviant ghettoes will be rigorously patrolled unless their populations swamp out over their borders. The inhabitants of Black and inner cities areas are more often the victims of crime and least often the recipients of police support. When those areas also become new reservations for the deviant, policing is likely to become even more token.[85]

1. Among the welfare programs adopted since World War II are: (1) in England — expansion of the state old-age and widows' pension systems, improved unemployment insurance and the provision of so-called National Assistance, compensation for industrial injuries, and state supported health care; (2) for the U.S.A., expansion of old age and survivors' insurance, expanded social security coverage and unemployment insurance, workmen's compensation and public assistance, and state supported health care for the elderly and a portion of the poor.

2. See O'Connor 1973. Such problems have been felt most acutely on the local, city, and (in the United States) state levels, but have also become increasingly evident at the central level (O'Connor 1973: esp. 211ff.).

3. Gough 1975: 76, emphasis in the original.

4. Marshall 1920: 229.

5. In England, for example, the Beveridge Report (which laid down the outlines of the British Welfare State), the so-called White Paper on Full Employment, and the 1944 Education Act, "were consciously seen as a necessary part of the war effort by integrating all classes and alleviating discontent" Gough 1975: 75.

6. Gough 1975: 69.

7. Gough 1975: 65, emphasis in the original.

8. Polanyi 1944.

9. Gough 1975: 67. The necessity of state intervention derives from the nature of much of the needed investment, which takes the form of collective or semi-collective goods. For example, since the benefits of a more highly educated workforce are *generally* shared, it is in the interest of no *individual* employer to provide such a service. Collective provision circumvents this dilemma, and has the added advantage of allowing the costs to be met be taxation falling on the population at large.

10. See O'Connor 1973: 17.

11. Nicolaus 1967: 37.

12. Marx 1967: Vol. I: 632.

13. O'Connor 1970: 3.

14. Nicolaus 1967: 37.

15. Gough 1975: 53.

16. Gough 1975: 61.

17. Gough 1975: 76.

18. Mencher 1967: 316.

19. Gough 1975: 76. Between 1955 and 1969, for example, the proportion of elderly in the population rose in every O.E.C.D. country, and it is apparent that this trend will continue for at least the next decade.

20. Dingman 1974: 48.

21. Greenblatt 1974: 8.

22. Rothman (1973) suggests that at least some advocates of decarceration have recognized and consciously exploited this situation. As he puts it:

> They believe that the number of individuals incarcerated makes standards of the type imposed [in Wyatt v. Stickney] too expensive to implement. They anticipate that a state, rather than upgrading its institutions, will recoil at the cost and abdicate its responsibility. Convinced that asylums are no more effective than prisons, they welcome this abdication; it would bring, at the very least, a drastic reduction in the number of people incarcerated for mental illness.

23. Dingman 1974: 48.

24. Greenblatt 1974: 8, emphasis in the original.

25. See Brill and Patton 1959: 495.

26. Myers and Bean 1968: 55–56.

27. See Chu and Trotter 1974: 42; Horizon House 1975: 143.

28. See National Association for Mental Health 1961: 4–10; Home Office 1968: para 339; M.I.N.D. 1971; Jones 1972: Ch. 13, esp. 326. By 1971 mental hospital populations in England and Wales had fallen by approximately 50,000; yet in the entire country there were less than 3,300 people in local authority provided facilities for care in the community.

29. Chase 1973: 18; Segal 1974: 141.

30. Epstein and Simon 1968: 958.

31. Chu and Trotter 1974: 43; Segal 1974: 141. In addition, discharged mental patients in California were given the "right" not to seek aftercare, enabling the state to disguise neglect as humane concern for the rights of the deviant. Seriously deteriorated cases have been incapable of seeking such assistance, and even those who have tried to obtain it have often found it is not available anyway. Chase 1973: 17.

32. This involved extending the principle embodied in the earlier Short-Doyle Act along lines similar to those of the Probation Subsidy Program, which was adopted to encourage the decarceration of criminals and juvenile delinquents. (See Smith 1971, which provides compelling evidence of the degree to which decarceration on a massive basis followed on careful assessments of the relative costs of de- and in-carceration.) In essence, the scheme depended on developing an estimate of how many beds a county would need in the coming year, based on its prior usage and estimated trends of the overall decline in hospital populations. A county which used less than its allocation would then be rewarded with a payment of $15 a day per patient involved — but the following year would find its bed allotment reduced accordingly. Conversely, if a county used more than its "share" of mental hospital beds, it would suffer a financial penalty in the form of reduced state assistance with its budget. Chase 1973: 16

33. Chu and Trotter 1974: 42–43; *Sacramento Union,* March 19, 1974: 9; Greenblatt 1974: 4.

34. For discussion of these developments, see Vorenberg and Vorenberg 1973; and Chapter Three above. Significantly, all this occurred in the absence of any clear-cut demonstration of the rehabilitative potential of community corrections — indeed, this still remains to be demonstrated.

35. For some nineteenth century comments on this phenomenon, see Massachusetts State Board of Health, Lunacy, and Charity, Vol. III, 1881: xcix; *Edinburgh Review* 1870: 221; Arlidge 1859: 7.

36. Nunally 1961: Cumming and Cumming 1957.

37. Wolpert and Wolpert 1974: 35; *New York Times* March 22, 1974: 40; Segal 1974: 143ff.

38. See Greenberg 1975: 28ff.; Coates and Miller 1973: 67.

39. Coates and Miller 1973: 78–79. As this article indicates, the state has been highly manipulative in an effort to secure acquiescence in such policies.

40. Wolpert and Wolpert 1974: 33, 38.

41. *New York Times* February 1, 1974: 33; Anspacher 1972; Schumach 1974; Trotter 1974; Aviram and Segal 1973: 130–131; California State Employees' Association 1972: 8–9; Chase 1973: 19; Reich and Siegal 1973: 42ff.

42. In San Jose, for example, "in a 20 square block area — an area also heavily peopled by alcoholics, drug users and prostitutes live over 1,100 of the mentally disordered" (Chase 1973: 19).

43. See Greenberg 1975: esp. 7.

44. "What is so terribly disturbing is that this policy was developed by the state without planning by the state for facilities in the community to care for these patients. the fact of the matter is that these facilities are just not available. What happens is that the individuals roam the streets, helpless victims of assault" Dr. Alexander Thomas, director of the Bellevue psychiatric wards, quoted in *The New York Times*, March 18, 1974: 17. © 1974 by The New York Times Company. Reprinted by permission.

45. Wolpert and Wolpert 1974: 22.

46. Stewart *et al.* 1968: 87 — in a study reporting on the progress of decarceration in Saskatchewan, Canada. See also Hall 1970; M.I.N.D. 1971; Bardach 1972: 31 and Chapter 5, *passim*.

In a number of instances, the complaints provoked by this situation have grown so vociferous as to force the slowdown or halting of the release program. (In California, the state has "postponed" an earlier plan to close all remaining state hospitals [see Wolpert and Wolpert 1974: 54–55]; similarly the New York program was ordered slowed recently [*New York Times*, April 26, 1974: 1, 32.] Ex-patients' families have rarely been involved in this process. The new policies have led to "a considerable burden being placed on the health, leisure, and finances of the families. . . . It is true that many relatives do not complain very much but this does not mean that there is nothing to complain about" (Wing 1971: 189). Brown indicates the probable source of such reticence: "Relatives are not in a strong position to complain — they are not experts, they may be ashamed to talk about their problems, and they have come to the conclusion that no help can be offered which will substantially reduce their difficulties" (Brown *et al.* 1966: 209). Similar constraints fail to operate, however, on those lacking such intimate ties to the ex-patients. Witnessing, or hearing eye-witness reports "of mental patients wandering helplessly in the streets, urinating and defecating in public, exposing themselves before women and children, terrifying apartment dwellers by riding up and down in automatic elevators, cursing pedestrians, collapsing from intoxication" (*New York Times*, January 21, 1974: 31. © 1974 by the New York Times Company. Reprinted by permission.), their protests have made temporization politically advisable. The depth and persistence of this opposition, and the increasingly hard-core character of the remaining candidates for community release, are likely to remain major constraints on further expansion of existing programs.

47. See Bakal 1973.

48. *Task Force Report: Corrections:* 1967: 4–5.

49. Glaser 1973: 99; see also Clark 1970: 237.

50. In California, the ratio of institutional costs to foster family reimbursement costs is approximately 5:1 (Koshel 1973: 39). In New York, "the cost of . . . care appears to be about five times the expense a family on a low cost budget would incur in rearing its own child." In some cases, the costs of providing for a single family's children via insitutionalization may ultimately run to over $500,000 (Fanshell and Shin 1972: 21–22, 30, and Appendix A).

51. Here, institutionalization is generally at least ten times as expensive. Recent English figures indicate that prison there costs £30 to £35 a week versus £2 for probation (Younger Report 1974: 39). In the United States, "state institutional cost is about six times that of parole and about 14 times that of probation" (*Task Force Report: Corrections:* 1967: 194, 10; see also Flynn 1973: 54). In California, where a careful study was made of the comparative cost of the two approaches prior to the widespread use of decarceration, "legislators learned . . . that the total minimum cost of an inmate who served an average term in prison and on parole was $5,700 (the figure by 1971 was estimated to be 'in excess of $10,000'). The comparative cost for treating an offender on probation under the supervision of a probation officer with a maximum of 50 cases was $142" (Ward 1973: 200).

52. Again a number of experimental programs demonstrated the savings available before the policy was widely adopted. In California, costs per inmate per year in the probation subsidy program were $142 compared with $4,500 for the institutional approach (Smith 1971: 11). In the Provo experiment in Utah, cost per boy was $200 for probation, $609 for a more "intensive" program of supervision in the community, and $2,015 for incarceration (Empey 1973: 46). Another California program, the Silverlake experiment, indicated that community treatment produced savings of almost $2 million for every 1,000 offenders (Empey and Lubeck 1971: 310).

53. E.g., Chien and Cole (1973) describe an experimental community treatment program involving more intensive (and expensive) supervision than most ex-patients receive. The per patient-year cost of the community approach was $2,183; at the local state mental hospital, the comparable cost would have been $10,307.

A more elaborate breakdown of the cost savings produced by community care, based on California data, is presented in Table 8-5. As these figures show (and as one would expect), the amount saved varies with the degree of disability (and hence care), but is always substantial. Moreover, the figures given tend to understate the actual savings realized, since the Community Service Divisions's calculations include administrative, placement, service, and Medi-Cal costs, while the Department of Mental Hygiene figures for state hospital costs fail to include all administrative costs.

TABLE 8-5
Cost Savings in California through Transfer to Community Facilities in 1970

Minimum to moderate care		
Age		
18–64	State Hospital ($16.25/day)	$5,691.25
	Boarding Home ($7.13/day)	1,391.06
	Net savings per patient year	$4,300.19
0–17	State Hospital ($16.25/day)	$5,691.25
	Family Care ($5.33/day)	2,151.32
	Net savings per patient year	$3,539.93
Intermediate Care		
Age		
0–17	State Hospital ($16.25/day)	$5,691.25
	Private Institution ($9.00/day)	3,578.00
	Net savings per patient year	$2,113.25
Nursing Care		
Age		
65+	State Hospital ($19.25/day)	$7,026.25
	Nursing Home ($12.04/day)	4,394.60
	Net savings per patient year	$2,631.65

SOURCE: California Department of Mental Hygiene Data, Sacramento, California, 1971.

54. This paragraph draws on the analysis presented in Lerman 1975.

55. This last point is often overlooked by outside analysts. It is, for example, missed in Greenberg's (1975: 7–8) otherwise useful review of the cost-benefit question. But to the states which would otherwise have been compelled to embark on a major expansion and renovation of the institutional sector, it was obvious. In 1954, for example, the California Department of Finance was confronted with the necessity of embarking on a massive capital investment program to expand existing mental hospitals and build new ones to accomodate rising numbers of patients. The following year legislation was introduced (eventually passed as the 1957 Short-Doyle Act) to encourage community responses to the mentally ill, explicitly on the grounds that this approach would allow the state "to brake rising needs for capital outlay and for large hospital payrolls . . ." (Bardach 1972: 27–30). See also *Task Force Report: Corrections:* 1967: 1976: "The population increase means more convictions and, unless the commitment rate is sharply reduced, vastly greater expenditures for prison construction. The way to reduce that rate is to increase the effective use of probation. Economy demands it."

Some idea of the magnitude of the savings decarceration has thus "invisibly" produced in the capital budget alone can be gleaned from the fact that as long ago as 1967, prison costs per bed exceeded $20,000 (*Task Force Report: Corrections:* 1967: 28). On a similar basis, the state of California calculated in 1965 that planned expansion of just its prison system would cost in the neighborhood of $90 million over the next decade. Shortly thereafter, it introduced a massive decarceration program for criminals (Smith 1971) which spared it the necessity of this capital investment.

For documentation of the consideration of cost savings (especially on capital account) in recommendations for a shift away from incarcertion of the mentally defective, see California Assembly 1963–65; ENKI 1972: 11.

56. See Jones 1972: Chs. 12 and 13; Bardach 1972: 27–30.

57. See Powell in National Association for Mental Health 1961; Brill and Patton 1959: 495.

58. Smith 1971: 69ff. An early experimental version of the same program "obviated the investment of $6 to $8 million" (*Task Force Report Corrections:* 1967: 42).

59. Gough 1975: 63.

60. An important caveat should be added here: obviously, one needs to know whether decreases in expenditures on mental hospitals have been partially offset by associated rises in state expenditures elsewhere (e.g., on welfare, or community treatment programs). Regrettably, for the United States (as for England) "on a nationwide basis only speculation is possible" about this question (Wolpert and Wolpert 1974: 22–23). However, where data do exist, as in the case of California, they demonstrate that the financial advantages do persist even when these other factors are taken into account. Table 8–6 shows that incorporating expenditures on local (noninstitutional) mental health programs still leaves a substantial downward trend of state outlays in this area. (See also footnote 53 above.)

61. See Conrad 1973: 433:

In a world in which the costs of incarceration have reached annual per capita costs which far exceed average citizen incomes, the future of incarceration must be constrained by a policy of rigorous selectivity. The informed opinion that coerced rehabilitation is an impractical objective is equally welcome to humane liberals and fiscal conservatives. *The task of research is to collect the information which will support the strategy of change* [my emphasis].

The curious view of the goals of social science research implied here has obviously been one widely shared among those "objectively" engaged in studying decarceration. Usually, however, those operating on such assumptions are not so naive as to state them publicly.

TABLE 8-6

**California Mental Health Budget, Including Local
(Short-Doyle) Programs, as a Percentage
of the Total State Budget**

Fiscal Year	Percent	Fiscal Year	Percent
1959–1960	2.58	1965–1966	2.12
1960–1961	2.53	1966–1967	2.00
1961–1962	2.46	1967–1968	1.80
1962–1963	2.39	1968–1969	1.63
1963–1964	2.15	1969–1970	1.71
1964–1965	2.26		

SOURCE: Calculated from figures in ENKI Research Institute, *A Study of California's New Mental Health Law*. Chatsworth, California, 1972, by permission.

62. "The fiscal conservatives have not been convinced that such institutions [state hospitals] are cost effective given the increase in wages and other costs, and despite the apparent scale economies. Furthermore, the budgetary process was being subverted through the long-term retention of clients who no longer needed the full range of services that can be provided at such large-scale facilities" (Wolpert and Wolpert 1976). [–i.e., who could be "dumped" elsewhere more cheaply.]

63. Wing 1971: 190.

64. Though since obsolescence on grounds of senescence comes ever earlier under advanced capitalism, this group also includes those in their late fifties and early sixties.

65. Pollack and Taube 1973: 14.

66. Figures calculated from N.I.M.H. Statistical Note #107. From 1968 to 1972, the fall in over-65 admissions was still more dramatic, from 26,594 to 14, 490, or 46 percent, while all other admissions fell by only 9 percent. See also N.I.M.H. Statistical Note #14. "Only in the 65 and over age-group did first admission rates show a general decline."

67. N.I.M.H. Statistical Note #1: 1.

68. Wolpert and Wolpert 1974: 27.

69. Pollack and Taube 1973: 12, 13.

70. N.I.M.H. Statistical Note #107: 2–3, 6.

71. Ahmed 1974.

72. N.I.M.H. Statistical Note #107: 6–7. See also Collins *et al.* 1967; Hefferin and Wilner 1971; Epstein and Simon 1968; Markson *et al.* 1971; Sharfstein 1974; Marlowe 1974.

73. Frankfather n.d.: 78.

74. N.I.M.H. Statistical Note #107: 6.

75. See Spitzer 1975.

76. Fanshell and Shinn 1972: 3; for the growth of this "industry" in New York City, cf. 6–7.

77. E.g., Beverly Enterprises, created in 1964, which has grown from three "convalescent" facilities to own more than sixty board and care facilities across the United States (including 38 in California), bringing in *net* revenues of $79.5 million in 1972 (Chase 1973: 17). There are also, of course, numerous smaller, often family-run enterprises.

78. In Pennsylvania, such places were once subject to inspection. Interestingly enough, "the same year the state stopped inspecting boarding homes — 1967 — the state also began

a massive deinstitutionalization program aimed at moving patients out of mental hospitals into community programs . . ." — that is, in many cases, into boarding homes. For the resulting conditions, see *Philadelphia Inquirer* September 21, 1975: 1B, 2B. Public institutions are scarcely known for their luxury, yet in New York, the private child care institutions used by the city cost *at most* $26 a day; while the *least* a public shelter costs is $42 a day, with others costing up to $52 (Fanshell and Shinn 1972: 10). Savings of this magnitude provide us with some clue of the level and type of "service" these operators provide for their "clients."

79. See for example, the activities of Bernard Bergman in New York (as reported in the *New York Times,* Jan. 18, 1975: 26, 21: 20, 22: 45, Feb. 4, 1975: 42, 5: 1, 6: 30), or Beverly Enterprises in California (Chase 1973: 17).

80. *New York Times* January 21, 1974: 31. © 1974 by The New York Times Company. Reprinted by permission.

81. Cited in *New York Times* March 22, 1974: 40. © 1974 by The New York Times Company. Reprinted by permission.

82. For a summary of expanding U.S. welfare provisions in this period, see Rimlinger 1971: 237–243.

83. Cf. Vorenberg and Vorenberg 1973: 163ff.; and Chapter Three above.

84. For example: "The trend away from institutionalization gained momentum in 1963 when the State of California, following national guidelines, redefined disability to include severe mental illness. Mentally ill persons would now return to the community as welfare recipients, under the Aid to the Total Dependent (AID) Program, if no purpose would be served by further institutionalization" (Wolpert and Wolpert 1974: 52).

85. Paul Rock, personal communication to the author.

PART FOUR

Afterword: 1983

He must have a very despicable opinion of mankind indeed who can conceive them to be imposed on, as often as they appear to be so. The truth is, they are in the same situation as the readers of romances who, though they know the whole to be one entire fiction, nevertheless agree to be deceived; and, as these find amusement, so do the others find ease and convenience in this concurrence.   HENRY FIELDING
Jonathan Wild the Great

The fortunate and the proud wonder at the insolence of human wretchedness, that it should dare to present itself before them, and with the loathsome aspect of its misery presume to disturb the serenity of their happiness.

ADAM SMITH
The Theory of Moral Sentiments

I

When I completed the first edition of this book, towards the end of 1975, the advocates of deinstitutionalization clearly dominated public debate in the United States about the proper approach to the mad and the bad. Indeed, even in Europe where – outside the sphere of mental health – the idea of abolishing or creating alternatives to incarceration had been much slower to take hold, such notions had begun to circulate freely. Opposition, if not silent, was fragmented and muted, and often could simply be dismissed as self-interested. Among the public at large, it took the form of protest by residents of particular communities against the placement of ex-inmates of any kind in *their* neighbourhood. Sometimes this involved harassment, threats of vigilante action, even arson, but in the politically more sophisticated and better organized communities, the favorite tactic was exclusionary zoning.[1] Such particularistic activities were simply designed to protect the parochial concerns of residents, who clearly wished to minimize contact with the very deviants whom they should eagerly be embracing, according to the decarceration ideology. Limited opposition of this sort, by its very nature, was not likely to coalesce into a more broadly based attack on the policy *tout court*. Provided the burden could be shifted elsewhere, to other less vociferous, less powerful populations, the discontent could readily be defused without serious modification of the underlying program. These complaints just reinforced other pressures to deposit the decarcerated in the poorest, most deteriorated, and least desirable of urban locations.

Attempts to stimulate a general repudiation of the movement were largely the work of state employee unions.[2] They sought to create moral panics[3] among the general population by skilled manipulation of "exemplary tales" concerning the squalor of the conditions in which ex-inmates were living and the violence to which they were prone, and the deleterious effects of these on both property values and public order. But though such efforts were not without their successes (see Chapter Four) they were vulnerable to the accusation that they expressed no more than the vested interest of those with direct responsibility for the shortcomings of the institutional alternative.

Within the past few years, of course, the situation has changed rather markedly. Concentrating for the moment on the mentally ill, the main focus of my earlier analysis, one notable feature has been the recognition even in "the heart of darkness", that community care is not all sweetness and light. Though there is an understandable reluctance in many quarters to acknowledge the full extent of "the demise of state responsibility for the seriously mentally ill and the current crisis of abandonment,"[4] even government officials and leading figures within the psychiatric establishment now concede that there is a profound disjuncture between the myth and the reality of "community care". The failures of contemporary policy have become the occasion for scathing critiques by politicians[5] and government bureaucrats,[6] not to mention a Maudsley lecture to the Royal College of Psychiatrists.[7] They have prompted denunciations in the *New England Journal of Medicine*[8] and complaints about "the wholesale neglect of the mentally ill, especially the chronic patient and the deinstitutionalized" from the President of the American Psychiatric Association.[9] And three leading journals concerned with the analysis of social policy have devoted entire issues to the topic.[10]

One or two of my early critics[11] argued that my portrait of the failures of contemporary policy was overdrawn. Such claims seem implausible now. Studies of deinstitutionalized patients show that "few live with biological or social relatives,"[12] and that even in this minority of cases, families grow restive under the serious and cumulative burden they represent, ultimately spurning and rejecting them.[13] In the United States, in particular, board and care homes and nursing homes have increasingly become "the dominant force in the residential care system [of the mentally ill]."[14]

One important consequence of this massive relocation program is that "the return of the patients to the community has, in many ways, extended the philosophy of custodialism into the community rather than ending it at the gates of the state hospital."[15] State and federal payments to the burgeoning entrepreneurial class "servicing" the chronically mentally disabled are scarcely munificent, after all, and at best would suffice to purchase the most basic forms of custodial care. Data from a number of studies suggest that survival level subsistence is indeed the best that discharged patients can hope for. In the words of a recent Oregon study, "a typical day for a mentally ill person in a nursing home was sleeping, eating, watching television, smoking cigarettes, sitting in groups in the largest room, or looking out the window, there was no evidence of an organized plan to meet their needs."[16]

On a nationwide basis, the National Institute of Mental Health (NIMH) has reported that "as the level of provided service declines – from nursing care homes to personal care homes – the admissions from mental hospitals as a percentage of total admissions to these homes increases."[17] Meanwhile, trends within the boarding home industry also suggest a declining quality of care. A shift is under way towards larger, more heavily capitalized units, and away from small, family-run homes, "which are marginal economical operations, providing many relatively low-income people with a source of additional money. The larger homes, in contrast, are clear-cut business enterprises requiring substantial amounts of capital investment, and are highly concerned with costs and profits."[18] This development is unlikely to meet with serious resistance from the states, since these larger "board and care homes require fewer [state] support services in order to function, a critical advantage in an era of cutbacks in state funding and direct services."[19]

Under the conditions that currently prevail, market failure is structurally guaranteed. A large number of atomized, uninformed consumers, whose mental condition renders them all-but incapable of initiative or of exercising meaningful choice, have been discharged into a hostile community and left to cope as best they can – in the virtual absence of state supported aftercare or follow-up services.[20] As I suggested in the first edition of this book, their plight has created a fertile ground for a new trade in lunacy, an entrepreneurial industry resembling the private madhouses of eighteenth-century England[21] which remains almost wholly unregulated by the state. Indeed, in a double sense, the state can hardly *afford* to regulate this industry in anything but a purely cosmetic fashion. First, of course, a serious effort to provide regulation would demand the commitment of substantial resources, and even then I would remain sceptical of its effectiveness.[22] Second, if the state attempted to insist on adequate standards of care, in all probability, given current levels of reimbursement, it would simply dry up the supply of beds. Thus, the US Senate's finding that only three states make a serious attempt to supervise board and care homes is wholly unsurprising.[23] The income of those speculating in this species of human misery is almost wholly inelastic (being fixed by the welfare payments that are their "clients" principal source of income), so that profits are strictly dependent upon successfully paring costs. Since the volume of profit is inversely proportional to the amount expended on the inmates, the logic of the marketplace ensures that the operators have every incentive to warehouse their charges as cheaply as possible.[24]

The mere size of the community facilities within which many of the mentally disabled are housed provides *prima facie* evidence that they have simply been transferred from public to private warehouses. As Lerman notes, "public discussions and modern terminology often refer to a 200-bed home for the aged or a 100-bed residential treatment center for disturbed youth as a 'community' not an 'institutional' residential facility"[25] – a piece of verbal sleight of hand designed to obfuscate the fact that, according to the National Center for Health Statistics, more than 50% of those placed in nursing homes were in facilities with more than 100 beds, and a further 15% were in facilities housing more than 200 at a time. In the course of its investigations in Michigan, the General Accounting Office found one such home that specialized in "the mentally disabled had 440 beds while another had 330."[26] In Massachusetts, its investigators were informed that it was standard state practice "to place formerly institutionalized persons in those nursing homes where the quality of care was poorer and safety standards not complied with as rigidly as in other nursing homes. . . .

Generally speaking, the more ex-mental patients there were in a facility, the worse the conditions."[27] Similarly, in New York, there have been repeated media exposés of the massive concentrations of ex-inmates in the squalid single-room occupancy hotels on the Upper West Side of Manhattan, and in homes run by former hospital employees in the Long Island communities surrounding Pilgrim and Central Islip State Hospitals.[28]

Such developments have not occurred without implicit and explicit state sponsorship and encouragement. In New York State, the scandals over the connections between the board and care industry and the political establishment eventually forced a full-scale official inquiry and subsequent prosecutions.[29] Hawaii faced a massive shortage of beds in licensed boarding homes when it adopted a policy of accelerated discharge. The problem was resolved, with unusual bureaucratic flexibility, through "the proliferation, with the explicit encouragement of the state mental health division, of unlicensed boarding homes for the placement of ex-hospitalized patients."[30] Nebraska at first shied away from such a *laissez-faire* approach, deciding apparently that some form of state oversight was called for. Accordingly, in a splendidly original variation on the ancient practice of treating the mad like cattle, the state placed the licensing and inspection of board and care homes in the hands of its state Department of Agriculture. Subsequent citizens' complaints about the resultant conditions led to second thoughts about the desirability of taking official notice of board and care operators' practices, so the state withdrew the licenses, *but not the patients*, "from an estimated 320 of these homes, leaving them without state supervision or regulation."[31] Missouri simply noted the existence of some "755 unlicensed facilities in [the] State housing more than 10,000 patients"[32] and continued to dispense the state funds on which their operators depended. Still other states, like Maryland and Oregon, opted for perhaps the safest course of all – no follow-up of those they released, and hence a blissful official ignorance about their subsequent fate.[33]

Intended as a cheap alternative to the state hospital, these board and care homes have instead become a poor alternative to living. They constitute perhaps the most extreme example of "the failure of deinstitutionalization policies to provide even minimally adequate aftercare and community support services anywhere in the nation."[34] Given this "almost unanimous abdication from the task of proposing and securing any provision for a humane and continuous form of care for those mental patients who need something rather more than short-term therapy for an acute phase of their illness"[35] it should come as no surprise to learn that decarceration "has not succeeded in ameliorating precisely those alleged results of institutionalization that [supposedly] led to it: the sociocultural and interpersonal isolation, degeneration and stigmatization of patients; the assymetrical [sic] dependency and vast power differences between patients and non-patients; the encouragement of chronicity contained in the treatment system and related social policies." [36]

In view of the depths of misery and maltreatment associated with recent American mental health policy, Kathleen Jones's claim that "so far the United States has made a much better job of the business of deinstitutionalization" [37] would, if accurate, constitute an even more damning indictment of British practice than she perhaps intended. Apparently, what led her to make this unfortunate assertion was the combination of a relatively intimate knowledge of the failures of British policies with a rather naive acceptance at face value of the claims made by American advocates of deinstitutionalization. [38] Certainly, at the level of rhetoric, Americans have by and large been more active and shameless. Practically, however, the British experience has not (yet?) been quite so awful.

In part, this is simply because deinstitutionalization has not been as rapid or far-reaching in Britain. This discrepancy was evident even by 1970, as a comparison of Tables 4 – 2 and 4 – 3 reveals (see pp. 68, 70), but it has become still more marked over the past decade. The population of English mental hospitals has continued to decline by a relatively modest average of just over 3% a year (see Table A – 1). As Tables A – 2 and A – 3 reveal, however, during the late 1960s the decline in the American mental hospital census was consistently larger than this, and the discrepancy only widened during the 1970s. Overall, while the inpatient census of English mental hospitals has declined by approximately one-half since the mid 1950s, the American mental hospital population has fallen to less than a quarter of what it was then.

The pattern of events during the 1970s amply confirms my suggestion, in the first edition of this book, that the major source of the more rapid decline in US mental hospital populations was the fragmentation of the American political structure, and the opportunities decarceration opened up for states to transfer costs to the federal level. As Lerman has noted, [39] just as the accelerated discharge of the elderly in the late 1960s was brought about by the advent of Medicare and Medicaid (together with Old Age Assistance, Aid to the Permanently and Totally Disabled, and Old Age and Survivor Insurance), so the further acceleration in 1972 and thereafter reflected "the availability of new welfare

TABLE A – 1

Average Daily Number of Inpatients in Mental Hospitals in England, and Annual Decrease in Patient Population, 1970 – 1980

Year	Number	% Decrease	Year	Number	% Decrease
1970	106,000		1976	83,800	3.68
1971	103,000	2.83	1977	80,800	3.58
1972	100,000	2.91	1978	78,200	3.22
1973	94,000	6.00	1979	76,500	2.17
1974	90,000	4.44	1980	75,200	1.70
1975	87,000	3.33			

SOURCE: Department of Health and Social Security: *Health and Personal Social Services Statistics for England.* London: Her Majesty's Stationery Office. (All figures rounded.)

TABLE A – 2

Rate of Decline of United States Mental Hospital Populations, Selected Periods, 1955 – 1976

Period	% Decline Per Year
1955 – 1960	0.8
1960 – 1964	2.1
1964 – 1972	5.5
1972 – 1974	10.8
1974 – 1977	10.2

SOURCE: National Institute of Mental Health, Bethesda, Maryland.

TABLE A – 3

United States State and County Mental Hospitals, Resident Patients on December 31, and Annual Decrease in Patient Population, 1970 – 1980

Year	Number	% Decrease	Year	Number	% Decrease
1970	339,000		1976	171,500	10.40
1971	309,000	8.85	1977	159,523	7.00
1972	276,000	10.68	1978	153,544	3.77
1973	255,000	7.61	1979	140,355	8.53
1974	215,600	15.45	1980	132,164	5.84
1975	191,400	11.22			

SOURCE: National Institute of Mental Health, Bethesda, Maryland.

resources," in this case the passage of new legislation authorizing the new SSI (Supplemental Security Income) Program. Of utmost importance, the new program offered "the unprecedented opportunity to transfer traditional state costs on to a 100%, permanent federal funding, source. None of the earlier federal programs had offered this type of long-term incentive."[40] Hence the rapidity and enthusiasm with which states seized the opportunity to implement further cutbacks in inpatient populations. In Britain, however, in the absence of this additional incentive, the rush to empty mental hospitals has been understandably less headlong.

Ex-patients in Britain have also for the most part been spared the excesses associated with the "new trade in lunacy."[41] The chains of private board and care homes and the dilapidated "welfare hotels", which we have seen are now so large a part of American mental health "services", have few precise British equivalents. In part, this probably reflects the somewhat lower numbers of chronic patients discharged. Undoubtedly, too, it mirrors the more entrepreneurial character of American capitalism, and the greater legitimacy accorded to the process of the privatization of state and welfare services[42] in a society still ideologically dominated by the myth of the benevolent "invisible hand."

Notwithstanding all of these qualifications, the British experience with community care remains dismal enough in all conscience. As Peter Sedgwick points out,

> in Britain no less than in the United States, "community care" and "the replacement of the mental hospital" were slogans which masked the growing depletion of real services for the mentally ill; the accumulating numbers of impaired, retarded, and demented males in the prisons and common lodging houses; the scarcity not only of local authority residential provisions for the mentally disabled, but of day-care centres and skilled social work resources; the jettisoning of mental patients in their thousands into the isolated, helpless environment of their families of origin, who appealed in vain for hospital admission (even for a temporary period of respite), for counselling or support, and even for basic information and advice. . . .[43]

Jones herself is not unaware of these catastrophic failures masquerading under the official guise of a "revolution" in psychiatric care. It is her awareness of the failures that prompts her bitter comparison of British policy with an idealized, indeed mythological portrait of American practices.[44] For her, much of the blame can be apportioned to administrative lapses. In particular, the reorganization of the British National

Health Service in 1973, which eliminated any distinctive organization for the mental health services, left "no administrative focus, no forum for policy debate, and no impetus to personal development. The result is that the British services are now fragmented and to a large extent the personnel are demoralised."[45]

But while low morale and administrative chaos have certainly contributed to worsening the situation, they are scarcely the major sources of current difficulties. More centrally important is the absence of the necessary infrastructure of services and financial supports without which talk about community care is simply a sham. During 1973 – 74, for example, while £300 million was spent on the mentally ill still receiving institutional treatment, a mere £6.5 million was spent on residential and day-care services for those "in the community." Local authority spending on residential facilities for the mentally ill was a derisory 0.04% of their total expenditures.[46] Three years later, 116 out of 170 local authorities still provided not a single residential place for the elderly mentally infirm,[47] and since then, the intensifying fiscal crisis of the Thatcher – Reaganite years has simply reinforced the existing conservative hostility to social welfare services, and made the prospect of providing even minimal levels of support services still more remote.[48]

II

It seems fair to say, then, that developments in the mental health sector over the past eight or nine years have involved the extension and intensification of the trends already visible in the mid-seventies, rather than any substantial modifications or changes of direction. To that extent, the descriptive account I provided in the first edition of this book has held up quite well. It remains the case that "evidence of benefits to [deinstitutionalized] psychiatric patients, especially those hospitalized over long periods, is not to be found anywhere in the professional literature"[49] and the priority of fiscal over therapeutic concerns has become even more apparent in the same period. Still, some re-examination of the specifics of the *explanation* I offered of deinstitutionalization seems in order.

One of the most controversial claims made in the first edition of this book was that the role of psychoactive drugs in bringing about decarceration had been grossly exaggerated. Given the coincidence between the downturn in mental hospital populations and the introduction of phenothiazines, one can readily understand why many simply assumed (and continue to assume)[50] that deinstitutionalization was no more than a reflex response to another technical breakthrough of modern medicine. But, as I showed in an earlier chapter, the attempts to provide detailed empirical support for this proposition are scientifically shoddy and largely fail to accomplish their purpose. I suggested then that, rather than being the primary reason for the changes we have observed, the drugs played only a secondary role, helping to persuade physicians of the feasibility of community treatment, and easing the management of patients by reducing florid symptomology. I further suggested that unless other pressures and incentives to deinstitutionalize had existed, the new technology would probably have been employed simply to ease internal management problems (very much as electroshock had previously been used), and not to precipitate mass discharges of elderly and chronic patients.[51]

A number of more recent detailed case studies have provided further support for these contentions.[52] Lerman's review of deinstitutionalization in California shows that the process did not get under way until several years after the use of ataraxic drugs had become widespread in the state hospital system, and concludes that "California required the hiring and promotion of new state hospital leaders [committed to deinstitutionalization] in order to utilize the new technology on behalf of pro-release, rather than institutional maintenance policies."[53] Likewise, Segal and Aviram's review of California data leads them to discount any major role for the phenothiazines: "It is our opinion that the provision of financial support through public assistance programs was primarily responsible for the mass emigration from state hospitals that began in California in 1962."[54] Noting the marked interstate variations in the speed with which deinstitutionalization took place, and the geographically variable patterns of rapidly accelerating discharges over time, the authors of a comparative epidemiological review of hospitalization rates in New York, Illinois, Texas, Virginia, and California pointedly remark, "It would be naive to claim that psychoactive drugs suddenly became more effective." Instead, they conclude that decarceration is indeed "best explained by the creation and implementation of specific programs aimed at reducing the number of hospitalized patients, either by control of admissions or by change of release policies or both."[55]

Perhaps the final nail in the coffin of the "medical" explanation of deinstitutionalization is provided by Peter Sedgwick's review of international data on the timing of the run-down of institutional populations in Western Europe. Were the switch to community treatment simply a response to the advent of effective antipsychotic medications, one would expect to see close similarities in the discharge patterns. Actually, the reverse is true: there are marked variations from one society to another in both the timing and the extent of the decline in mental hospital populations.

> Most damaging of all for the view that these new medications constitute a collective miracle drug which eradicates the worst psychotic symptoms and enables large-scale discharges into the community to take place as a direct result of their chemical action. . . [is] the relatively late point (1970) at which the in-patient numbers in French mental hospitals began to dip, following a post-war population explosion in the asylums which continued throughout the very period of the fifties and sixties that had been marked by a firm de-hospitalization in British and American psychiatry. It should be noted that chlorpromazine (Largactil), the most prominent of the new tranquillisers, had actually been first synthesised in France as early as December 1950, by the pharmaceuticals firm Rhône Polenc. It is not to be supposed that this lag of 20 years between the availability of the chemical First Cause and its effects on hospital practice was due to inactivity on the part of the merchandisers of Largactil in France.[56]

But the fact that mental hospital populations in France, West Germany, Italy, Spain, and elsewhere continued to grow into the 1960s and sometimes beyond, has serious implications, not just for the proponents of the "magic bullet" explanation of decarceration, but also for my own account. As a number of my critics have rightly pointed out,[57] my original argument presents the relationship between the adoption of a policy of deinstitutionalization on the one hand, and the advent of welfare capitalism and the growing fiscal crisis of the state apparatus on the other, as a necessary and essentially deterministic one. A larger comparative perspective unquestionably demonstrates that such a claim is an oversimplification. The existence of a well-developed system of social welfare services, and the intensifying fiscal crisis of the last decade and a half, certainly created powerful structural *pressures* to adopt a policy of deinstitutionalization and, as a growing body of research documents, they have profoundly shaped the implementation of "community care". But the Western European experience demonstrates that the connections are by no means as automatic and inevitable as I previously implied.[58]

In the long run, then, any fully adequate explanation of deinstitutionalization in the mental health sector must allow us to understand, not just its rapid and "successful" implementation in Britain and

North America, but also its much more erratic and halting progress in Western Europe. Unfortunately, we remain a long way from possessing such a unified account. Richard Warner's invocation of the conditions in the labor market,[59] while suggesting a possible explanation for some of the fluctuations over time in rehabilitation efforts and the recovery rates of schizophrenics, and for some of the variations in the outcomes for "schizophrenia" between industrial nations and non-wage-labor societies in the developing world,[60] gives us no adequate means of accounting for the differences between (for example) France, Italy, and England. No more persuasive is Peter Sedgwick's attempt to link variations in the "de-hospitalizing" movement to the development of a liberal social psychiatry, whose intellectual ancestry he traces back to "the progressive anti-fascist mobilisations of the forties."[61]

Gaining an adequate understanding of these cross-societal variations must surely be a major goal of future research in this area. I remain convinced, however, that a crucial part of the answer is to be found in the factors I previously identified. As I suggested in both *Museums of Madness*[62] and in the first edition of this book, the operations of different general systems of public assistance form the essential structural and political preconditions for the particular forms taken by the mental health systems of each epoch. In my earlier work, I identified two major factors prompting a shift away from a segregative "solution" to the problems posed by the chronically crazy. The first of these was the existence of welfare payments, guaranteeing at least a minimal maintenance to the poor living outside the institutions. The second major factor was the subsequent development, from the mid- to late-1960s onwards, of an intensifying fiscal crisis of the state apparatus – a crisis which has continued to worsen over the ensuing decade and a half.

To begin with, and indeed on a continuing basis, the construction of the infrastructure of a modern welfare state was the *necessary*, if not always a sufficient condition for the adoption of a policy of deinstitutionalization. Such programs not only made large-scale discharges possible, they also sharply raised the opportunity cost of not adopting a policy of this sort. As the research I have cited earlier in this chapter shows, the linkage between the extension of welfare programs and the contraction of state hospital populations has remained persistently close, particularly in the United States. Even in the halcyon days of the late 1950s, in the never-had-it-so-good heyday of postwar capitalist expansion, and long before, as Peter Sedgwick reminds us,[63] the "'fiscal crisis of the state' had been discovered by any economic researcher," there were powerful economic incentives to slow and, if possible, reverse the upward spiral in mental hospital populations. Admissions were already rising sharply, in both Britain and the United States, as they continued to do throughout the 1960s. (In both countries, they more than doubled between 1955 and 1970.)[64] Without a major decline in the average length of stay, an extraordinary expansion of the mental hospital system would have been required to house this influx. To make matters worse, the Victorian barracks inherited from the nineteenth century were in a terminal state of decay and dilapidation. As a British government spokeswoman concluded at the time, replacement of this "appalling legacy" was "not a question of a few million pounds . . . [but] a question of thousands of millions over many years."[65] Finally, unionization of state workers meant that they shared in the increase in wage rates after World War II, and contributed to the very sharp increases in the running costs of the existing hospitals. The subsequent fiscal crisis merely added to these pressures and made them far more intense and urgent, a situation I held primarily responsible for the rapid acceleration in discharge rates then observable.

The issue of whether (and to what extent) the decarceration of the mentally ill has produced cost savings has provoked considerable debate, though there has been widespread recognition that "the pivotal political assumption that appears to have motivated deinstitutionalization is that state tax dollars would be saved. . . ."[66] A variety of academic and governmental researchers have concluded that major savings have resulted.[67] Rose, for example, estimates "cost savings to the states in the ten-year period from 1965 to 1974 would be approximately \$5.4 billion. . .without regard to accelerated admissions rates and added capital construction costs."[68] Others, however, have been more sceptical, pointing to continuing rises in state mental health budgets and alleging that apparent cost savings in one sector have been at least partly offset by increased expenditures elsewhere.[69]

The methodological difficulties in this area are formidable. As the General Accounting Office recently acknowledged, "the state of the art of determining the costs in alternative long-term care settings is still in the early stages of development"[70] – with the result that elementary mistakes continue to be made. Rose, for example, appears to base his calculations of cost savings on the *average* cost rather than the marginal cost of hospitalization. If so, he seriously overstates the savings which have resulted, since, as I point out in Chapter Eight, in the short run at least, many of the costs of a mental hospital system are fixed and unchangeable, regardless of the number of inmates that occupy it.

On the other hand, those who are sceptical of the cost savings produced by decarceration are prone to errors that even more seriously *underestimate* the magnitude of the sums involved. In noting the continued rise in mental health budgets, they often fail to allow for the effects of inflation and, much more significantly, they do not incorporate into their analyses a whole series of factors which, in the absence of decarceration, would most certainly have produced a veritable explosion in expenditures on the mentally ill. I have already pointed out some of these, notably rapidly rising admissions rates, and the decay of the physical infrastructure of the hospital system.[71] To these must be added the substantial increase in the general population over the past three decades, and the growing numbers of the aged, a substantial proportion of whom were traditionally warehoused in public mental hospitals.[72] In assessing the savings resulting from decarceration, it simply will not do, therefore, to compare *actual* expenditure levels over time and to conclude that if they rise, cost savings have not resulted. Instead, the calculations must be based on the relevant counterfactual: what would be the approximate level of state expenditures on the mental health services had governments persisted with traditional segregative approaches to the problem, rather than adopting a program of massively accelerated deinstitutionalization and diversion?

While precise estimates are obviously unattainable, the basic financial impact of the new policies is surely not in doubt.[73] Nor can there be much doubt about the social impact of the new approach. Bitter experience ought by now to have taught us to scorn millenial claims that the adoption or rejection of the asylum will substantially ameliorate the mental patient's situation. We must recognize instead that neither institutional treatment nor community care is in any sense a panacea, and that both, if inadequately funded, provide ample opportunity for, and plenty of concrete examples of, squalor, neglect, abuse and inhumanity. Deinstitutionalization of the mentally ill, while securing the negative right to be free of organized interference in one's life, has all too often meant the denial of the positive right to care and attention. As a result, for the majority of those affected with chronic mental illness, what has changed is the packaging rather than the reality of their misery.

III

If developments in the mental health sector since I wrote the first edition of this book have involved no fundamental departures from the patterns

I originally described and analysed, the same can hardly be said of the so-called community corrections movement. On the ideological level, the 1970s witnessed a strong conservative backlash against anything smacking of leniency towards crime and criminals. The law and order issue was a favorite weapon of politicians on the right, and their electoral success with this tactic soon persuaded most of their opposition to fall into line. In the academic world, orthodox criminologists scurried to provide a mantle of scholarly respectability for such tactics as mandatory fixed sentences and longer terms of imprisonment,[74] with even liberals rediscovering the virtues of swiftness and certainty in punishment.[75]

Moreover, so far from matching the remorseless and, for much of the period, accelerating decline in mental hospital populations, our prison and jail censuses have once again increased (to record levels). Overcrowding is rife, and old and discarded buildings are being reopened and crammed with prisoners.[76] California has even resorted to housing

TABLE A – 4
Average Daily Prison and Borstal Population in England and Wales

Year	Number	Rate Per 100,000	Year	Number	Rate Per 100,000
1970	39,028	80.2	1976	41,443	84.3
1971	39,708	81.3	1977	41,570	84.6
1972	38,328	78.2	1978	41,796	85.1
1973	36,774	74.8	1979	42,220	85.9
1974	36,867	75.0	1980	42,264	85.8
1975	39,820	81.0	1981	43,311	87.8

SOURCE:*Annual Abstract of Statistics* 1983: 82. London: Her Majesty's Stationery Office.

its overflowing population of convicts in tents. As Table A – 4 reveals, the British prison population changed somewhat erratically, but generally declined between 1970 and 1974. Thereafter, however, it rose by just over 17% over the next seven years. Similarly, the populations of state and federal prisons in the United States levelled off at just over 190,000 in the late 1960s, and remained essentially static in the first years of the 1970s. Indeed, allowing for population change, the rate of imprisonment continued to fall every year until 1972. 1974, however, marked the first of a series of sharp increases in both the absolute numbers imprisoned and in the rate of imprisonment per 100,000 people. Here the percentage increase in the numbers imprisoned was

TABLE A – 5

United States: Federal and State Prisoners on December 31, 1970 – 1981

Year	Number	Rate Per 100,000	Year	Number	Rate Per 100,000
1970	196,429	96.7	1976	263,291	123.1
1971	198,061	96.4	1977	285,456	132.4
1972	196,183	94.6	1978	294,396	135.4
1973	204,211	97.8	1979	301,470	137.3
1974	218,466	103.6	1980	314,272	139.0
1975	240,593	113.3	1981	353,167	153.0

SOURCE: United States Bureau of Justice Statistics.

very much steeper than in England – an extraordinary 80.1% in the years from 1972 to 1981 (Table A – 5).

We need to bear in mind, of course, that long continued secular increases in crime rates have generated a much larger population eligible for the attentions of the criminal justice system. To an extent, therefore, one might reasonably argue that diversionary programs have enabled the authorities to avoid some of the expenditures for prison accommodation they would otherwise have incurred.[77] But obviously one can push this argument only so far, and in the United States in particular, the sheer size of the increase in prison populations, which has occurred alongside and despite a dramatic rise in the use of probation and other non-institutional forms of punishment, suggests the need for a fundamental reassessment of the significance of recent "reforms".

To begin with, my earlier conclusion that "community corrections" meant a further erosion of the sanctions imposed on criminals' conduct now seems much too crude to capture the complexities which the introduction of the new programs has entailed. With hindsight, one could argue that I fell victim to exactly the danger I warned of – that of taking reformist rhetoric at face value and, as a result, assuming that the *language* of radical non-intervention closely coincided with everyday practice.[78] Taking self-criticism a step further, notwithstanding my own criticisms of the "total institutions" literature in Chapter Six, it is now apparent that when I wrote the first edition of this book I remained "imprisoned" within one of the central assumptions of that research: that it made sense (and presented no analytic difficulties) to study prisons and asylums as a unitary phenomenon.[79] While I would still contend that such assimilation is sometimes theoretically and empirically justified, and that similar imperatives do explain the *origins* of the

drive to decarcerate prisoners and patients, I also recognize how
important it is to remain sensitive to crucial differences between the two
groups, and to the ways in which these serve to modify policy outcomes
over time.

   In the light of the developments that have taken place over the past
decade, the central question seems to be why, granted that governments were bent on finding "cheaper alternatives to
incarceration. . .decarceration has not turned out to be a cheaper form
of punishment. If anything, it seems to have been accompanied by a
substantial growth of the criminal control apparatus."[80] This in turn
has entailed a marked rise in expenditures on police and prisons, as well
as other, less visible parts of the criminal justice apparatus.

   Following the line of analysis adopted by David Rothman in his
discussion of progressive era reforms,[81] Chan and Ericson[82] have
suggested that to explain these patterns, we must look to the ways in
which the organizational interests of the professions running the
criminal justice system have ensured the transmogrification of yet
another generation of "reforms" in the directions dictated by administrative convenience and bureaucratic aggrandisement. Plausible as
this explanation is, however, it is clearly incomplete and insufficient as
it stands.[83] As James Jacobs has recently argued,[84] the suggestion that
correctional bureaucrats have an insatiable appetite for organizational
growth ignores the fact that, "historically, prison officials have been
more concerned with issues of 'control' that with capacity; prestige in
the profession has gone to those who could run a 'tight ship' rather than
to those who presided over the largest number of prisoners." To
comprehend why, on this occasion, they have moved in an expansionist
direction, and have secured a substantial amount of public and political
support for "widening the net,"[85] we must surely incorporate other
elements into the equation.

   Of quite central importance, I think, has been the accelerating
volume of crime over the past quarter century. Whether that increase
reflects shifts in society's age structure,[86] the dislocations and social
atomization characteristic of contemporary capitalism[87] or, more
doubtfully, is the artificial by-product of a "control wave",[88] its
existence provides powerful ammunition for those seeking a larger
commitment of resources to crime control. Indeed, there is substantial
evidence that the "fear of crime" has become an issue capable of
mobilizing powerful if somewhat confused pressures for "action"
among an otherwise fractured and fragmented public. It is an issue
which transcends standard ideological divisions to provide "strong

support for a fundamental change in punishment policy – one that
pushes toward greater severity and more frequent use of incarceration.''[89] The radical non-interventionism which had a powerful
appeal for the professoriate in the sixties and early seventies (and which
initially – though for rather different reasons – found some supporters among policy-makers as well), turns out to possess little
attraction for the proletariat or bourgeoisie, for whom the most vital
question remains, What is to be done?

As this suggests, in comprehending why decarceration for the criminal has meant heightened control rather than neglect, we need to attend
carefully to the character of the population to be controlled. The
importance of this factor is readily seen if we compare the criminal and
the mentally ill. It is one of the many ironies with which the sociology
of social control abounds that the casual dumping of the disoriented and
senile has been made easier by the fact that the measures designed to
dispose of them are ostensibly undertaken from a benevolent and
humanitarian concern for their welfare. However great the discrepancy
between the ideology and the reality of asylum existence – indeed,
precisely *because* of the magnitude of that discrepancy[90] – enormous
energy and substantial resources have been devoted for more than a
century and a half to elaborating, disseminating, and perpetuating
what has all too often been the illusion of concern with the inmate's
welfare.[91] As someone who is sick and therefore cannot be held responsible for his condition or situation, the mental patient is the recipient of
treatment ''for his own good''. If it is concluded that traditional
approaches are destructive and anti-therapeutic, then non-
intervention, dressed up as community treatment and promoted in the
name of the very virtues once attributed to the asylum, can be advocated on the grounds of its advantages to the client. But prisoners are
not clients, and pain, privation, and suffering are seen by many as
their just desserts. Because they ''chose'' to offend, retribution is in
order. The humanity of community corrections is thus its Achilles heel,
precisely the feature most likely to alienate (fiscal) conservatives and
indeed the public at large, who might otherwise be attracted by the
idea. Criminals recidivate because of an innate or acquired depravity,
and if prisons are unpleasant places, that is exactly what they should
be.[92]

Beyond the striking increases in prison populations, evidence is now
accumulating that the development of so-called ''diversionary
programs'' leads to ''a more voracious processing of deviant popu-

lations, albeit in new settings and by professionals with different names."[93] Thus, unlike the situation with the mentally ill, the decar-ceration of the criminal has, over time, meant the widening of the network of social control. Here, as Chan and Ericson put it, "people are not diverted *from*, but *into* and within the system."[94] Most subtly, this process has involved a more or less deliberate "blurring of the boundaries" of the network of social control.[95] Finding one's way through the maze of supervised release schemes, halfway houses, community correctional centers, group homes, foster homes, pre-trial release centers, deferred sentencing agencies and the like, requires a nice ability to make (increasingly meaningless) conceptual distinctions. At the extreme, "it becomes difficult to distinguish a very 'open' prison – with liberal provisions for work release, home release, outside educational programmes – from a very 'closed' halfway house." The "administrative surrealism" extends further, incorporating a system-atic obfuscation of the issue of guilt and innocence as it stretches to incorporate "preventive, diagnostic or screening enterprises aimed at potential, pre-delinquents, or high risk populations," and allowing program failure, the violation of agency norms rather than statutes, to become the basis of future punishment.[96]

Greenberg provides a striking example of how this can transform programs to "deinstitutionalize" status offenders, through

> the imposition of special conditions on probationers to facilitate revocation. Thus prostitutes [for example] will be forbidden for a two year period from being "parked in a motor vehicle with lone male motorists," cannot "approach male pedestrians or motorists or engage them in conversation upon a public street or in a public place" and must agree to "submit [her] person, vehicle, and place of residence to search and seizure at any time of the day or night, with or without a search warrant, whenever requested to do so by a peace officer." [The administrators of the penal system are thereby granted powerful new resources with which to coerce their "clients", since] probationers who are accused of involvement in a new crime but who refuse to plead guilty can still be imprisoned even if not convicted of a new offense in a criminal trial [through the simple administrative device of] a probation violation hearing in which the relevant standard is "preponderance of the evidence," a weaker requirement than the "reasonable doubt" standard required in a criminal trial.[97]

As with the implementation of an earlier generation of reforms in the first quarter of the twentieth century,[98] the outcome of changes ostensibly aimed at decreasing state intervention has all too often been the development of programs which expand the reach of social control agencies and expose new populations to their (generally unwelcome) attentions. In practice, "the meaning of 'diversion' has been shifted from diversion from to 'referral to' [with a consequent extension of] the costs, caseload, and system purview even further than had previously been the case." [99] Cressey and McDermott neatly capture the discrepancy between rhetoric and reality. Examining a whole series of "diversionary" schemes, they note:

> If "true" diversion occurs, the juvenile is safely out of the official realm of the juvenile justice system and he is immune from incurring the delinquent label or any of its variations – pre-delinquent, delinquent tendencies, bad guy, hard core, unreachable. Further, when he walks out of the door from the person diverting him, he is technically free to tell the diverter to go to hell. We found very little "true" diversion in the communities studied. [100]

This tendency is hardly surprising, for neglect has clear disadvantages as a social control strategy, as least when dealing with criminals and some delinquents. Although the advocates of diversion consistently ignore or play down the importance of the deterrent and retributive functions of punishment, to the extent that crime represents a "rational" form of activity, the erosion of sanctions threatens to elicit more of it. The crazy and senile can, by and large, be contained and isolated while being neglected. Even were we to grant the attractions of unpoliced ghettoes, however, the same result cannot be secured by releasing criminals. The targets they victimize are insufficiently selective and not adequately geographically concentrated or controllable. Moreover, a strategy of this sort creates serious ideological problems. To allow criminals to violate the law, with something approaching impunity, significantly weakens the incentives to conform while simultaneously provoking public outrage. It is likely to trigger vigilante responses, thus threatening the state's monopoly of legal violence. In the process, it exhibits an insidious yet powerful tendency to undermine the legitimacy of a social and political order that permits such developments.

We must appreciate, therefore, the advantages possessed by the crime control bureaucracies as they have sought to protect and extend their empires. By playing upon the fears and mobilizing the disquiet of the public, the correctional staff can readily justify a substantial expansion of the amount and intensity of professional involvement and activity. Thus one may anticipate that Lerman's [101] findings on the way the California Community Treatment Project has been manipulated by and in the interests of the correctional establishment will turn out to be applicable more generally.

This leaves unresolved, however, the issue of why the criminal justice bureaucracy has been so protective of its state supported activities, whereas most mental health professionals have cheerfully abandoned their concern with the chronically crazy.[102] I suggest that this paradox disappears when we bear in mind the structural constraints and opportunities facing these two groups of controllers. The advent of community psychiatry and the growing willingness of insurance carriers to provide some coverage for mental disorders (together with the existing private psychiatric sector) mean that the higher status mental health professionals have ample alternative markets for their skills. Furthermore, those markets offer significant advantages. Though often heavily subsidized by tax money, they are free of the stigma of publicly provided care. Rather than the hopeless, impoverished and often senile patients characteristic of public psychiatry, they attract the less disturbed and more readily treatable, and the social status of the new clients is often higher.[103] In terms of prestige, income, and closer assimilation to the patterns of conventional medical practice, these fields are clearly preferable to the meager rewards associated with institutional psychiatry. Once the more articulate and politically influential professionals have been bought off in this fashion, whatever opposition is generated by hospital rundowns naturally comes primarily from low status workers with little credibility.[104]

On the other hand, notwithstanding all their efforts to "professionalize", police and prison officers have few transferable skills and operate in a severely restricted market. The careers of even the senior ranks remain inextricably bound up with servicing a lower class clientele. Even in the context of a burgeoning private security industry,[105] their collective interests remain inseparably linked to the fortunes of the public sector, to a degree that simply does not hold for such groups as psychiatrists. Hence the vigor with which those running the system have sought to exploit their natural advantages to transform decarceration into a policy of more pervasive intervention and control.

The convergence created by the special problems involved in controlling crime – "the occupational interests of correctional and prison employees and administrators [and] public demands, partly instrumental and partly symbolic, for sterner measures to stop increasing crime,"[106] – merely reinforces the tendency towards greater intervention already signalled in the pervasive and uncritical stress on rehabilitation so deeply entrenched in the community corrections literature and practice. Battered by assaults on its constitutionality, effectiveness, and moral justification,[107] the therapeutic ethic now appears to be giving ground in institutional settings.[108] From both right and left, there are renewed calls for fixed sentencing based upon deterrent and retributive considerations rather than rehabilitation.[109] What seems to be happening, however, is that the self-same therapeutic rationalizations and practices are being re-invoked as the basis for the new community programs.[110] In substantial measure, it has been by exploiting the opportunities decarceration offers for blurring the boundaries between guilt and innocence, accentuating discretion, and promulgating an aggressive ideology of treatment and prevention, that the crime control bureaucracy has transformed something that promised to curtail their operations into the basis for a further expansion of their activities.

The discretionary decision-making that forms an integral part of any program of coercive "rehabilitation" is a crucial feature of community corrections at all levels of its operations. It is most obvious in decisions about who is eligible for community dispositions in lieu of the harsher sanction of imprisonment. The very sense that the former is less punitive (or even non-punitive), and can actually *prevent* more crime, diminishes concern with whether the "client" has actually committed the offence that nominally brought him to the attention of the authorities. Instead of an adjudication focused on prior conduct there is an assessment of whether the accused can benefit from the services offered by the program, a decision which often entails intentional avoidance of due process and of the whole issue of guilt and innocence. The whole approach thus brings with it the danger "of highly intrusive intervention concerning matters of personal choice that have no direct bearing on criminal activity."[111] To the extent that these features generate further perceptions of injustice or unfairness, the long-run tendency must be for them to undermine further the legitimacy of a criminal justice system already widely regarded as inequitable and arbitrary.

This outcome is in no sense an aberration. On the contrary, in "corrections" as in other social control systems, the more control comes to be legitimated in terms of diagnosis and treatment rather than rules, responsibility, and punishment, the more likely it is to intrude into the emotions, thought, and behavior of the individual and to be concerned with generalized behavioral problems rather than specific acts. The threat thus looms of a massive extension of official intervention into the lives who had previously escaped notice or attention –

all under the guise of "helping" them. In fact, "the more benign, attractive, and successful the programme is defined [as being]. . . the more it will be used and the wider it will cast its net."[112]

1. Coates and Miller 1973: 67; Segal 1974: 143ff; Greenberg 1975: 28ff.

2. For example, CSEA 1972; AFSCME 1975.

3. Cohen 1972.

4. Gruenberg and Archer 1979: 498. The reluctance is comprehensible since, after all, those now recognizing some of the defects of community care were often among the main cheerleaders of deinstitutionalization, and in some instances, at least, bear personal responsibility for the implementation of the new policy.

5. Senate Special Committee on Aging 1976.

6. General Accounting Office 1977.

7. Jones 1982.

8. Borus 1981; Mollica 1983.

9. Langsley 1980.

10. *Journal of Social Issues* 37, # 3, 1981; *American Behavioral Scientist* 24, # 6, 1981; *Milbank Memorial Fund Quarterly* 57, # 4, 1979.

11. See Kaplan 1978. Kaplan claims that part of the difficulty arises from my "middle class bias", which leads me to recoil from the conditions of existence in the ghetto. Apparently, what I perceive to be "truly horrible" is in fact a life "rich in social interaction and communal feeling", indeed, one often preferable to the "serialized" existence of the American middle class (pp. 193 – 194). I leave it to the reader to judge the merits of these claims.

12. Estroff 1981: 120. Talbott (1980: 44 – 45) reports that in the 1950s, 65% of deinstitutionalized patients returned to their families, compared with only 23% now, a figure which drops off sharply within a year or two of discharge. Based on NIMH data, Goldman et al. (1981) have recently estimated the number of chronically and seriously mentally disturbed people in the United States at 1.7 million. Of these, 150,000 were in State, County, and Veterans Administration psychiatric hospitals, and approximately 1.15 million were in nursing homes and board and care homes (750,000 and 400,000 respectively). Thus, all other community settings, ranging from welfare hotels to families of origin, housed about 400,000 of the chronically mentally disabled.

13. Cf. Davis et al. 1974: "Our data show that the majority of patients do not hold jobs nor do they function very well in their domestic roles; most patients ultimately alienate their families and are divorced or rejected by their primary groups." See also Arnhoff 1975; Wing 1978.

14. Emerson et al. 1981: 772. NIMH estimates are that by the mid-1970s, nursing homes had become "the largest single place of care for the mentally ill," absorbing some $4.3 billion, or 29.3% of the direct care costs associated with mental illness. Cited in General Accounting Office 1977: 11.

15. Kirk and Thierren 1975: 212.

16. General Accounting Office 1977: 15 – 16.

17. NIMH 1975: 6.

18. Emerson et al. 1981: 772.

19. Emerson et al. 1981: 774; see also Lerman 1982: 11 ff.

184 　afterword: 1983

20. As Borus points out, "The state hospital took responsibility not only for mental health care, but also for the patient's housing, food, finances, medical care, medications, work activities, and social relations. The deinstitutionalized patient's limited ability to cope is often overwhelmed when he or she is forced to seek these types of care from multiple, uncoordinated community agencies. . . .The wishful notion that these patients will require such supportive services only for a transitional period is not supported by the data, which show that the mentally ill need on-going care to maintain a reasonable level of function." (Borus 1981: 340) See also Davis et al. 1974; Stein and Test 1980; Test 1981. Since such continuing care is routinely absent in all but a handful of well-publicized but wholly unrepresentative demonstration projects, it is obvious why misery, morbidity, steady deterioration and loss of basic social capacities are so widespread. Note that even in the well-funded demonstration project studied by Soloman et al. (1980), with the attention of a special team, half the discharged patients were doing very little or nothing at all eighteen months after discharge.

21. Parry-Jones 1972.

22. There is, of course, a long history of regulatory bodies being captured by the very interest groups they are supposed to regulate (for the classic approach to this problem, see Stigler 1971; see also Posner 1974; Peltzman 1976; Levine 1981; Breyer 1982) and the previous attempt to control the excesses of a profit-oriented mad business through official inspection – in nineteenth century England – does not inspire confidence. It was in part the inability of inspection to counter the structural imperatives of the marketplace that led an earlier generation of reformers to urge the construction of the public asylum system. (Cf. Scull 1979; Jones 1955) I see no reason to believe that episodic visits by regulators will somehow suffice to protect the vulnerable from a situation in which the structure of economic incentives systematically rewards exploitation and neglect.

23. Cf. Lerman 1982: 9. We shall examine the consequences of this situation at more length below.

24. For the effects of this on daily operations, see Kielhofner 1980; Emerson et al. 1981.

25. Lerman 1982: 3.

26. General Accounting Office 1977: 16.

27. General Accounting Office 1977: 13 – 14.

28. See Hynes 1977; Mesnikoff 1978. For similar findings for New Jersey, see New Jersey State Commission 1978.

29. Hynes 1977.

30. Kirk and Thierren 1975: 211.

31. General Accounting Office 1977: 19.

32. Senate Committee on Aging 1976: 724.

33. General Accounting Office 1977: 95.

34. Rose 1979: 440. See also Bassuk and Gerson 1978; Van Putten and Spar 1979.

35. Sedgwick 1982: 38.

36. Estroff 1981: 116 – 117.

37. Jones 1979a, 567.

38. Cf. Jones 1979b and Mollica 1980.

39. Lerman 1982: 91 ff.

40. Lerman 1982: 104; see also Witkin 1976.

41. Cf. Scull 1981.

42. Spitzer and Scull 1977.

43. Sedgwick 1982: 193 – 194. See also Rollin 1970; Korer 1978; Ebringer and Christie-Brown 1980.

44. Particularly notable in this regard is her endorsement of American Community Mental Health Centers as the solution to the problems of delivering care to chronic mental patients, a suggestion that reflects a lack of acquaintance with the dismal role actually played by these facilities. Community Mental Health Centers have quite self consciously selected "less troubled patients", including very substantial numbers diagnosed as "not mentally ill" but merely "maladjusted" (Langsley 1980: 817) – and have deliberately avoided serving "the needs of those who have traditionally resided in state psychiatric institutions." Kirk and Thierren 1975: 210.

45. Jones 1979a: 565 – 566; see also Jones 1982 and Scull 1983a.

46. Sedgwick 1982: 251. Commenting on some of the results of this situation, Minto (1983: 169) rightly notes that "There can be few states more pathetic than the withdrawn, hallucinated, neglected, and sometimes starving schizophrenic, barely capable of existence let alone a decent quality of life, who is left to 'enjoy' his miserable state in the wholly spurious name of individual freedom".

47. *The Guardian* January 13, 1976. By way of comparison, in New York State in 1974, the average proportion of mental health budgets allocated to aftercare was 6.5%; for Pilgrim State Hospital, the largest state facility, the figure was 1.1% (General Accounting Office 1977: 207 – 208).

48. For the United States, note Mollica's pessimistic conclusion that "the financial pragmatism of the states appears to preclude any possibility of a unified mental health policy and to undermine public psychiatry's ability to guarantee adequate and effective treatment" (Mollica 1983: 369).

49. Rose 1979: 431.

50. For a recent example, see Davis 1981: 2257.

51. For a very similar assessment of the quite limited role of drug therapy (linked in this case with a much more optimistic evaluation of community care), see Minto 1983, esp. p. 167.

52. There is also growing recognition of another problem connected with drug treatment, to which I had earlier drawn attention: the immense amount of neurological damage we are busy doing to substantial segments of the population via long-term administration of the neuroleptics. Ominously, questions are now being raised in the psychiatric literature about whether "the cure is worse than the disease" (Gardos and Cole 1976; Teppe and Haas 1979; Jeste and Wyatt 1979). In the words of an eminent British psychiatrist, "the side effects occasioned by these drugs may be pretty intolerable. . . .There is a danger, as I see it, that the injudicious use (or abuse) of psychotropic or tranquillising drugs. . . .may be edging [us] back to the era of bromides and paraldehyde from which we escaped nearly half a century ago" (Rollin 1979: 1775).

53. Lerman 1982: 209.

54. Segal and Aviram 1978: 37. Cf. Aviram et al. 1976: 574: "The fact that the rate of decline in California accelerated significantly after 1963, almost a decade after the introduction of psychoactive drugs, and that the greatest decrease was in age groups and diagnostic categories which are usually less amenable to these drugs, clearly suggest that we should look for other factors besides chemotherapy as the ones responsible for this change."

55. Aviram et al. 1976: 574. For a more extended review demonstrating that "the trend to community care is largely independent of drug therapy. . .[and that] recovery rates and levels of functioning in schizophrenia have not improved overall since the intro-

duction of these drugs, see Warner, forthcoming, Ch. 11.

56. Sedgwick 1982: 198.

57. Sedgwick 1982; Goldstein 1982; Matthews 1979; Warner forthcoming.

58. Note, however, that Odegard's study suggests that the later advent of deinstitutionalization in Norway is intimately bound up with the development of a "new and improved pension system for persons incapacitated by illness, which was introduced in 1960 and which includes psychotic invalids. . . . This has made possible the discharge of many psychotic invalids and is probably the main reason why the rates of discharge as 'not cured' did not show any great increase until after 1960." (Odegard 1967: 819.)

59. Warner, forthcoming, esp. Chs 2, 3, 4, 6, 7, 8.

60. Cf. World Health Organization 1979.

61. Sedgwick 1982: 205 – 213.

62. Scull 1979 (1982).

63. Sedgwick 1982: 202.

64. Cf. p. 67 and Table 8 – 1, p. 145 in this book.

65. Patricia Hornsby Smith, Parliamentary Secretary to the Minister of Health, in *Hansard* February 19, 1954, Vol. 523, Col. 2371.

66. Borus 1981: 340.

67. See, for example, General Accounting Office 1977; Murphy and Datel 1976; Sheehan and Atkinson 1974.

68. Rose 1979: 448.

69. See Matthews 1979; Borus 1981; Lerman 1982: Ch. 6.

70. General Accounting Office 1977: 6.

71. The potential impact of the latter problem in the United States has been greatly exacerbated by two further developments: the rash of lawsuits (most famously *Wyatt* v. *Stickney*, 344 Fed. Supp. 373 (Northern District, Alabama, 1972), over the so-called right to treatment, which have led the courts to attempt to define a required "minimum quality of care" associated with much higher staff – patient ratios, the provision of a "more humane psychological environment," and generally higher per patient expenditures; and the requirement to upgrade hospital facilities in order to meet the standards of the Joint Commission on the Accreditation of Hospitals, an essential step in order to be eligible for major non-state funding of the hospital system.

72. See Grob 1983. Note that the rise in mental hospital admission rates occurred despite the development as an act of deliberate state policy of screening programs designed to cut down on geriatric admissions to the state hospital system (Senate Special Committee on Aging, November 1971: 61 – 75); and, in later years, explicit changes in commitment laws aimed at excluding the "senile" from state hospitals altogether (Cf. Scull 1981a: 745 – 746).

73. Lerman's (1982: Ch. 6) discussion of the origins of deinstitutionalization in California is in general one of the more sophisticated attempts to grapple with these issues, and does at least begin to recognize the existence of "hidden" savings and their impact on public policy; but having identified some of the underlying factors that enter into the equation, he shies away from recognizing their fundamental significance. He does, however, suggest a plausible reason for the marked inter-state discrepancies in the speed with which decarceration was implemented, the differential sophistication of the state mental health bureaucracies. He argues that short-run costs generally increased in the early stages of deinstitutionalization, since states had to supply matching funds in order to capture federal subsidies. In consequence, "States whose leaders exhibited entre-

preneurial skills, and who were supported by executives and legislators willing to risk increased spending in order to gain long-term fiscal benefits via deferred construction and maintenance of facilities, displayed marked population reductions by 1969. Laggard states waited until Supplemental Security Income [allowing 100% federal financing of the decarcerated] was passed in 1972'' (Lerman 1982: 209).

74. Wilson 1975, 1981; Fogel 1975.

75. Martinson 1974; see generally Greenberg and Humphries 1979.

76. Flynn 1978: 131 – 132.

77. I emphasized this point in the first edition of this book (see pp. 56 – 57 above), and Anthony Bottoms (1983: 166 – 167, 182 – 184) has also recently deplored the tendency to focus only on prison numbers and rates per 100,000 which has the unfortunate corollary that "data on the *proportion* of convicted offenders given imprisonment or probation are given little or no attention" and the sharp decline in the proportion of convicted defendants given imprisonment is simply overlooked.

78. In mitigation, I would plead that in 1975 the contradictions between social control talk and action (Cohen 1979, 1983) were far less blatant in this area than they have now become.

79. Kaplan 1978: 205 – 206 correctly takes me to task for this.

80. Chan and Ericson 1981: 47, 39.

81. Rothman 1980.

82. Chan and Ericson 1981.

83. For a related critique of Rothman's original argument, see Scull 1981b.

84. Jacobs 1983b.

85. Cohen 1979.

86. Greenberg 1977.

87. Hall et al. 1978; see also Bottoms 1983: 193 – 194.

88. Ditton 1979.

89. Jacobs 1983b. Compare, in this regard, Jacobs 1983a: 115 – 132, which analyses the defeat of a recent New York prison bond by the electorate. Notwithstanding the fact that "The prison bond's opponents were traditionally liberal organizations, predominantly based in New York City," Jacobs notes the "powerful irony. . . .[that] New York City voters, traditionally the most liberal in the state, strongly *supported* prison expansion"; and the votes defeating the bond issue came from conservative, Republican, law-and-order voters of upstate New York. Partly, this may have relected unwillingness to "pay to lock up New York City's problems." More centrally, the crucial determinant of voting patterns seems to have been the degree of fear and concern about crime, itself a quite direct reflection of the local crime rate.

90. Orlans 1948; Deutsch 1973; Rawls 1980.

91. That many of those employed to run such places are not hypocrites but true believers does not detract from the falsity of these beliefs. The benefits of such mythologies accrue largely to those who perpetrate them, not to their alleged beneficiaries. Inmates are generally all too aware of the emperor's missing clothes, save where sharing the illusion makes their lives more bearable. Arnold Hauser has pointed out that this is not atypical of ideological constructs:

> What most sharply distinguishes a propagandistic from an ideological presentation and interpretation of the facts is. . . .that its falsification and mystification of the truth is always conscious and intentional. Ideology, on the other hand, is mere

deception – in essence self deception – never simply lies and deceit. It obscures truth in order not so much to mislead others as to maintain and increase the self-confidence of those who express and benefit from such deceptions. (Quoted in Muraskin 1976: 559)

92. Compare California Governor Deukmejian's claim to be "delighted" by over-crowded prisons "because it keeps criminals out of the way of the law-abiding public"; and an anonymous legislator's claim that voters would like to see convicts "locked up sixteen to a cell." *Los Angeles Times* September 8, 1983, Section 2, p. 14. And note the studious avoidance of the question of the welfare of prisoners by proponents of the recent New York prison bond. As James Jacobs notes, in this connection "humanitarianism apparently had little political appeal" (Jacobs 1983a: 118).

93. Cohen 1979: 350. See Lerman 1975; Klein (ed.) 1976; Rutherford and Bengur 1976; Messinger 1976; Blomberg 1977; Warren 1981; Lerman 1980, 1982; Downs 1978.

94. Chan and Ericson 1981: 55. For extensive documentation of this point, see Austin and Krisberg 1981, 1982; Hylton 1981a, 1981b, 1981c, 1982; Blomberg 1980; and for a trenchant overview of the whole net-widening phenomenon, see Cohen, forth-coming 1984, Ch. 2.

95. Cohen 1979.

96. Cohen 1979.

97. Greenberg 1975: 10 – 11. For a description of a program of this sort, see Wold and Mendes 1974.

98. Rothman 1980; Scull 1981.

99. Klein et al. 1976: 10.

100. Cressey and McDermott 1974: 3 – 4.

101. Lerman 1975.

102. In Minto's words (1983: 168 – 169), "The mental hospital scene has been one of steady and increasing resistance to the provision of psychiatric treatment and long-term support to a group of sick people who do not respond to current treatment. . . .It is almost as though the patient's inability to be cured has become a personal insult to his treaters, who respond to his continuing disability as if it were a specific act of non-cooperation in the treatment process rather than a distressingly constant malady over which the patient has little control." We are witnessing, then, "the disowning of the chronic schizophrenic patient by the psychiatric services. . . .more and more psychiatric resources have been applied to patient groups least needing medical care, whilst the serious neglect of an overtly ill group of patients continues to exist."

103. Chu and Trotter 1974.

104. Moreover, many even of these workers have found an alternative source of income, as operators of the board and care homes to which mental patients have now been discharged.

105. Spitzer and Scull 1977; Shearing and Stenning 1981.

106. Greenberg 1975: 16.

107. American Friends Service Committee 1972; Leifer 1969; Kittrie 1972; Gaylin 1974.

108. See Allen 1981. This applies, of course, to institutional settings in general, including those, such as mental hospitals, whose nominal justification is self-consciously therapeutic. The growing willingness of courts to intervene to secure "patients' rights" has necessarily involved considerable legalistic circumscription of the behavior and

judgments of therapeutic staff. By thus sharply limiting professional autonomy (Freidson 1970), ''legalization'' has made institutional psychiatry even less attractive to professionals.

109. Fogel 1975; Von Hirsch 1976; Wilson 1975: Van den Haag 1975.

110. This transfer of the therapeutic rationalization from the sphere of formal incarceration to that of community corrections obviously deserves more extended treatment than I can give it here. One of the most critical questions it raises, of course, is why this flip-flop is occurring. Richard Abel (personal communication) has suggested one plausible explanation – that community dispositions are both less visible and, because they are less imbued with state action, less subject to constitutional scrutiny. Elsewhere, he has made an analogous point about the relationship between the distribution of bias in the criminal justice system and the visibility of that bias in the behavior of official agents. See Abel 1978.

111. Greenberg 1975: 6.

112. Cohen 1979: 348. For a more extended critique of recent developments in community corrections than I have had space for here, see Scull 1983b.

Bibliography

CHAPTERS 1 – 8

ABEL-SMITH, BRIAN. *The Hospitals 1800—1948*. Cambridge, Mass.: Harvard University Press, 1964.

Advisory Council of Judges, National Council on Crime and Delinquency. "Model Sentencing Act," *Crime and Delinquency*, 9 (1963), 339–369.

AHMED, PAUL. "New Thrusts in Unified Mental Health Care Systems, and the Status of State Mental Hospitals," in *Where is My Home?* Mimeographed. Scottsdale, Arizona: N.T.I.S., 1974.

ALBEE, G. "The Uncertain Future of Clinical Psychology." *American Psychologist*, 25 (1970), 1071–1080.

ALCOCK, THOMAS. *Observations on the Defects of the Poor Laws*. London, 1752.

ALPER, BENEDICT S. Foreword to Y. Bakal, ed. *Closing Correctional Institutions*. Lexington, Mass.: Lexington Books, D.C. Heath and Company, 1973, pp. vii–x.

American Federation of State, County, and Municipal Employees. *Out of their Beds and into the Streets*. Washington D.C.: A.F.S.C.M.E., 1975.

American Friends Service Committee. *Struggle for Justice*. Philadelphia: Hill and Wang, 1971.

ANON. *An Account of Several Workhouses*. London, 1725.

ANON. *On the Present State of Lunatic Asylums: With Suggestions for their Improvement*. London: Drury, 1839.

ANSPACHER, C. "What Happens to Ex-Mental Patients." *San Francisco Chronicle*, September 4, 1972: 4.

ARLIDGE, JOHN T. *On the State of Lunacy and the Legal Provision for the Insane* . . . London: Churchill, 1859.

AVIRAM, U. and S. SEGAL. "Exclusion of the Mentally Ill: A reflection on an old problem in a new context." *Archives of General Psychiatry*. 29 (1973), 126–131.

BAILEY, WILLIAM. *A Treatise on the Better Employment and More Comfortable Support of the Poor in Workhouses.* London, 1758.

BAKAL, YITZAK, ed. *Closing Correctional Institutions: New Strategies for Youth Services.* Lexington: Lexington Books, D.C. Heath and Company, 1973.

BALDWIN, J. "How Many Beds? A Critical Discussion of Some Approaches to Hospital Planning: II Mental Hospitals." *Health Bulletin*, 26 (1968), 1.

BALTER, M. B. and J. LEVINE. "The Nature and Extent of Psychotropic Drug Usage in the United States." *Psychopharmacological Bulletin*, 5 (1969), 3–13.

BARDACH, E. *The Skill Factor in Politics.* Berkeley: University of California Press, 1972.

BARNES, HARRY E. *A History of New Jersey Penal Institutions.* n.p.: MacCrellish and Quigley, n.d.

——— *The Evolution of Penology in Pennsylvania.* Indianapolis: Bobbs-Merrill Inc., 1927.

BARON, ROGER, FLOYD FEENEY and WARREN THORNTON. "Preventing Delinquency through Diversion: The Sacramento County 601 Diversion Project." *Federal Probation* 37 (March 1973), 13–18.

BARRABEE, PAUL S. "A Study of a Mental Hospital; the Effect of its Social Structure on its Functions." Unpublished Ph.D. dissertation, Harvard University, 1951.

BARTON, RUSSELL. *Institutional Neurosis.* 2nd edition. Bristol: Wright, 1965.

Bay Area Research Unit. "Open Letter to the Editor: Correctional News Brief." *The Outlaw*, 3 (1974), 3.

BECKER, HOWARD S. *Outsiders: Studies in the Sociology of Deviance.* Glencoe, Illinois: Free Press, 1963.

——— "Labelling Theory Reconsidered," in Paul Rock and Mary McIntosh, eds. *Deviance and Social Control.* London: Tavistock, 1974.

BELKNAP, IVAN. *Human Problems of a State Mental Hospital.* New York: McGraw-Hill, 1956.

BELLERS, JOHN. *Proposals for Raising a College of Industry of All Useful Trades and Husbandry.* London, 1696.

BENNETT, I.F. "Chemotherapy in Psychiatric Hospitals: Critical Review of the Literature and Research Trends." *Transactions of the First Research Conference on Chemotherapy in Psychiatry.* Washington D.C.: Veterans Administration, 1956.

BENTHAM, JEREMY, *Panopticon: or the Inspection House* . . . London: Payne, 1791.

——— *Pauper Management.* London, 1797.

——— *Works.* Edited by J. Bowring. Edinburgh: Tait, 1843.

BLAIR, D. and D. M. BRADY. "Recent Advances in the Treatment of Schizo-phrenia: Group Training and Tranquillizers." *Journal of Mental Science,* 104 (1958), 625–664.

BLUMER, HERBERT. "Society as Symbolic Interaction." *Human Behavior and Social Processes.* Edited by Arnold M. Rose. Boston: Houghton Mifflin, 1962, 179–192.

BLUMSTEIN, ALFRED and JACQUELINE COHEN. "A Theory of the Stability of Punishment." *Journal of Criminal Law and Criminology,* 64 (1973), 198–207.

Board of Directors, National Council of Crime and Delinquency. "The Non-Dangerous Offender Should not be Imprisoned: A Policy Statement." in *Crime and Delinquency,* 19 (1973), 449–556.

Boston Prison Discipline Society. *Annual Reports 1827–1833.* Boston.

BRACE, C. L. *The Dangerous Classes of New York and Twenty Years Work Among Them.* New York: Wyncoop and Hallenbeck, 1872.

BRILL, H. and ROBERT E. PATTON. "Analysis of 1955-56 Population Fall in New York State Mental Hospitals during the First Year of Large-Scale Use of Tranquillizing Drugs." *American Journal of Psychiatry,* 114 (1957), 509–517.

————· "Analysis of Population Reduction in New York State Mental Hospitals During the First Four Years of Large Scale Therapy with Psychotropic Drugs." *American Journal of Insanity,* 116 (1959), 495–508.

————· "Clinical Statistical Analysis of Population Changes in New York State Mental Hospitals Since the Introduction of Psychotropic Drugs." *American Journal of Psychiatry,* 119 (1962), 20–35.

————· "Psychopharmacology and the Current Revolution in Mental Health Services." *Proceedings of the Fourth World Congress of Psychiatry.* Part One. Amsterdam: Exerpta Medica Foundation, 1966, 288–295.

BROOKE, E. M. "Factors Affecting the Demand for Psychiatric Beds." *The Lancet* (December 8, 1962), 1211–1213.

BROWN, G. W. "Length of Hospital Stay and Schizophrenia: A Review of Statis-tical Studies." *Acta Psychiatrica et Neurologica Scandinavia,* 35 (1960), 414–430.

————· M. BONE, B. DALISON, and J. K. WING. *Schizophrenia and Social Care.* London: Oxford University Press, 1966.

BROWNE, W. A. F. *What Asylums Were, Are, and Ought to Be . . .* Edinburgh: Black, 1837.

BRYANT, J. H., B. M. MOSS, and F. R. HINE. "Drug Therapy—A Survey of the Literature." Research Report #3, Department of Institutions, Baton Rouge, Louisiana, 1956.

BUCKNILL, JOHN CHARLES. *The Care of the Insane and their Legal Control.* London: MacMillan, 1880.

California Department of Mental Hygiene. *A Long-Range Plan for Mental Health Services in California.* Sacramento, 1962.

———· *A Study of Successful Treatment.* Sacramento, 1972.

California State Employees' Association. *Where Have All the Patients Gone? A CSEA Report on the Crisis in Mental Health Care in California.* Sacramento, 1972.

California State Governor's Budget 1972–1973. Sacramento: 1972.

CAUDILL, WILLIAM. *The Psychiatric Hospital as a Small Society.* Cambridge, Mass.: Harvard University Press, 1958.

CHADWICK, EDWIN. *Report on the Sanitary Conditions of the Labouring Population of Great Britain . . .* London, 1842.

CHAMBLISS, W. "A Sociological Analysis of the Law of Vagrancy." *Social Problems,* 12 (1964), 67–77.

CHASE, J. "Where Have All the Patients Gone?" *Human Behavior* (October 1973), 14–21.

Chief Medical Officer's Report. *Report of the Ministry of Health for the Year 1959, Part II: On the State of the Public Health.* London: Her Majesty's Stationery Office, Command 1207, 1959.

CHIEN, C. and J. O. COLE. "Landlord Supervised Cooperative Apartments: a New Modality for Community-Based Treatment." in *American Journal of Psychiatry,* 130 (1973), 156–159.

CHITTICK, R. A., G. W. BROOKS, and W. N. DEANE. *Vermont Project for the Rehabilitation of Chronic Schizophrenic Patients: Progress Report.* Vermont State Hospital, February 1959.

CHU, F., and S. TROTTER. *The Madness Establishment.* New York: Grossman, 1974.

CICOUREL, A. *The Social Organization of Juvenile Justice.* New York: Wiley, 1968.

CLARK, SIR JAMES. *A Memoir of John Conolly, M.D. . . .* London: John Murray, 1869.

CLARK, L. D., "Evaluation of the Therapeutic Effects of Drugs in Psychiatric Patients." *Diseases of the Nervous System,* 17 (1956), 282–286.

CLARK, RAMSAY. *Crime in America.* New York: Simon and Schuster, 1970.

CLAY, R. M. *The Mediaeval Hospitals of England.* London: Methuen, 1909.

CLEMMER, D. *The Prison Community.* New York: Rinehart, 1938.

COATES, R. B. and A. MILLER. "Neutralization of Community Resistance to Group Homes." in Y. Bakal, ed. *Closing Correctional Institutions.* Lexington, Mass.: Lexington Books, D.C. Heath and Company, 1973, 67–84.

———· ———· and L. OHLIN. "A Strategic Innovation in the Process of Deinstitutionalization: The University of Massachusetts Conference." in Y. Bakal, ed. *Closing Correctional Institutions.* Lexington, Mass.: Lexington Books, D.C. Heath and Company, 127–148.

COHEN, S. "Criminology and the Sociology of Deviance in Britain." in P. Rock and M. McIntosh, eds. *Deviance and Social Control.* London: Tavistock, 1974, 1–40.

COLE, G. F. "The Decision to Prosecute." *Law and Society Review,* 4 (1970), 331–343.

COLLINS, J. A., B. A. STOTSKY, and J. R. DOMINICK. "Is the Nursing Home the Mental Hospital's Back Ward in the Community?" *Journal of the American Geriatric Society,* 15 (1967); 75–81.

CONOLLY, JOHN. *An Inquiry Concerning the Indications of Insanity . . .* London: Taylor, 1830.

CONRAD, J. P. "Corrections and Simple Justice." *Journal of Criminal Law and Criminology,* 64 (1973), 208–217.

Council of Judges, "Model Sentencing Act," *Crime and Delinquency,* 18 (1972), 335–370.

CRANE, GEORGE E. "Clinical Psychopharmacology in its Twentieth Year." *Science,* 181 (July 13, 1973), 124–128. Copyright 1973 by the American Association for the Advancement of Science.

CRESSEY, D. "Adult Felons in Prison." in L. Ohlin, ed. *Prisoners in America.* Englewood Cliffs, N.J.: Prentice-Hall Inc., 1973, 117–150.

CUMMING, E. and J. CUMMING. *Closed Ranks.* Cambridge, Mass.: Harvard University Press, 1957.

DAVIS, J. M. "Efficacy of Tranquilizing and Anti-depressant Drugs." *Archives of General Psychiatry,* 13 (1965), 552–572.

DEFOE, D. *A Tour Through the Whole Island of Great Britain . . .* London: G. Strahan, 1724–26. (London: Penguin edition, 1971).

DE GRAZIA, E. "Report on Pre-trial Diversion of Accused Offenders to Community Mental Health Treatment Programs." Washington D.C.: Georgetown University Department of Psychiatry, 1972.

Department of Health and Social Security. *On the State of the Public Health: Report of the Chief Medical Officer.* London: Her Majesty's Stationery Office, 1969.

———. *Psychiatric Hospitals and Units in England and Wales.* Statistical Report Series #11. London: Her Majesty's Stationery Office, 1970.

———. *Better Services for the Mentally Handicapped.* London: Her Majesty's Stationery Office, Command 4683, 1971.

DEUTSCH, A. *The Mentally Ill in America.* 2nd ed. New York: Columbia University Press, 1949.

DICKSON, D. "Bureaucracy and Morality: An Organizational Perspective on a Moral Crusade." *Social Problems,* 16 (1968), 143–156.

DINGMAN, P. R. "The Case for the State Hospital." *Where is my Home?* Mimeographed. Scottsdale, Arizona: N.T.I.S. 1974, 28–52.

DOBB, M. *Studies in the Development of Capitalism.* New York: International Publishers, 1963.

DOLESCHAL, E. "Criminal Justice Programs in Model Cities." National Council on Crime and Delinquency, Hackensack, N.J., June 1972.

DONAHUE, H. H. "The Oklahoma Program." *Where is my Home?* Mimeographed. Scottsdale, Arizona: N.T.I.S., 1974, 74–85.

DOUGLAS, J. D. *Deviance and Respectability.* New York: Basic Books, 1970.

EARLE, PLINY, PAPERS. At the American Antiquarian Society, Worcester, Massachusetts.

EATON, D. B. "Despotism in Lunatic Asylums." *North American Review,* 132 (1881), 263–275.

EDGERTON, R. *Cloak of Competence: Stigma in the Lives of the Retarded.* Berkeley: University of California Press, 1967.

Edinburgh Review. "Non-restraint in the Treatment of the Mentally Ill." 131 (1870) 215–231.

EDSALL, N. C. *The Anti-Poor Law Movement 1834–44.* Manchester: University of Manchester Press, 1971.

ELKES, J. and C. ELKES. "Effects of Chlorpromazine on the Behaviour of Chronically Over-active Psychotic Patients." *British Medical Journal,* 2 (1954), 560–565.

ELLIS, HAVELOCK. *The Criminal.* New York: Scribners, 1900.

EMPEY, L. T. "Juvenile Justice Reform: Diversion, Due Process, and Deinstitutionalization." L. Ohlin, ed. *Prisoners in America.* Englewood Cliffs, N.J.: Prentice-Hall Inc., 1973, 13–48.

———· and S.G. LUBECK. *The Silverlake Experiment.* Chicago: Aldine, 1971.

ENGELHARDT, D. M., N. FREEDMAN, B. GLICK, L. HANKOFF, D. MANN, R. MARGOLIS. "Prevention of Psychiatric Hospitalization with the Use of Psychopharmacological Agents." *Journal of the American Medical Association,* 173 (1960), 147–149.

———· "Phenothiazines in Prevention of Hospitalization: II Duration of Treatment Exposure." *Journal of the American Medical Association,* 186 (1963), 981–983.

———· "Phenothiazines in Prevention of Psychiatric Hospitalization: III Delay or Prevention of Hospitalization." *Archives of General Psychiatry,* 11 (1964), 162–169.

———· "Phenothiazines in Prevention of Psychiatric Hospitalization: IV Delay or Prevention of Hospitalization—A Re-evaluation." *Archives of General Psychiatry,* 16 (January 1967), 98–101.

ENGELS, FREDERICK. *The Condition of the Working Class in England.* London: Panther Books, 1969.

ENKI Research Institute. *A Study of California's New Mental Health Law.* Chatsworth, California: ENKI, 1972.

EPSTEIN, L. J., R. D. MORGAN, and L. REYNOLDS. "An Approach to the Effect of Ataraxic Drugs on Hospital Release Rates." *American Journal of Psychiatry*, 119 (1962), 36–47.

————, and A. SIMON. "Alternatives to State Hospitalization for the Geriatric Mentally Ill." *American Journal of Psychiatry*, 124 (1968), 955–961.

ERIKSON, KAI. "Notes on the Sociology of Deviance," H.S. Becker, ed. *The Other Side*. New York: Free Press. 1964.

FANSHELL, D. and E. SHINN. *Dollars and Sense in the Foster Care of Children: A Look at Cost Factors*. New York: Child Welfare League of America, 1972.

FESSLER, A. "The Management of Lunacy in Seventeenth Century England." *Proceedings of the Royal Society of Medicine, Historical Section*, 49 (1956), 901–907.

FINK, ARTHUR E. *Causes of Crime*. New York: Barnes, 1962.

FLETCHER, R. "The New School of Criminal Anthropology," *American Anthropologist*, 4 (1891), 201–236.

Florida Parole and Probation Commission. *34th Annual Report*, 1974.

FLYNN, E. E. "Jails and Criminal Justice." in L. Ohlin, ed. *Prisoners in America*. Englewood Cliffs, N.J.: Prentice-Hall, Inc., 1973, 49–88.

FOSTER, R. M. "Youth Service Systems: New Criteria." in Y. Bakal, ed., *Closing Correctional Institutions*. Lexington, Mass.; Lexington Books, 1973, D.C. Heath and Company, 1973, 33–38.

FOUCAULT, MICHEL. *Madness and Civilization*. New York: Mentor Books, 1965.

FOULDS, G. A. "Clinical Research in Psychiatry." *Journal of Mental Science*, 104 (1958), 259–265.

FOX, B. "The Investigation of the Effects of Psychiatric Treatment." *Journal of Mental Science*, 107 (1961), 493–502.

FRANKFATHER, D. Background and Position Paper on Mental Health Care for the Elderly. Unpublished final report for the Planning Branch, Office of Program Planning and Evaluation, NIMH, Rockville, Maryland.

FRANKLIN, BENJAMIN. *Some Account of the Pennsylvania Hospital* . . . Philadelphia, 1754.

FREIDSON, E. *Profession of Medicine*. New York: Dodd, Mead and Co., 1970.

FURNISS, EDGAR S. *The Position of the Laborer in a System of Nationalism*. New York: Kelly, 1965.

GANS, H. Preface to *The Great School Legend*, by Colin Greer. New York: Basic Books Inc., 1971.

GAYLIN, WILLARD. *Partial Justice: A Study of Bias in Sentencing*. New York: Knopf, 1974.

General Accounting Office. *Controls on the Use of Psychotherapeutic Drugs and Improved Psychiatrist Staffing are Needed in Veterans Administration Hospitals*. Washington D.C.: Government Printing Office, April 18, 1975.

GEORGE, M. DOROTHY. *London Life in the Eighteenth Century.* London: Kegan Paul, 1925 (London: Penguin edition 1965).

Georgia Law Review. "Addict Diversion: An Alternative Approach for the Criminal Justice System." 60 (1972), 667.

GITTLEMAN, R. K., D. F. KLEIN, and M. POLLACK. "Effects of Psychotropic Drugs on Long-term Adjustment: A Review." *Psychopharmacology,* 5 (1964), 317–338. Amsterdam: Elsevier, 1965.

GLASER, D. "Correction of Adult Offenders in the Community." in L. Ohlin, ed. *Prisoners in America.* Englewood Cliffs, N.J.: Prentice-Hall Inc., 1973, 89–116.

GLICK, B. and R. MARGOLIS. "A Study of the Influence of Experimental Design on Clinical Outcome in Drug Research." *American Journal of Psychiatry,* 118 (1962) 1087–1096.

GOFFMAN, ERVING. *Asylums: Essays on the Social Situation of Mental Patients and Other Inmates.* Garden City, N.Y.: Doubleday, 1961.

GOODMAN, LOUIS S., and ALFRED S. GILMAN. *The Pharmacological Basis of Therapeutics.* 4th edition. New York: MacMillan, 1969.

GOUGH, IAN. "State Expenditure in Advanced Capitalism." *New Left Review,* 92 (July-August 1975), 53–92.

GOULDNER, ALVIN W. "The Sociologist as Partisan: Sociology and the Welfare State." *American Sociologist* 3 (1968), 103–116.

———· *The Coming Crisis of Western Sociology.* New York: Avon Books, 1970.

GOULDSMITH, RICHARD. *Some Considerations on Trade.* London, 1725.

GRANVILLE, JOSEPH MORTIMER. *The Care and Cure of the Insane . . .* 2 vols. London: Hardwicke and Bogue, 1877.

GREENBERG, DAVID F. "Problems in Community Corrections." *Issues in Criminology,* 10 (1975); 1–34.

GREENBLATT, M. "Historical Forces Affecting the Closing of State Mental Hospitals." *Where is my Home?* Mimeographed. Scottsdale, Arizona: N.T.I.S., 1974.

———· R.H. YORK, and E. L. BROWN. *From Custodial to Therapeutic Patient Care in Mental Hospitals.* New York: Russell Sage Foundation, 1955.

GREENLEY, J. R. "Exit from a Mental Hosptial." Unpublished Ph.D. dissertation, Yale University, 1970.

———· "Alternative Views of the Psychiatrist's Role." *Social Problems,* 20 (1972), 252–262.

GREER, COLIN. *The Great School Legend.* New York: Basic Books Inc., 1972.

GRINSPOON, L. and P. HEDBLOM. *The Speed Culture: Amphetamine Use and Abuse in America.* Cambridge, Mass.: Harvard University Press, 1974.

GROB, GERALD N. *The State and the Mentally Ill. A History of Worcester State Hospital in Massachusetts, 1830–1920.* Chapel Hill, N.C.: University of North Carolina Press, 1966.

————· *Mental Institutions in America: Social Policy to 1875*. New York: Free Press, 1973.

GULA, M. "Community Services and Residential Institutions for Children." in Y. Bakal, ed. *Closing Correctional Institutions*. Lexington, Mass.: Lexington Books, D.C. Heath and Company, 1973, 13–18.

GUSFIELD, JOSEPH. *Symbolic Crusade*. Urbana, Ill.: University of Illinois Press, 1963.

HACKER, ANDREW. *The Triumph of American Capitalism*. New York: 1940.

HALEVY, ELI. *England in 1815*. London: Benn, 1949.

HALL, CHARLES P. "The Economics of Mental Health." *Hospital and Community Psychiatry*, 21 (1970), 105–110.

HALL, JEROME. *Theft, Law, and Society*. Indianapolis: Bobbs Merrill Inc., 1935.

HALLER, M. H. *Eugenics: Hereditarian Attitudes in American Thought*. New Brunswick, N.J.: Rutgers University Press, 1964.

HAMILTON, E. J. "Origin and Growth of the National Debt in Western Europe." *American Economic Review*, 37 (1947), 118–130.

HAMMOND, WILLIAM A. *Insane Asylum Reform I: The Non-Asylum Treatment of the Insane*. New York: Putnam, 1879.

HANDLIN, O. *Boston's Immigrants 1790–1880*. New York: Atheneum, 1968.

HANSARD'S *Parliamentary Debates*. London.

HANWELL ASYLUM, *Annual Reports*. London, 1846–1890.

HARE, J. and J. WILCOX. "Do Psychiatric Inpatients take their Drugs?" *British Journal of Psychiatry*, 3 (1967), 1435–1439.

HARLOW, ELEANOR. "Diversion from the Criminal Justice System." National Council on Crime and Delinquency, Hackensack, N.J., April 1970.

HARTFORD RETREAT, *Annual Reports*, 1825–1890. Hartford, Connecticut.

HARTLEDGE, L. C. "Effects of Chlorpromazine on Learning." *Psychological Bulletin*, 64 (1965), 235–245.

HAWES, JOSEPH M. *Children in Urban Society. Juvenile Delinquency in Nineteenth Century America*. New York: Oxford University Press, 1971.

HAWKINS, K. "Young Adult Offenders: III The Problems of Discretion." *British Journal of Criminology*, 14 (1974), 399–403.

HECKER, A. O. "The Demise of Large State Hospitals. *Hospital and Community Psychiatry*, 21 (1970), 261–263.

HECKSCHER, ELI F. *Mercantilism*. 2 vols. New York: Macmillan, 1955.

HEFFERIN, E. A., and WILNER, D. N. "Opinions About Geriatric Patients in Public Mental Hospitals." *HSMHA Reports*, 86, No. 5 (1971), 457–471.

HENDERSON, C. R. *Introduction to the Study of the Dependent, Defective and Delinquent Classes*. Boston: Heath, 1901.

HIGHAM, JOHN. *Strangers in the Land: Patterns of American Nativism 1860–1925.* New Brunswick, N.J.: Rutgers University Press, 1955.

HILL, GEORGE NESSE. *An Essay on the Prevention and Cure of Insanity.* London: Longman, Hurst, Rees, Orme, and Brown, 1814.

HOBSBAWM, ERIC J. *Industry and Empire.* London: Penguin, 1968.

———· and RUDE, GEORGE. *Captain Swing.* London: Penguin, 1969.

HOENIG, J. and M. W. HAMILTON. "Extramural Care of Psychiatric Patients." *The Lancet,* (June 19, 1965), 1322–1325.

———· *The Desegregation of the Mentally Ill.* London: Routledge and Kegan Paul, 1969.

HOFSTADTER, R. *Social Darwinism in American Thought.* Boston: Beacon, 1944.

Home Office. *Criminal Statistics, England and Wales 1958.* London: Her Majesty's Stationery Office, Command 803, 1959.

———· *Criminal Statistics, England and Wales 1972.* London: Her Majesty's Stationery Office, Command 5402, 1973.

———· *Report of the Committee on Local Authority and Allied Personal Social Services.* London: Her Majesty's Stationery Office, 1968.

HOOD, ROGER. "Young Adult Offenders: I The Custodial Sector." *British Journal of Criminology,* 14 (October 1974), 388–395.

Horizon House Institute for Research and Development. *The Future Role of State Mental Hospitals.* Philadelphia; Horizon House, July 1975.

House of Commons. *Report of the Select Committee on the Operation of the Lunacy Law, so far as Regards Security Afforded by it Against Violations of Personal Liberty,* Hansard: London, 1877.

HOWE, S. G. *A Letter to J. H. Wilkins, H. B. Rogers and F. B. Fay, Commissioners of Massachusetts for the State Reform School for Girls.* Boston, 1854.

———· "The Insane and their Treatment Past and Present." *National Quarterly Review,* 7 (September 1863), 207–232.

———· A Corrected Copy of Dr. Howe's Letter in the *Daily Advertizer*, October 30, Entitled 'A Plea, Alike in Behalf of our Pauper Lunatics and our Taxpayers.' Boston: n. p., 1871.

———· *Letters and Journals of Samuel Gridley Howe.* 2 vols. Edited by his daughter Laura E. Richards with notes by F. B. Sanborn. Boston: Dana Estes, 1909. Reprint New York: AMS, 1973.

HUNT, R. C. "Ingredients of a Rehabilitation Program." *Proceedings of the 34th Annual Conference of the Milbank Memorial Fund,* New York: Milbank Memorial Fund, 1957.

HURD, HENRY M., ed. *The Institutional Care of the Insane in the United States and Canada.* 4 vols. Baltimore: Johns Hopkins Press, 1916–1917.

Indiana Department of Mental Health. *Outline of the Department of Mental Health's Program for Delivery of Services 1975–1981.* January 27, 1975.

Joint Commission on Mental Illness and Health. *Action for Mental Health.* New York: Basic Books, 1961.

JONES, K. *Lunacy, Law, and Conscience 1744–1845. The Social History of the Care of the Insane.* London: Routledge and Kegan Paul, 1955.

————· *Mental Health and Social Policy 1845–1959.* London: Routledge and Kegan Paul, 1960.

————· *A History of the Mental Health Services.* London: Routledge and Kegan Paul, 1972.

————· and R. SIDEBOTHAM. *Mental Hospitals at Work.* London: Routledge and Kegan Paul, 1962.

JONES, PETER D. *An Economic History of the United States Since 1783.* London: Routledge and Kegan Paul, 1956.

JORDAN, W. K. *Philanthropy in England 1480–1660. A Study of the Changing Pattern of English Social Aspirations.* New York: Russell Sage Foundation, 1959.

————· *The Charities of London 1480–1660. The Aspirations and the Achievements of the Urban Society.* New York: Russell Sage Foundation, 1960.

————· *The Charities of Rural England.* New York: Russell Sage Foundation, 1961.

KALINOWSKI, L. B. "An Appraisal of the 'Tranquillizers' and their Influence on Other Somatic Treatments in Psychiatry." *American Journal of Psychiatry,* 115 (1958), 294–300.

KEENAN, BRIAN. "The Modesto State Hospital Closing: A Case Study of the Impacted Employee and the Community." *Where is my Home?* Mimeographed. Scottsdale, Arizona; N.T.I.S., 1974, 125–140.

KELSO, R. W. *The History of Public Poor Relief in Massachusetts 1620–1920.* Boston and New York: Houghton-Mifflin, 1922.

KIRKBRIDE, THOMAS S. *On the Construction, Organization, and General Arrangements of Hospitals for the Insane, with some Remarks on Insanity and its Treatment.* 2nd ed. Philadelphia: Lippincott, 1880.

KITTRIE, NICHOLAS. *The Right to be Different: Deviance and Enforced Therapy.* Baltimore: Johns Hopkins University Press, 1971.

KLEIN, D. F. and J. M. DAVIS. *Diagnosis and Drug Treatment of Psychiatric Disorders.* Baltimore: Williams and Wilkens, 1969.

KLERMAN, G. "Psychotropic Hedonism vs. Pharmacological Calvinism." *Hastings Center Report,* 2 (1972), 1–3.

————· "Psychotropic Drugs as Therapeutic Agents." *Hastings Center Studies,* 2, No. 1 (January 1974), 81–93.

KOSHEL, JEFFREY. *Deinstitutionalization—Dependent and Neglected Children.* Washington D.C.: The Urban Institute, 1973.

KRAMER, M. and POLLACK, E. S. "Problems in the Interpretation of Trends in the Population Movement of the Public Mental Hospitals." *American Journal of Public Health,* 48 (1958), 1003–1019.

LA FAVE, W. R. *Arrest: The Decision to Take a Suspect into Custody.* Boston: Little, Brown, 1964.

LAMB, H. R. and V. GOERTZEL. "Discharged Mental Patients — Are They Really in the Community?" *Archives of General Psychiatry,* 24 (1971), 29–34.

——— · "The Demise of the State Hospital — A Premature Obituary?" *International Journal of Psychiatry,* 11 (1973), 239–256.

Leavesden Asylum, *Annual Reports,* 1876–85.

LEHMANN, H. E. and G. E. HANRAHAN. "Chlorpromazine: New Inhibiting Agent for Psychomotor Excitement and Manic States." *Archives of Neurology and Psychiatry,* 71 (1954), 227–237.

LEMERT, EDWIN. *Social Pathology.* New York: McGraw-Hill, 1951.

——— · *Human Deviance, Social Problems, and Social Control.* Englewood Cliffs, N.J.: Prentice-Hall Inc., 1967. 2nd ed. 1972.

——— · *Instead of Court: Diversion in Juvenile Justice.* Washington D.C.: U.S. Public Health Service, Publication # 2127, 1971.

LENTZ, R. J., G. L. PAUL, and J. F. CALHOUN. "Reliability and Validity of Three Measures of Functioning with 'Hard-Core' Chronic Mental Patients." *Journal of Abnormal Psychology,* 78 (1971), 69–76.

LEONARD, E. M. *The Early History of English Poor Relief.* Cambridge: Cambridge University Press, 1900.

LERMAN, P. "Evaluating Studies of Institutions for Delinquents: Implications for Research and Social Policy." *Social Work,* 13 (1968), 55–64.

——— · *Community Treatment and Social Control.* Chicago: University of Chicago Press, 1975.

LEVETON, A. F., "The Evaluation and Testing of Psychopharmaceutical Drugs." *American Journal of Psychiatry,* 115 (1958), 232–238.

LEWIS, AUBREY. in P. B. Bradley, P. Deniker, and C. Raducco-Thomas, eds. *Neuropsychopharmacology Vol. 1.* Amsterdam: Elsevier, 1959, 207–212.

LEWIS, O. F. *The Development of American Prisons and Prison Customs, 1776–1845.* New York: Prison Association of New York, 1922. Reprinted Montclair, N.J.: Patterson-Smith, 1967.

LEWIS, W. D. *From Newgate to Dannemora: The Rise of the Penitentiary in New York, 1796–1848.* Ithaca: Cornell University Press, 1965.

LIAZOS, A. "The Poverty of the Sociology of Deviance: Nuts, Sluts, and Preverts." *Social Problems,* 20 (1972), 103–120.

——— · "Class Oppression: The Functions of Juvenile Justice." *The Insurgent Sociologist,* 5 (Fall 1974), 2–24.

LINDESMITH, A. *The Addict and the Law.* New York: Vintage Books, 1965.

LINN, E. L. "Drug Therapy, Milieu Change, and Release from a Mental Hospital." *A.M.A. Archives of Neurology,* 81 (1959), 785–794.

LORBER, J. "Deviance as Performance: The Case of Illness." *Social Problems,* 14 (1967), 302–310.

LUBOVE, R. *The Professional Altruist*. New York: Atheneum, 1971.

LUKES, STEVEN. "Methodological Individualism Reconsidered." *British Journal of Sociology*, 19 (1968), 119–129.

———· *Individualism*. Oxford: Blackwell, 1973.

MACFARLAN, JOHN. *Inquiries Concerning the Poor*. Edinburgh: Longman and Dickson, 1782.

MALTHUS, T. R. *An Essay on the Principle of Population*. London: Johnson, 1798. (London: Penguin edition 1970; also 6th edition, London: Murray, 1826).

MANTOUX, PAUL. *The Industrial Revolution in the Eighteenth Century*. London: Cape, 1928.

MARKSON, E. and J. H. CUMMING. "The Post-Transfer Fate of Relocated Patients in New York." *Where is my Home?* Mimeographed. Scottsdale, Arizona; N.T.I.S., 1974, 98–107.

———· A. KWOH, and E. CUMMING. "Alternatives to Hospitalization for Psychiatrically Ill Geriatric Patients." *American Journal of Psychiatry*, 127 (1971), 1055–1062.

MARLOWE, R. A. "When they Closed the Doors at Modesto." *Where is my Home?* Mimeographed. Scottsdale, Arizona; N.T.I.S., 1974, 110–124.

MARSHALL, ALFRED. *Principles of Economics*. 8th ed. New York: MacMillan, 1920.

MARSHALL, DOROTHY. *The English Poor in the Eighteenth Century*. London: Routledge, 1926.

MARX, KARL. *Capital*. 3 vols. New York: International Publishers, 1967.

———· and FREDERICK ENGELS. "The Communist Manifesto." *Selected Works*. New York: International Publishers, 1968.

MASON, A., I. S. FORREST, and F. M. FORREST. "Adherence to Maintenance Therapy and Rehospitalization." *Diseases of the Nervous System*, 24 (1963), 103–104.

Massachusetts State Board of Charities, *Annual Reports*, 1864–1878.

Massachusetts State Board of Health, Lunacy, and Charity, *Annual Reports* 1879–1885. Boston: Wright and Potter.

MASSIE, JOSEPH. *Plan for the Establishment of Charity Houses*. London, 1758.

MATZA, DAVID. *Becoming Deviant*. Englewood Cliffs, N.J.: Prentice-Hall, Inc., 1969.

MAUDSLEY, HENRY. *The Physiology and Pathology of the Mind*. London: 1867. American Edition. New York: Appleton, 1871.

MCKELVEY. B. *American Prisons: A Study in American Social History Prior to 1915*. Chicago: University of Chicago Press, 1936.

MECHANIC, DAVID. "Some Factors in Identifying and Defining Mental Illness." *Mental Hygiene*, 46 (1962), 66–74.

————· *Mental Health and Social Policy.* Englewood Cliffs, N.J.: Prentice-Hall Inc., 1969.

MENCHER, S. *Poor Law to Poverty Program: Economic Security Policy in Britain and the United States.* Pittsburgh: The University of Pittsburgh Press, 1967.

MENDEL, WERNER M. "Dismantling the Mental Hospital." *Where is my Home?* Mimeographed. Scottsdale, Arizona; N.T.I.S., 1974, 18–27.

MENNEL, R. M. *Thorns and Thistles: Juvenile Delinquents in the States 1825–1940.* Hanover, N.H.: University Press of New England, 1973.

MESSINGER, SHELDON. "Strategies of Control." Unpublished Ph.D. dissertation, University of California, Berkeley, 1968.

MEYERS, MARVIN. *The Jacksonian Persuasion.* Stanford: Stanford University Press. 1957.

MILLER, ALAN D. "New York in Action." *Where is my Home?* Mimeographed. Scottsdale, Arizona; N.T.I.S., 1974, 53–60.

MILLER, JEROME. "The Politics of Change: Correctional Reform." in Y. Bakal, ed. *Closing Correctional Institutions.* Lexington: Lexington Books, 1973, 3–8.

MILLER, MARTIN B. "At Hard Labor: Rediscovering the Nineteenth Century Prison." *Issues in Criminology,* 9 (1974), 91–114.

MILLS, C. WRIGHT. "The Professional Ideology of Social Pathologists." *American Journal of Sociology,* 49 (1943), 165–180.

M.I.N.D. *Community Care Provisions for the Mentally Ill.* M.I.N.D. Report # 4, National Association for Mental Health. London, 1971.

MITCHELL, S. WEIR. "Address before the American Medico-Psychological Association." Philadelphia, 1894.

MOFFETT, JOHN. "Bureaucracy and Social Control: A Study of the Progressive Regimentation of the Western Social Order." Unpublished Ph.D. dissertation, Columbia University, 1971.

MOUNTNEY, G. "Local Authority Psychiatric Hostels." *British Journal of Psychiatric Social Work,* 10 (1965), 20–26.

MULHEARN, JOHN. "Closing State Hospitals: Accreditation as a Factor." *Where is my Home?* Mimeographed. Scottsdale, Arizona: N.T.I.S., 1974, 151–159.

MYERS, J. and L. BEAN. *A Decade Later: A Follow-up of Social Class and Mental Disorder.* New York: John Wiley, 1968.

National Advisory Commission on Criminal Justice Standards and Goals. *Report on Corrections.* Washington D.C.: Government Printing Office, 1973.

National Association for Mental Health, *Report of the Annual Conference,* London: M.I.N.D., 1961.

National Institute of Law Enforcement and Criminal Justice. *Community Based Corrections in Des Moines.* Washington D.C.: U.S. Department of Justice, n.d.

National Prisoner Statistics. *Prisoners in State and Federal Institutions for Adult Felons 1967.* Washington D.C.: U.S. Department of Justice, July 1969.

N.I.M.H. Pharmacology Service Center, Collaborative Study Group. "Pheno-thiazine Treatment in Acute Schizophrenia—Effectiveness." *Archives of General Psychiatry,* 10 (1964), 246–261.

N.I.M.H. *Statistical Notes # 1 - # 114.* Rockville, Maryland, N.I.M.H. 1968–1975.

NICOLAUS, M. "Proletariat and Middle Class in Marx." *Studies on the Left,* 7 (January–February 1967), 22–49.

NIMMER, RAYMOND. *Two Million Unnecessary Arrests.* Washington D.C.: American Bar Foundation, n.d.

NORTH, D. *The Economic Growth of the United States, 1790–1860.* Englewood Cliffs, N.J.: Prentice-Hall Inc., 1961.

North American Review. "Statistics of Insanity in Massachusetts." 82 (1856), 78–100.

NUNALLY, J. C. *Popular Conceptions of Mental Health.* New York: Holt, 1961.

O'CONNOR, JAMES. "Some Contradictions of Advanced U.S. Capitalism." *Social Theory and Practice,* 1 (Spring 1970), 1–11.

————· *The Fiscal Crisis of the State.* New York: St. Martin's Press, 1973.

O.E.C.D. "Public Expenditure Trends." *Occasional Studies,* July 1970.

OHLIN, L. *Prisoners in America.* Englewood Cliffs, N.J.: Prentice-Hall Inc., 1973.

OWEN, D. *English Philanthropy 1660–1960.* Cambridge, Mass.: Harvard University Press, 1964.

OXLEY, G. W. *Poor Relief in England and Wales 1601–1834.* Newton Abbot: David and Charles, 1974.

PARRY-JONES, W. Ll. *The Trade in Lunacy: A Study of Private Madhouses in England in the Eighteenth and Nineteenth Centuries.* London: Routledge and Kegan Paul, 1972.

PAUL, G. L., L. L. TOBIAS, and B. L. HOLLY. "Maintenance Psychotropic Drugs in the Presence of Active Treatment Programs. A 'Triple-Blind' Withdrawal Study with Long-Term Mental Patients." *Archives of General Psychiatry,* 27 (1972), 106–115.

Pennsylvania. *Annual Reports of the Board of Commissioners of Public Charities of the State of Pennsylvania.* Harrisburg, Pa.: 1870.

PERKIN, H. *The Origins of Modern English Society 1780–1880.* London: Routledge and Kegan Paul, 1969.

PESSEN. E. *Jacksonian America: Society, Personality, and Politics.* Homewood, Ill.: Dorsey, 1969.

PETTIBONE, J. M. "Community-Based Programs: Catching up with Yesterday and Planning for Tomorrow." *Federal Probation,* 37 (1973), 3–8.

PHILLIPS, ERASMUS. *The State of the Nation.* London, 1725.

PIVEN, F. and R. CLOWARD. *Regulating the Poor.* New York: Random House, 1971.

PLATT, ANTHONY M. *The Child-Savers: The Invention of Delinquency.* Chicago: University of Chicago Press, 1969.

POLANYI, KARL. *The Great Transformation.* New York: Rinehart, 1944. Paperback edition, Boston: Beacon, 1957.

POLLACK, E. S. and C. A. TAUBE. "Trends and Projections in State Hospital Use." Mimeographed. Paper presented at the Symposium on the Future Role of the State Mental Hospital, SUNY Buffalo, October 11, 1973.

POLSKY, H. "Vision and Process: The Quality of Life in Community Group Homes." in Y. Bakal, ed. *Closing Correctional Institutions.* Lexington: Lexington Books, D.C. Heath and Company, 1973, 59–66.

POMERANTZ, S. I. *New York—An American City 1783–1803. A Study of Urban Life.* New York: Columbia University Press, 1938.

Poor Law Report. *Report of the Royal Commission on the Poor Laws.* London, 1834.

POTTER, ROBERT. *Observations on the Poor Laws.* London, 1775.

PUGH, R. B. *Imprisonment in Medieval England.* Cambridge: Cambridge University Press, 1968.

RAPPAPORT, MAURICE, H.K. HOPKINS, K. HALL, T. BELLEZA, J. SILVERSTEIN. "Schizophrenics for whom Phenothiazines may be Contraindicated or Unnecessary." Mimeographed. Langley Porter Neuropsychiatric Institute, University of California, 1975.

RAY, ISAAC. *Mental Hygiene.* Boston: Ticknor and Fields, 1863.

REES, T. P. "Some Observations on the Psychiatric Patient, the Mental Hospital, and the Community." in M. Greenblatt, D. J. Levinson, and R. H. Williams, eds. *The Patient and the Mental Hospital.* Glencoe, Ill.: Free Press, 1957, 527–529.

REHIN, G. and F. M. MARTIN. *Psychiatric Services in 1975.* PEP vol. 29, No. 468, 1963.

REICH, ROBERT and LLOYD SIEGAL. "Psychiatry under Seige: The Chronic Mentally Ill Shuffle to Oblivion." in *Psychiatric Annals,* 3 (1973), 37–55.

REID, JOHN. *Essays on Insanity, Hypochondriacal and Other Nervous Affections.* London: Longman, Hurst, Rees, Orme, and Brown, 1816.

RIMLINGER, GASTON. "Welfare Policy and Economic Development: A Comparative Historical Perspective." *Journal of Economic History,* 26 (1966), 556–571.

———· *Welfare Policy and Industrialization in Europe, America, and Russia.* New York: Wiley, 1971.

ROBERTSON, ANDREW G. "The California Plan." *Where is my Home?* Mimeographed. Scottsdale, Arizona: N.T.I.S. 1974, 61–73.

ROBINSON, W. H., P. SMITH and J. WOLF. *Prison Populations and Costs— Illustrative Projections to 1980.* Washington D.C.: Library of Congress, Congressional Research Service, April 24, 1974.

ROBISON, J. and G. SMITH. "The Effectiveness of Correctional Programs." *Crime and Delinquency*, 17 (1971), 67–80.

ROCK, PAUL. "The Sociology of Deviancy and Conceptions of Moral Order." *British Journal of Criminology*, 14 (1974), 139–149.

———· and MARY MCINTOSH, eds. *Deviance and Social Control.* London: Tavistock, 1974.

ROSENBERG, CHARLES. *The Trial of the Assassin Guiteau.* Chicago: University of Chicago Press, 1968.

ROTHMAN, DAVID. *The Discovery of the Asylum.* Boston: Little Brown, 1971.

———· "Decarcerating Prisoners and Patients." *The Civil Liberties Review*, 1 (1973), 8–30.

Royal College of Physicians. *Report by the Committee on Psychological Medicine of the Royal College of Physicians.* London, January 1963.

RUBINGTON, E. and M. WEINBERG, eds. *Deviance: The Interactionist Perspective.* New York: MacMillan, 1968.

RUSCHE, G. and O. KIRCHHEIMER. *Punishment and Social Structure.* New York: Russell and Russell, 1968.

RYAN, M. V. *California Prisoners 1969.* Sacramento: California Department of Corrections, n.d.

SAINZ, A., N. BIGELOW and C. BARWISE. "On a Methodology for the Clinical Evaluation of Phrenopraxic Drugs." *Psychiatric Quarterly*, 31 (1957), 10–16.

SANBOURNE, F.B. *Dr. S. G. Howe—The Philanthropist.* New York: Funk and Wagnalls, 1891.

SCHEFF, T. *Being Mentally Ill: A Sociological Theory.* Chicago: Aldine, 1966.

SCHRAG, PETER and DIANE DIVORKY. *The Myth of the Hyperactive Child and Other Means of Child Control.* New York: Pantheon, 1975.

SCHULBERG, H. C. "From Institutions to Human Services." in Y. Bakal, ed. *Closing Correctional Institutions.* Lexington Mass.: Lexington Books, D.C. Heath and Company 1973, 39–48.

SCHUMACH, M. "Halfway Houses for Former Mental Patients Create Serious Problems for City's Residential Communities." *New York Times*, January 21, 1974: 31, Columns 1–4.

SCHUR, EDWIN. *Labeling Deviant Behavior: Its Sociological Implications.* New York: Harper and Row, 1971.

SCOTT, R. A. *The Making of Blind Men.* New York: Russell Sage, 1969.

SCULL, ANDREW T. "Museums of Madness: The Social Organization of Insanity in Nineteenth Century England." Unpublished Ph.D. dissertation, Princeton University, 1974.

————· "From Madness to Mental Illness: Medical Men as Moral Entrepreneurs." *European Journal of Sociology*, 16 (Fall 1975a), 218–261.

————· "Cyclical Trends in Psychiatric Practices: The Case of Bettelheim and Tuke." *Social Science and Medicine*, 9 (1975b), 633–640.

Second Convention of Managers and Superintendents of Houses of Refuge and Schools of Reform, *Proceedings*, 1859.

SEGAL, S. P. "Life in Board and Care: Its Political and Social Context." *Where is my Home?* Mimeographed. Scottsdale, Arizona; N.T.I.S. 1974, 141–150.

SHARFSTEIN, S. "Mentally Ill Aged and Neighborhood Health Centers." Paper presented at the 127th Annual Meeting of the American Psychiatric Association, New York: May 1974.

SHRYOCK, R. *Medicine and Society in America 1660–1860*. New York: New York University Press, 1960.

SILBERSTEIN, S. O. *A Survery of the Mental Health Functions of the Systems of Residential Home Care for the Mentally Ill and Retarded in the Sacramento Area*. Mimeographed 1969.

SILVER, A. "The Demand for Order in Civil Society: A Review of Some Themes in the History of Urban Crime, Police, and Riot." in D. Bordua, ed. *The Police*. New York: Wiley, 1967.

SILVER, MORRIS. "Punishment, Deterrence and Police Effectiveness: A Survey and Critical Interpretation of the Recent Econometric Literature." A Report Prepared for the Crime Deterrence and Offender Career Project. New York, 1974.

SKOLNICK, J. *Justice Without Trial*. New York: John Wiley, 1966.

SMITH, ADAM. *The Wealth of Nations*. London: Original edition 1776. New York: Modern Library, 1937.

SMITH, ROBERT. *A Quiet Revolution—Probation Subsidy*. Washington D.C.: U.S. Department of Health, Education, and Welfare, 1971.

SPENCER, HERBERT. *Social Statics*. London: Williams and Norgate, 1868.

SPITZER, STEVEN. "Toward a Marxian Theory of Deviance." *Social Problems*, 22 (1975), 638–651.

————· *Deviance and Control in American Society: A Critical Perspective*. Englewood Cliffs, N.J.: Prentice-Hall, forthcoming.

SROUFFE, L. A. and M. A. STEWART. "Treating Problem Children with Stimulant Drugs." *New England Journal of Medicine*, 289 (August 23, 1973), 407–412.

STALLARD, J. H. "Pauper Lunatics and their Treatment." *Transactions of the National Association for the Promotion of Social Science*, (1870), 465–477.

STANTON, A. H. and M. S. SCHWARTZ. *The Mental Hospital: A Study of Institutional Participation in Psychiatric Illness and Treatment.* New York: Basic Books Inc., 1954.

STARK, W. *Remarks on the Construction of Public Hospitals for the Cure of Mental Derangement.* Glasgow: Hedderwick, 1810.

STEER, D. "Young Adult Offenders: II Control in the Community." *British Journal of Criminology,* 14 (1974), 396–399.

STEPHEN, LESLIE. *The English Utiltarians.* 2 vols. London: Duckworth, 1900.

STEWART, A., H. G. LAFAVE, F. GRUNBERG, and M. HERJANIC. "Problems in Phasing out a Large Psychiatric Hospital." *American Journal of Psychiatry,* 125 (1968), 82–88.

STOKES, H. K. *The Finances and Administration of Providence.* Baltimore: Johns Hopkins, 1903.

SUDNOW, DAVID. "Normal Crimes: Sociological Features of the Penal Code in a Public Defender Office." *Social Problems,* 12 (1965), 255–276.

SYKES, GRESHAM. *Society of Captives.* Princeton, N.J.: Princeton University Press, 1958.

SWAZEY, JUDITH. *Chlorpromazine in Psychiatry: A Study of Therapeutic Innovation.* Cambridge, Mass.: M.I.T. Press, 1974.

SZASZ, T. *Law, Liberty, and Psychiatry.* New York: MacMillan, 1963.

———. *Psychiatric Justice.* New York: MacMillan, 1965.

TAKAGI, PAUL. "The Correctional System." *Crime and Social Justice,* 2 (1974), 82–89.

Task Force Report: Corrections. The President's Commission on Law Enforcement and the Administration of Justice. Washington D.C.: U.S. Government Printing Office, 1967.

TAYLOR, I., P. WALTON, and J. YOUNG. *The New Criminology.* New York: Harper and Row, 1973.

TAYLOR, L. and TAYLOR I. "We are all Deviants Now." *International Socialism,* 34 (1968), 28–32.

TEMPLE, WILLIAM. *An Essay on Trade and Commerce.* London, 1770.

THOMAS, KEITH. *Religion and the Decline of Magic.* London: Penguin, 1971.

THOMPSON, E. P. *The Making of the English Working Class.* New York: Vintage Books, 1963.

TOOTH, G. C. and E. M. BROOKE. "Trends in the Mental Hospital Population and their Effect on Future Planning." *The Lancet,* (April 1, 1961), 710–713.

[TOWNSEND, JOSEPH]. *A Dissertation on the Poor Laws, by a Well-wisher of Mankind.* London, 1786.

TROTTER, S. "The Mentally Ill: From Back Wards to Back Alleys." *The Washington Post,* February 24, 1974: 19.

U.S. Bureau of the Census, *Statistical Abstract of the United States.* Washington D.C.: Government Printing Office, 1970.

U.S. Department of Commerce, Bureau of the Census. *Pharmaceutical Preparations, Except Biologicals, 1969.* Washington D.C.: 1971.

Vera Institute of Justice, *Ten Year Report, 1961–1971.* New York: May 1972.

VORENBERG, E. and J. VORENBERG. "Early Diversion From the Criminal Justice System: Practice in Search of a Theory." in L. Ohlin, ed. *Prisoners in America.* Englewood Cliffs, N.J.: Prentice-Hall Inc., 1973, 151–183.

WAKEFIELD, E. "Plan of an Asylum for Lunatics, Etc." *The Philanthropist,* 2 (1812), 226–229.

WALLERSTEIN, IMMANUEL. *The Modern World System.* New York: Academic Press, 1974.

WARD, D. "Evaluative Research for Corrections." in L. Ohlin, ed. *Prisoners in America.* Englewood Cliffs, N.J.: Prentice-Hall Inc., 1973, 184–206.

WATT, D. and D. BUGLASS. "The Effects of Clinical and Social Factors on the Discharge of Chronic Psychiatric Patients." *Social Psychiatry,* 1 (1966), 57–63.

WEBB, BEATRICE and SIDNEY WEBB. *English Prisons Under Local Government.* London, Longmans, Green, 1922.

———· *English Poor Law History, Part I: The Old Poor Law.* Longmans, Green, London, 1927.

WEBER, ADNA FERRIN. *The Growth of Cities in the Nineteenth Century: A Study in Statistics.* New York: Columbia University Studies in History, Economics, and Public Law No. 11, 1899.

WEBER, MAX. *The Protestant Ethic and the Spirit of Capitalism.* London: Allen and Unwin, 1930.

———· *From Max Weber: Essays in Sociology.* London: Oxford University Press, 1946.

———· *General Economic History.* New York: Collier, 1961.

———· *Economy and Society.* 3 vols. Totowa, N.J.: Bedminster Press, 1968.

WEINER, S. "The Impact on Staff and Community of a State Hospital Closing." *Where is my Home?* Mimeographed. Scottsdale, Arizona: N.T.I.S., 1974, 87–97.

WEIR, JAMES. "Criminal Anthropology." *Medical Record,* 45 (January 13, 1894), 42–45.

WEST, D. J. "Report of the Parole Board for 1971." *British Journal of Criminology,* 13 (1973), 56–59.

Where is my Home? Proceedings of a Conference on the Closing of State Mental Hospitals. Scottsdale, Arizona; N.T.I.S., 1974.

WILKINS, E. T. *Insanity and Insane Asylums: Report of E. T. Wilkins M.D., Commissioner in Lunacy for the State of California.* Sacramento: T. A. Springer, 1872.

WILLS, GARY. "The Human Sewer." *The New York Review of Books,* 22 (April 3, 1975), 3–8.

WING, J. K. "Institutionalism in Mental Hospitals." *British Journal of Social and Clinical Psychology,* 1 (1962), 38.

―――. "How Many Psychiatric Beds?" *Psychological Medicine,* 1 (1971), 188–190. New York: Cambridge University Press.

―――· and G. W. BROWN. *Institutionalism and Schizophrenia.* Cambridge: Cambridge University Press, 1970.

WING, J. K., J. DENHAM, and A. B. MONRO. "The Duration of Stay in Hospital of Patients Suffering From Schizophrenia." *Journal of Preventive and Social Medicine,* 13 (1959), 145.

WOLFGANG, MARVIN E. "Cesare Lombroso." in Herman Mannheim, ed. *Pioneers in Criminology.* London: Stevens, 1960, 168–227.

WOLPERT, JULIAN and EILEEN R. WOLPERT. "The Relocation of Released Mental Hospital Patients into Residential Communities." Mimeographed. Princeton: Princeton University, 1974.

―――· "The Relocation of Released Mental Hospital Patients into Residential Communities." *Policy Sciences* (Spring 1976).

Worcester State Lunatic Hospital, *Annual Reports.* 1865–75.

Younger Report. *Young Adult Offenders: Report of the Advisory Council on the Penal System.* London: Her Majesty's Stationery Office, 1974.

ZINBERG, N. E. "Unsafe at Any Speed." *New York Review of Books,* (October 30, 1975), 32–33.

AFTERWORD

A.F.S.C.M.E. *Out of Their Beds and Into the Streets.* Washington D.C.: American Federation of State, County, and Municipal Employees, 1975.

ABEL, RICHARD. "From the Editor." *Law and Society Review,* 12 (1978), 333.

ALLEN, FRANCIS. *The Decline of the Rehabilitative Ideal: Penal Policy and Social Purpose.* New Haven: Yale University Press, 1981.

American Behavioral Scientist. Special Issue on New Forms of Social Control: The Myth of Deinstitutionalization. 24, # 6 (1981).

American Friends Service Committee. *Struggle for Justice.* New York: Hill and Wang, 1972.

ARNHOFF, F. "Social Consequences of Policy Toward Mental Illness." *Science,* 188 (1975), 1277 – 1281.

AUSTIN, JAMES and KRISBERG, BARRY. "Wider, Stronger, and Different Nets: The Dialectics of Criminal Justice Reform." *Journal of Research in Crime and Delinquency,* 18 (1981), 165 – 196.

―――· . "The Unmet Promise of Alternatives to Incarceration." *Crime and Delinquency,* 28 (1982), 374 – 409.

AVIRAM, URI, SYME, S.L., COHEN, J.B. "The Effects of Policies and Programs on Reduction of Mental Hospitalization." *Social Science and Medicine*, 10 (1976), 571 – 577.

BASSUK, E. and GERSON, S. "Deinstitutionalization and the Mental Health Services." *Scientific American*, 238 (1978), 46 – 53.

BAYER, RONALD. "Crime, Punishment, and the Decline of Liberal Optimism." *Crime and Delinquency*, (1981), 169 – 190.

BLOMBERG, T. "Diversion and Accelerated Social Control." *Journal of Criminal Law and Criminology*, 68 (1977), 274 – 282.

———— . "Widening the Net: An Anomaly in the Evaluation of Diversion Programs" in Malcolm Klein and Katherine Teilmann (eds) *Handbook of Criminal Justice Evaluation* Beverley Hills, California: Sage, 1980.

BORUS, J.F. "Deinstitutionalization of the Chronically Mentally Ill." *New England Journal of Medicine*, 305 # 6 (1981), 339 – 342.

BOTTOMS, ANTHONY E. "Neglected Features of Contemporary Penal Systems." in David Garland and Peter Young (eds) *The Power to Punish*. London: Heinemann/New York: Humanities Press, 1983, 166 – 202.

BREYER, STEPHEN. *Regulation and its Reform*. Cambridge, Mass.: Harvard University Press, 1982.

C.S.E.A. *Where Have All the Patients Gone?* Sacramento: California State Employees Association, 1972.

CHAN, JANET and ERICSON, RICHARD. *Decarceration and the Economy of Penal Reform*. Toronto: Research Report # 14, University of Toronto Centre of Criminology, 1981.

CHU, FRANKLIN and TROTTER, SHARLAND. *The Madness Establishment*. New York: Grossman, 1974.

COATES, ROBERT and MILLER, ALDEN. "Neutralization of Community Resistance to Group Homes." in Y. Bakal (ed.) *Closing Correctional Institutions*. Lexington, Mass.: Lexington Books, 1973.

COHEN, STANLEY. *Folk Devils and Moral Panics*. London: Paladin, 1972.

———— . "The Punitive City: Notes on the Dispersal of Social Control." *Contemporary Crises*, 3 (1979), 339 – 363.

———— . "Social Control Talk: Telling Stories About Correctional Change." in David Garland and Peter Young (eds) *The Power to Punish*. London: Heinemann, 1983.

———— . *The Future of Social Control* Oxford: Martin Robertson, forthcoming 1984.

CRESSEY, D. and McDERMOTT, R. *Diversion from the Juvenile Justice System*. Washington, D.C.: National Institute of Law Enforcement and Criminal Justice, 1974.

DAVIS, J.M. "Organic Therapies." in H.I. Kaplan, A.M. Freedman, and B.J. Sadock (eds) *Comprehensive Textbook of Psychiatry III* Baltimore: Williams and Wilkins, 1981.

DAVIS, A., DINITZ, S., and PASAMANICK, B. *Schizophrenics in the New Custodial Community*. Columbus: Ohio State University Press, 1974.

DEUTSCH, ALBERT, *The Shame of the States*, New York: Arno, 1973.

DITTON, JASON, *CONTROLOLOGY*, London: Macmillan, 1979.

DOWNS, G. *Bureaucracy, Innovation, and Social Policy*. Lexington, Mass.: Lexington Books, 1978.

EBRINGER, L. and CHRISTIE-BROWN, J.R.W. "Social Deprivation among Short Stay Psychiatric Patients." *British Journal of Psychiatry*, 136 (1980), 46 – 52.

EBRINGER, L. and CHRISTIE-BROWN, J.R.W. "Social Deprivation among Short Stay Psychiatric Patients." *British Journal of Psychiatry*, 136 (1980), 46 – 52.

EMERSON, ROBERT, ROCHFORD, E.B., and SHAW, LINDA L. "Economics and Enterprise in Board and Care Homes for the Mentally Ill." *American Behavioral Scientist*, 24 (1981), 771 – 785.

ESTROFF, SUE. "Psychiatric Deinstitutionalization: A Socio-Cultural Analysis." *Journal of Social Issues*, 37 # 3 (1981), 116 – 132.

FLYNN, E.E. "Classification for Risk and Supervision: A Preliminary Conceptualization." in John Freeman (ed.) *Prisons Past and Future*. London: Heinemann, 1978.

FOGEL, D. *We Are the Living Proof: The Justice Model for Corrections*. Cincinnati: Anderson, 1975.

FREIDSON, ELIOT. *Profession of Medicine*, New York: Dodd, Mead, 1970.

GARDOS, G. and COLE, J. "Maintenance Antipsychotic Therapy: Is the Cure Worse Than the Disease?" *American Journal of Psychiatry*, 133 (1976), 32 – 36.

GAYLIN, WILLARD. *Partial Justice*. New York: Knopf, 1974.

General Accounting Office. *The Mentally Ill in the Community: Government Needs To Do More*. Washington, D.C.: Government Printing Office, 1977.

GOLDMAN, H.H., GATTOZZI, A.A., and TAUBE, C.A. "Defining and Counting the Chronically Mentally Ill." *Hospital and Community Psychiatry*, 32 (1981), 21 – 27.

GOLDSTEIN, MICHAEL. Review of Andrew Scull's, *Decarceration. Contemporary Sociology*, 11 (1982).

GREENBERG, DAVID. "Problems in Community Corrections." *Issues in Criminology*, 19 (1975), 1 – 34.

——— . "Delinquency and the Age Structure of Society." *Contemporary Crises*, 1 (1977).

——— . and HUMPHRIES, DREW. "The Cooptation of Fixed Sentencing Reform." *Crime and Delinquency*, 26 (1979), 206 – 225.

GROB, GERALD. *Mental Illness and American Society 1875 – 1940*. Princeton, New Jersey: Princeton University Press, 1983.

GRUENBERG, E. and ARCHER, J. "Abandonment of Responsibility for the Seriously Mentally Ill." *Milbank Memorial Fund Quarterly*, 57 (1979), 485 – 506.

HALL, S., CRITCHLEY, C., JEFFERSON, A., CLARKE, S., and ROBERT, B. *Policing the Crisis: Mugging, the State, Law and Order*. London: Macmillan, 1978.

HYLTON, JOHN. "The Growth of Punishment: Imprisonment and Community Corrections in Canada." *Crime and Social Justice*, 15 (1981a), 18 – 28.

——— . *Reintegrating the Offender: Assessing the Impact of Community Corrections* Washington, D.C.: University Press of America, 1981b.

——— . "Community Corrections and Social Control: The Case of Saskatchewan, Canada." *Contemporary Crises*, 5 (1981c), 193 – 215.

——— . "Rhetoric and Reality; A Critical Appraisal of Community Correctional Programs." *Crime and Delinquency*, 26 (1982), 341 – 373.

HYNES, C. *Private Proprietary Homes for Adults: Their Administration, Management, Control, Operation, Supervision, Funding, and Quality*, New York: Deputy Attorney General's Office, 1977.

JACOBS, JAMES. *New Perspectives on Prisons and Imprisonment*. Ithaca: Cornell University Press, 1983a.

——— . "The Politics of Prison Construction" *Review of Law and Social Change*, (1983b) in press.

JESTE, D.V. and WYATT, R.J. "In Search of Treatment for Tardive Dyskinesia: A Review of the Literature." *Schizophrenia Bulletin*, 5 (1979), 251 – 293.

JONES, KATHLEEN. *Lunacy, Law, and Conscience, 1744 – 1845*. London: Routledge and Kegan Paul, 1955.

——— . "Deinstitutionalization in Context." *Milbank Memorial Fund Quarterly*, 57 (1979a), 552 – 569.

——— . "Integration of Disintegration in the Mental Health Services" *Journal of the Royal Society of Medicine*, 72 (1979b), 640 – 648.

——— . "Scull's Dilemma." *British Journal of Psychiatry*, 141 (1982).

Journal of Social Issues. Special Issue on Institutions and Alternatives. 37, # 3 (1981).

KAPLAN, LEONARD. "State Control of Deviant Behavior: A Critical Essay on Scull's Critique of Community Treatment and Deinstitutionalization." *Arizona Law Review* 20 (1978), 189 – 232.

KIELHOFNER, G. *Evaluating Deinstitutionalization: An Ethnographic Study of Social Policy*. Ph.D. dissertation, School of Public Health, University of California, Los Angeles, 1980.

KIRK, S. and THIERREN, M. "Community Mental Health Myths and the Fate of Former Hospitalized Patients." *Psychiatry*, 38 (1975), 209 – 217.

KITTRIE, NICHOLAS. *The Right to be Different*. Baltimore: Penguin, 1972.

KLEIN, MALCOLM (ed.) *The Juvenile Justice System*. Beverley Hills, California: Sage, 1976.

KORER, J. *Not the Same as You: The Social Situation of 190 Schizophrenics Living in the Community*. London: Psychiatric Rehabilitation Association, 1978.

LANGSLEY, DONALD G. "The Community Mental Health Center: Does It Treat Patients." *Hospital and Community Psychiatry*, 31 (1980), 815 – 819.

LEIFER, RONALD. *In the Name of Mental Health*. New York: Aronson, 1969.

LERMAN, PAUL. *Community Treatment and Social Control*. Chicago: University of Chicago Press, 1975.

——— . "Trends and Issues in the Deinstitutionalization of Youth in Trouble." *Crime and Delinquency*, 2 (1980), 281 – 298.

——— . *Deinstitutionalization and the Welfare State*. New Brunswick, New Jersey: Rutgers University Press, 1982.

LEVINE, MICHAEL. "Revisionism Revisited? Airline De-Regulation and the Public Interest." *Journal of Law and Contemporary Problems*, 44 (1981).

MARTINSON, ROBERT. "What Works? Questions and Answers About Prison Reform." *The Public Interest*, 35, 1974.

MATTHEWS, ROGER. *"Decarceration and the Fiscal Crisis."* in B. Fine et al. (eds) *Capitalism and the Rule of Law*. London: Hutchinson, 1979.

MESNIKOFF, A. "Barriers to the Delivery of Mental Health Services: The New York City Experience." *Hospital and Community Psychiatry*, 29 (1978), 373 – 378.

MESSINGER, SHELDON. "Confinement in the Community." *Journal of Research in Crime and Delinquency*, 13 (1976), 82 – 92.

Milbank Memorial Fund Quarterly. Special Issue on Deciphering Deinstitutionalization. 57 (1979).

MINTO, ALFRED. "Changing Clinical Practice, 1950 – 1980." in Philip Bean (ed.) *Mental Illness: Changes and Trends*. Chichester: John Wiley, 1983.

MOLLICA, RICHARD. "Community Mental Health Centres: An American Response to Kathleen Jones." *Journal of the Royal Society of Medicine*, 73 (1980), 863 – 870.

——— . "From Asylum to Community: The Threatened Disintegration of Public Psychiatry." *New England Journal of Medicine*, 308 (1983), 367 – 373.

MURASKIN, WILLIAM. "The Social Control Theory of History" *Journal of Social History*, 9 (1976), 559 – 565.

MURPHY, J. and DATEL, W. "A Cost-Benefit Analysis of Community Versus Institutional Living." *Hospital and Community Psychiatry*, 25 (1976), 165 – 170.

National Institute of Mental Health. *Statistical Notes*. Rockville, Maryland, 1975.

New Jersey State Commission of Investigation. *Abuses and Irregularities in New Jersey's Boarding Home Industry* Trenton, New Jersey: State Commission of Investigation, 1978.

ODEGARD, O. "Changes in the Prognosis of Functional Psychosis since the Days of Kraepelin." *British Journal of Psychiatry*, 113 (1967), 813 – 822.

ORLANS, H. "An American Death Camp." *Politics*, 5 (1948), 162 – 168.

PARRY-JONES, WILLIAM. *The Trade in Lunacy*. London: Routledge and Kegan Paul, 1972.

PELTZMAN, S. "Toward a More General Theory of Regulation." *Journal of Law and Economics*, 14 (1976).

POSNER, RICHARD. "Theories of Economic Regulation." *Bell Journal of Economics and Management Science*, 5 (1974).

RAWLS, WENDELL. *Cold Storage*. New York: Simon and Schuster, 1980.

ROLLIN, H. "From Patients Into Vagrants." *New Society*, January 15 (1970), 90 – 93.

——— . *British Medical Journal*, 1 (1979), 1775.

ROSE, S. "Deciphering Deinstitutionalization." *Milbank Memorial Fund Quarterly*, 57 (1979), 429 – 460.

ROTHMAN, DAVID *Conscience and Convenience: The Asylum and Its Alternatives in Progressive America*. Boston: Little, Brown, 1980.

RUTHERFORD, A. and BENGUR, O. *Community Based Alternatives to Juvenile Incarceration*. Washington, D.C.: Law Enforcement Assistance Administration, 1976.

SCULL, ANDREW. *Museums of Madness*. London: Allen Lane/New York: St Martin's Press, 1979.

——— . "A New Trade in Lunacy: The Recommodification of the Mental Patient." *American Behavioral Scientist*, 24 (1981a), 741 – 754.

——— . "Progressive Dreams, Progressive Nightmares: Social Control in Twentieth Century America" *Stanford Law Review*, 33 (1981b), 575 – 590.

——— . "Whose Dilemma? The Crisis of the Mental Health Services." *British Journal of Psychiatry*, 142 (1983a), 98.

——— . "Community Corrections: Panacea, Progress, or Pretence?" in David Garland and Peter Young (eds) *The Power to Punish*. London: Heinemann/New York: Humanities Press, 1983b.

SEDGWICK, PETER. *Psychopolitics*. London: Pluto Press, 1982.

SEGAL, S. "Life in Board and Care: Its Political and Social Context." in *Where is my Home?* Scottsdale, Arizona: NTIS, mimeographed, 1974.

——— . and AVIRAM, U. *The Mentally Ill in Community Based Sheltered Care*.

New York: Wiley, 1978.

SENATE SPECIAL COMMITTEE ON AGING. *Trends in Long Term Care: Hearings* Washington, D.C.: Government Printing Office, 1971.

——— . *The Role of Nursing Homes in Caring for Discharged Mental Patients.* Washington, D.C.: Government Printing Office, 1976.

SHEARING, C.D. and STENNING, P.C. "Modern Private Security: Its Growth and Implications." in M. Tonry and N. Morris (eds) *Crime and Justice: An Annual Review of Research*, Vol. 3. Chicago: University of Chicago Press, 1981.

SHEEHAN, D.N. and ATKINSON, J. "Comparative Cost of State Hospitals and Community Based Inpatient Care in Texas." *Hospital and Community Psychiatry*, 25 (1974), 242 – 244.

SOLOMAN, E.B., BAIRD, R., and EVERSTINE, L. "Assessing the Community Care of Chronic Psychotic Patients." *Hospital and Community Psychiatry*, 31 (1980), 113 – 116.

SPITZER, STEVEN and SCULL, ANDREW. "Privatization and State Control: The Case of the Private Police." *Social Problems*, 25 (1977), 18 – 29.

STEIN, L.I. and TEST, M.A. "Alternatives to Mental Hospital Treatment." *Archives of General Psychiatry*, 37 (1980), 392 – 397.

STIGLER, GEORGE. "The Theory of Economic Regulation." *Bell Journal of Economics and Management Science*, 2 (1971).

TALBOTT, J.A. "Toward a Public Policy on the Chronic Mental Patient." *American Journal of Orthopsychiatry*, 50 (1980), 43 – 53.

TEPPE, S.J. and HAAS, J.F. "Prevalence of Tardive Dyskinesia." *Journal of Clinical Psychiatry*, 40 (1979), 508 – 516.

TEST, M.A. "Effective Community Treatment of the Chronically Mentally Ill: What is Necessary?" *Journal of Social Issues*, 37 (1981), 71 – 86.

VAN DEN HAAG, E. *Punishing Criminals.* New York: Basic Books, 1975.

VAN, PUTTEN, T. and SPAR, J.E. "The Board and Care Home: Does it Deserve a Bad Press?" *Hospital and Community Psychiatry*, 30 (1979), 461 – 464.

VON HIRSCH, ANDREW. *Doing Justice.* New York: Hill and Wang, 1976.

WARNER, RICHARD. *Recovery from Schizophrenia.* New York: John Wiley, forthcoming.

WARREN, CAROL. "New Forms of Social Control: The Myth of Deinstitutionalization." *American Behavioral Scientist*, 24 (1981), 724 – 740.

WILSON, JAMES Q. *Thinking About Crime.* New York: Basic Books, 1975.

——— . "What Works? Revisited: New Findings on Criminal Rehabilitation." *The Public Interest*, 61 (1981), 3 – 17.

WING, JOHN K. "Planning and Evaluating Services for Chronically Handicapped Psychiatric Patients in the United Kingdom." in L.I. Stein and M.A. Test (eds) *Alternatives to Mental Hospital Treatment.* New York: Plenum, 1978.

WITKIN, M. *State and County Mental Hospitals, United States, 1973 – 74.* Washington, D.C.: Government Printing Office, 1976.

WOLD, J.T. and MENDES, R.G. "Innovation in an Inner City Arraignment Court." *Judicature,* 57 (1974).

World Health Organization. *Schizophrenia: An International Follow-Up Study.* New York: John Wiley, 1979.

Index

Able-bodied poor, 26 – 29
Act of Settlement of 1662, 19, 153
Aftercare facilities, 142
Aid to the Permanently and Totally
    Disabled, 166
Almshouses, 20
Alper, Benedict S., 43
Arlidge, John T., 106
Arrests, 44, 46
Asylums, *see* Mental hospitals
Ataraxic drugs, *see* Psychoactive
    drugs

Beard, 106
Becker, Howard S., 10 – 11
Bemis, 113
Boarding homes, 102, 103, 163 – 65
Bridewell, 16
Brill, H., 83 – 84
Bryant, J.H., 87
Bureaucratization of systems of
    social control, 29, 31

California, 50, 54 – 56, 69, 72 – 73,
    84 – 85, 100, 101, 143, 170,
    175
California Community Treatment
    Program, 100, 101, 143, 180
California Probation Subsidy
    Program, 50, 54 – 56, 143
Capitalism, 16, 24 – 27, 30 – 32,
    129, 131, 136 – 38, 152

Charity asylums, 21
Chlorpromazine, 80, 86, 87, 88,
    171
Clark, Sir James, 106
Classical liberalism, 129, 131
Clemmer, D., 97
Colonial America, 19 – 20
Community care, 161 – 62,
    168 – 69
Community psychiatrists, 98, 181
Community Treatment Programs,
    California, 100, 101, 103
Conolly, John, 107, 112
Cottage plan, 113
Cotton production, 23
Crime
    control, 175 – 83
    rates, 46, 100, 175 – 76, 177
Cure rates of mentally ill, 67, 106

Defoe, D., 20
Diagnostic parole, 48
Dickson, D., 10
Differentiation of deviance, 29
Diversionary schemes, 180
Drug companies, 80 – 81
Drug therapy, 77, 78, 79 – 89

Earle, Pliny, 127
Ecclesiastical responsibility, 18 – 19
Epstein, L. J., 84, 102
Erikson, Kai, 10

Ethnomethodological/
    phenomenological cult, 9

Federal Drug Administration, 80
Felonies, 45, 46, 48
Florida Parole and Probation
    Commission, 46 – 48
Foster care, 150
Foucault, Michel, 16

Gaols, *see* Prisons
Geriatric patients, 102 – 3, 140,
    148 – 51
Glick, B., 87
Goffman, Erving, 95, 96, 97, 104,
    107, 123
Gough, Ian, 136
Gouldner, Alvin W., 9, 43
Granville, Joseph Mortimer, 106,
    111
Greenblatt, M., 73
Group homes, 141

Halfway houses, 77, 150, 153, 179
Hamilton, M. W., 95
Hammond, William A., 106, 111
Hawaii, 165
Hill, George Nesse, 107, 112
Hoenig, J., 95
Hospitals
    decay of superstructure, 173 – 74
    in eighteenth century, 20
Howe, Samuel Gridley, 106, 112,
    113
Hurd, Henry M., 113

Industrial Revolution, 23
Insanity, *see* Mentally ill
Institutional peonage, 139
Institutionalization of social control
    systems, 20 – 22, 24 – 26,
    29 – 33
Insurance cover for mental
    disorders, 181

Joint Commission on Mental Illness
    and Health (1961), 81, 102

Jones, Maxwell, 52
Juvenile delinquents, 48, 50 – 56,
    58 – 59, 99 – 102, 109 – 10,
    124, 141

Kirchheimer, 0., 16

Labeling (societal reaction) theory,
    4 – 11
Lanterman Petris-Short Act (1967),
    140
Law Enforcement Assistance
    Administration, 45, 50
Lemert, Edwin, 5, 7 – 8, 11
Lewis, Aubrey, 82

Macmillan, Duncan, 96
Madhouses, 21
Mantoux, Paul, 24
Margolis, R., 87
Marijuana, 44
Marx, Karl, 25, 26, 137
Massachusetts
    mental hospitals, 111, 113 – 14
    nursing homes, 164
    reform schools, 50 – 53, 101, 142
Maudsley, Henry, 106, 125
Mead, George Herbert, 6
Mechanic, David, 22, 82
Medicaid, 166
Medicare, 150, 151, 166
Medieval period, 16 – 18
Mental hospitals
    admission policies, 148
    expenditures, 144 – 47
    failure of 19th century
        decarceration movement,
        124 – 31
    length of stay, 147, 148
    populations, 65 – 70, 144 – 45,
        149, 166 – 68, 169 – 73
    total institution, critique of,
        95 – 97, 99 – 100, 102,
        104 – 14
    welfare state and, 138 – 41, 144,
        147 – 48
Mentally ill, 30, 64 – 73, 77

cure rates, 67, 100
drug therapy, 79 – 89
Michigan, 150, 164
Miller, Jerome, 51 – 52, 53
Minimum security prisons, 45
Misdemeanors, 45, 46
Missouri, 165
Mitchell, S. Weir, 106, 108
Moffett, John, 27

National Health Service (UK),
    168 – 69
Nebraska, 165
New York State, 69, 165
Non-able-bodied poor, 26, 27
Nursing homes, 103, 148, 149,
    163 – 65

Old Age and Survivor Insurance,
    166
Old Age Assistance, 166
Old-age homes, 153
Open hospital, concept of, 96

Parole, 44 – 45, 46, 48, 57, 77, 100,
    101 – 2
Patton, Robert E., 83 – 84
Paul, G. L., 87
Personal care homes, 149, 150
Phenomenalism, 9
Phenothiazines, 170
Plea-bargaining, 44
Polanyi, Karl, 28
Political fragmentation, 53, 54
Poor Law Act of 1601, 18, 26, 27
Population
    of mental hospitals, 65 – 70,
        144 – 45, 149
    of prisons, 56 – 58
Powell, Enoch, 70
Power, role of, 11
President's Commission on Law
    Enforcement and the
    Administration of Justice
    (1967), 46, 48, 50
Pretrial detention, 46
Primary deviation, 5, 6

Prisons, 97, 124 – 25, 130, 143,
    144,
    colonial, 19 – 20, 21
    eighteenth century, 21
    medieval period, 17
    populations, 56 – 58, 175 – 76
Probation, 44 – 48, 77, 101 – 2, 179
Probation subsidy, 50, 54 – 56, 143
Professionalization of social control
    systems, 22 – 23, 29 – 30, 181
Psychiatrists, 29
Psychoactive drugs, 77, 79 – 89,
    139, 169 – 71

Rappaport, Maurice, 86, 88
Ray, Isaac, 128
Reagan, Ronald, 73, 147
Recidivism rates, 8, 51, 78,
    100 – 1, 125
Rees, T. P., 96
Reform schools, 50 – 53, 101,
    124 – 25, 130, 142
Rehabilitation, 30, 31, 33, 45, 100,
    106, 143, 181 – 82
Rock, Paul, 153
Rothman, David, 42, 43
Rule creator, 10
Rule making process, 10, 11
Rusche, G., 16

Schizophrenia, 81, 82, 84 – 85, 86,
    87, 172
Secondary deviation, 5
Secular rationalization of society,
    30
Simon, A., 102
Societal reaction theory, 4 – 11
Spitzka, 106
State
    fiscal crisis, 171, 172 – 73
    involvement, 15, 16, 21,
        31 – 32, 164 – 66
Statute of Artificers (1563), 27
Supplemental Security Income
    Program (SSI), 168
Suspended sentences, 44 – 45
Sykes, Gresham, 97

Symbolic-interactionist view of
    society, 6, 8

Temple, William, 26
Theft Act of 1968, 57
Thorazine, 80, 81
Total institution, critique of,
    95 – 114, 176
Townsend, Joseph, 28

Urbanization, 22 – 24, 25

Vagrancy laws, 26

Ward attendants, 71 – 72
Weber, Max, 26, 30

Welfare, 129 – 31, 134 – 51, 152,
    171 – 72
Wills, Gary, 97
Wisconsin, 69
Wolpert, Eileen R., 99
Wolpert, Julian, 99
Workhouses, 16, 20, 21, 28, 129,
    130
Wyatt v. Stickney (1972), 139

Youth Development and
    Delinquency Prevention
    Administration (HEW), 50
Youth services system, 50

Zoning regulation, 141, 153